HALFBREED

A True Story of Defeat, Faith and Triumph
By Duane Garvais Lawrence

ISBN-13: 978-1976418402

ISBN-10: 1976418402

Halfbreed is a spiritually powerful book that embraces you and takes you on a trip in someone else's shoes. If you like books filled with inspiration and wisdom, this book is for you.

– Lil Mike & FunnyBone

Halfbreed is a "Powerfully Inspirational Journey" … a great awakening of the Native American people is here!

–Ron Hazard, Former Administrator of
Beth Israel/ The Jerusalem Center

After reading the riveting story of "Halfbreed" you'll be entertained, encouraged and edified. I recommend this book to anyone who wants to grow in wisdom, knowledge and understanding. Be blessed.

–Gerry Borromeo aka: Prawphit On Point

Cover photo by Spirit Peoples

Forward
By John "Jay" Goss, Jr.

John the Baptist was baptizing in the name of Lord, when Roman Soldiers (Police officers of the day) *asked John the Baptist and what do you say we should do? And John said unto them, "Do violence to no man, neither accuse anyone falsely; and be content with your wages."*
– (King James Version) Luke 3:14

Every law enforcement officer should live by John's recommendation, for if they did, controversy would not lead the headlines.

I watched and was unable to prevent what I knew to be misrepresentation of truth for political favor by those sworn to uphold truth. The Bureau of Indian Affairs Law Enforcement Divisions internal investigations had been used as a political tool for an outcome, rather than the finder of truth. I have known Duane from the start of his career and I know him to be a hard-working, ethical police officer. I had the opportunity to read and review the criminal investigations of the Bureau of Indian Affairs alleging dishonesty, and it was clear that at best it was a work of fiction, biased presentation of what the investigator wished had happened rather than what happened, it was no wonder the United States Attorney's Office refused to prosecute, as the United States Attorney's knew it was necessary that there first be a crime to prosecute a crime.

From the start of his career in law enforcement I, respected his dedication to serve his tribal heritage, by connecting with and for his people of the Colville and Cree. When Duane first entered my office, he looked very much the US Marine, in appearance and the way he maintained his police uniform. Upon his graduation from the Washington State Police Academy, this young Native American Police Officer took top honors in physical fitness. As his Chief, I was proud of the way he represented the department. I task Duane with representing our department in the drug task force as he had the character to stand in what I knew would be a difficult assignment, the removal of internal and external drug cartels from the Colville Reservation. The drug problems of the reservation reached into the governing body of the tribe and the fallout of successful investigation was going to cause dissention with the tribe and for the person who brought it to an end. Duane took this same fighting spirit into his new assignment with the BIA; bring to justice drug dealers on the Spokane Reservation and breaking up corruption, which again entered into the governing body. Had Duane chosen to give into political corruption, pretended no thefts took place by his fellow law enforcement officers, he would today be a Special Agent-in-Charge or a Deputy Chief with a corrupted conscience with the BIA. Duane's clear path, the honest path, a truthful path, brought a test of strength and difficulty in his and his family's life, and at the end of years of struggle vindication in a United States Court for Duane. But more importantly brought him to a personal commitment to our Father and Creator, the Lord most high, and into the arms of his and our Savior Jesus.

Duane with this same fighting spirit and strength of the Holy Spirit continues to work with his wife and family to ensure all tribal people come to know the salvation found in the arms of Jesus and the special connection with God's chosen people Israel.

In God's Service, Your Friend.
J.A. Goss, Jr. Chief of Police
Federal Agent Retired

Some names in *Halfbreed* have been changed

Table of Contents

Chapter 1: Prayers for the Nation

Yod Hey Wav Hey is my shepherd, I do not lack. He makes me to lie down in green pastures. He leads me beside still waters. He turns back my being, He leads me in paths of righteousness, For his Name's sake, when I walk through the valley of the shadow of death, I fear no evil, For You are with me; Your Rod and STAFF they comfort me. You spread before a table in the face of my enemies; You have anointed my head with oil, My cup runs over, Only goodness and loving commitment follow me, All the days of my life; And I shall dwell in the House of YHWH To the length of days!
    – Tehillim (Psalms) 23

LoVina Louie traversed the streets between Fulton and Vesey Streets in Lower Manhattan, in search of even one available parking spot near St. Paul's Chapel. The rental van, filled to capacity with the most precious cargo I can imagine, dodged impatient drivers and taxi operators. Car horns honked, sometimes at other drivers, and often at us. Riding shotgun, I kept watch for anything resembling a vacancy for us to park, but by this time, our options became clear. Every turn and every corner brought the same familiar sights we had seen just minutes earlier; we were driving in circles.

Winner of the 1990 Miss Indian World competition, a motivational speaker, and currently the Director of the Benewah Wellness Center on the Coeur d'Alene Indian Reservation, LoVina has been my friend in our Covenant marriage since 2005. She stood by my side faithfully through trials and hardships that most women would not have endured. Now she was here with me to see nothing less than a sign from the times of the Historical Jesus, and a modern day miracle for a Nation in sin and distress.

We were at *Ground Zero*. I was here once before–on September 11, 2001–when I was in training as a federal agent. I will never forget that day when terrorists attacked and killed thousands of innocent people from all races, destroying the World Trade Center by flying jet airliners into the Twin Towers in an evil, cowardly attack upon innocent human beings. The landscape has changed since that day, and just like ancient Israel, our leaders chose to build bigger, to use *hewn stone* for rebuilding the ruins of an enemy attack.

Like the leaders of ancient Israel, America's politicians refused to humble themselves and repent for the good of their people and the United States of America. Shaking their fist at God in defiance, American leaders, and Israelite leaders both failed to recognize the progressively more devastating warnings as clearly outlined in Rabbi Jonathan Cahn's bestselling book, *The Harbinger*. We have the benefit of reading how that worked out for Israel, yet with all our accumulated knowledge, we lack the wisdom and spiritual fortitude necessary to change our ways.

Built in 1756, St. Paul's Chapel, was the church that George Washington attended every Sunday, and where the Founding Fathers dedicated the United States of America to God and the historical Jesus. On April 30, 1789, President Washington and the government of the United States walked to what is now 209 Broadway for the dedication ceremony. This small stone building, with a Sycamore tree growing on the property, stood across the street from the Twin Towers. This Sycamore tree miraculously survived the most destructive attack on American soil since Pearl Harbor. Four towering columns guarded the entrance to this nondenominational place of worship. The architectural style, influenced by Byzantine, Italian Renaissance, and Gothic, perfectly complemented the stained glass windows on the ceiling and behind the altar. Wrought iron gates inside the chapel originated from the North Dutch Church at Fulton and William Streets in lower Manhattan.

As LoVina guided the rental van through busy traffic, I reflected on our journey from a very different landscape and tradition. The passengers in our van were a select group–each person was here to complete a task so important to our nation that we sacrificed personal expense, putting our full faith into this mission. Unlike my experiences in the Marine Corps, or even as a Federal Agent, or Chief of Police, this excursion required an entirely different kind of training and discipline–*spiritual* discipline, dedication, and focus.

I felt so proud to see my oldest daughter, Daisy Marie Garvais Lawrence, among our group. She was my daughter, my first-born blessing from a previous marriage and a recent high school graduate. Daisy remained a strong Native woman, who had returned to our sacred language, and chose to join us on this trip to pray and repent for her one and only High School senior trip. While many high school seniors opt for a week of partying with friends in Cancun, Daisy chose to spend her week with us, praying, repenting, and asking God to forgive our nation.

Tina Cline, of the *Pretty Eagle Clan,* and a member of the Crow Tribe, was first introduced to me in a vision, and became even closer to me in the role of friend, mentor, and adopted mother. As a respected elder of the Crow Indian Nation, Tina was instrumental in helping each of us complete this very important and sacred task. In the traditions of Native American Tribes, the elders are revered and sacred. Tina was no different; however, she preferred to avoid attention for herself–instead, she was quick to give all praise and glory to God. As my adopted mother, Tina played a huge role in getting us to this pivotal moment in the history of our great nation–a spiritual crossroads for our country and the sovereign Indian nations. Sitting next to Tina was my teenage niece, Mariah Boyd–pretty, athletic, and carrying the same trademark smile and spirit as her late mother, Dolly Louie. Our oldest daughter, NorthStar Mary Jean Lawrence, was so much like her mother, LoVina. She lived every moment of her life to the fullest and was not about to miss this opportunity.

Sensing I was deep in thought, LoVina continued around the block one last time before suggesting the only viable plan. "I'll pull up to St. Paul's. Everyone be ready to jump out–I'll join you inside once I park."

As we readied ourselves to exit the van, I thought back to the day I first had the vision. It was in the small town of Worley, Idaho on the Coeur d'Alene Indian Reservation. A few weeks earlier, we had attended a Sabbath gathering, held at the home of our friend, Ed Casey in the city of Coeur d'Alene. As a small group, we watched a video, *The Harbinger* (2012) by Rabbi Jonathan Cahn. Rabbi Cahn cited a passage from Isaiah chapter nine from which he drew parallels between ancient Israel and modern day America.

The harbingers, described by Isaiah, warned Israel to turn from its sins and repent. A devastating invasion had already torn the northern kingdom brick upon brick, scattering the ten northern tribes to the nations. Israel failed to recognize that this was a lesser judgment requiring full repentance in order to avoid greater judgments to come. The leaders of ancient Israel refused to repent, and the nation was conquered–sending the two tribes of Judah and the whole twelve Hebrew tribes into exile. The Rabbi's message resonated within me. I thought about my wife, my family, and my four daughters. What kind of life would they live? If our nation did not repent, what would America look like when my daughters were grown adults?

Twelve years earlier, the same day the Twin Towers collapsed from an enemy terrorist attack, I was in class while attending *Command College* at the FBI Academy. Our entire class of BIA Special Agents was rerouted to provide additional security and protection for the second half of President George W. Bush's cabinet at an unknown location, which I now believe to be Camp David.

Now less than a week after viewing Rabbi Cahn's video, I had stopped by Ed's house for coffee. We blew the shofar and prayed for direction regarding the warnings Rabbi Cahn had described from Isaiah chapter nine. Clearly, I was not alone in seeing that there is a very tangible threat looming over our nation. God has shown throughout Israel's history that He will use an evil king or nation to punish Israel by allowing them to prevail in their assault. God later punished the Assyrians for their sins, but in terms of judgment–He allowed, and still does allow, judgment to come upon His people when they turn their back on Him and refuse to repent.

I thanked Ed for the coffee and got back into my car. Having just dropped my daughters off at school before stopping at Ed's house, I still had some errands to run. One of those errands involved putting gas in my tank–a task I should have completed much earlier! That day, I was playing the *gas game*, and as I sat at the red light in Coeur d'Alene, I thought that I was going to be on the losing side without a doubt. The gas gauge was on *E*, but even worse, the more accurate digital gauge read, "miles *to empty–zero."* The nearest gas station was out of reach no matter how I tried to map it out. I prayed, and the words that I heard myself saying were not the words that I thought I would be praying. "Creator God, if you want us to do something, to help our nation and the Native American Indian Reservations, to repent and pray for our future generations, then please give me a sign *so profound* that I know it's from you, and not of my desire or will. In *Yahushua's,* the historical Jesus' name, I pray, *Aho Amen Shalom."*

As I sat there, waiting for the light to change, I watched my gas gauge go from the left side of *empty* to the right. The miles-to-empty digital readout showed that it had changed from *zero* to *fourteen* in front of my eyes once I had completed the prayer. When the light finally changed to green, my first instinct was to locate the first gas station. I realized, though, that God had given me enough gas to get to where I needed to go, and that His answer to my prayer was right there in front of me. I had asked for a sign so profound that I would know it was from Him. I *got* that sign.

4

I turned the car around and headed right back to Ed's house. He had to be a little amused when I jumped out of my car and exclaimed, *"Ed! I have gas!"* Once I explained what had happened, we prayed that God would continue giving us signs for direction, and confirmation that we were doing His will. Ed decided to do some research about my gas tank, while I returned to my home on the CDA Indian Reservation. Later that evening I decided it was time to go to bed. It was like any other night and I went to sleep.

That was the night I had the vision dream. I drifted off that night without difficulty, and I soon found myself landing on top of an enormous mountain–unlike any other. It was sacred. *Different.* I could feel the presence of God nearby–to my right, but up much higher. I looked to my left and saw about fifteen to twenty figures lying upon their backs, arms crossed over their chests as if they were sleeping. They had their feet straight out, and I could begin to see regalia. They had full war bonnets with eagle feathers, buckskin leggings, and moccasins. I asked the Creator, "What are they all doing? Lying there like that?" I saw *Crazy Horse, Chief Joseph, Tecumseh, Sitting Bull, Geronimo, Black Elk*, and others; great tribal chiefs from the Indian Nations. The Creator replied that they are resting. He was getting ready to wake them up for a time such as this for His plans and purposes–to win the battle through spiritual warfare. The Creator then told me to look across the mountaintop.

I looked across and saw two houses sitting on the far end. In the spirit, I was whisked away and my presence was in front of the first house. Both houses looked the same; however, the first house had inferior construction. The foundation was unstable and the wood and stone was uneven and weak. I saw a large piece of pavement next to the house, which extended to the edge of the mountaintop. There was a gold fence at the edge. At that moment, I heard a cry. Looking back, I could see a person running toward the edge of the mountaintop. The person had no facial features. In fact, this person had no face. I watched as the person ran screaming toward the gold fence, jumped upon it, then leapt into the blackness beyond.

I turned to the Creator and asked what I had just seen. The Creator replied in a sad voice," *This* is what happens when my children take their lives. There is *nothing* I can do for them."

The Creator then directed me to the poorly built house. Once inside, I saw a round, grey stone in the center. The Creator asked me to pray, smudge, and sing. Pulling out my shofar, my sage tobacco, and sweet grass, I placed them on the big round stone. As I watched, nothing happened. I began to pray and sing.

Once I had completed my prayers, the Creator directed me to go to the second house. It was the same as the first, except that its foundation was even. The stone and woodwork were square and built from sturdy materials. The same grey stone from the first house was in front of me here in the second house. I removed my smudge, sage, tobacco, and sweet grass and placed them on the center of the stone. This time, they caught fire. As the smudge drifted toward the ceiling, I began to pray and sing. Soon, I could hear a vast chorus of angels rejoicing–voices saying that I was singing and praising in the Indian language.

Once I completed the song, the Creator directed me back outside the house, and pointed to a map in the far distance. This was a map of the United States, as one might expect to see in a history book. He told me to look closely. I could see small grey dots throughout the United States. I asked the Creator what they were. He replied that they are the sovereign Indian reservations, and that He has hidden away the people for such a time as this.

The Creator pointed to the Pine Ridge Indian Reservation, which was in the shape of an "L." He said to watch that Indian Nation very closely, as it is very sacred and very important to Him. At that point, I woke up suddenly.

I called Ed immediately, and told him about the dream. I explained that I had the sense I was on Mount Sinai while I was in the dream. Ed agreed to do some research, and told me he would call me back soon.

Two days later, Ed called. He said that he located the place where the Founding Fathers dedicated the United States of America to God–*St Paul's Chapel in New York City*. A statue of Mount Sinai, inscribed with God's original Hebrew name on top–Yod Hey Vah Hey–stood inside the chapel! Ed also outlined the meaning of the number "14." As stated before, the original language our Creator God spoke and the same language the Hebrew Chief Cornerstone spoke, taught, and prayed by, was the Hebrew language. This was a tribal language comprised of numbers, letters, and pictures. Much has been lost either intentionally, or unintentionally, in the translations and the meanings of the Bible verses.

The Hebrew number, *fourteen*, and the Hebrew calendar, (which is set by the New Moon sighting), references Moses' prayers for rebellious

Israel and Moses' intercessory Prayer for Israel in the Book of Numbers (14:1-20). There we were, ready to do the same for the United States of America–a nation steeped in sins, a nation on the brink of collapse, a nation that needed to repent.

We stood on the sidewalk of New York City–and it felt like New York was looking right back at us. Maybe it was seeing a group of Native Americans in full regalia; one guy standing with a prayer shawl, the Staff of Moses, the Shirt-Wearer's shirt of Chief Crazy Horse, and a shofar, surrounded by Native American women from child to elder. Once LoVina joined us, we joined in prayer before we entered the chapel. Our spiritual mom, Tina Cline had taught us long ago the battle must be won in the spirit before it can manifest victory in the physical. This was no exception. We approached our Creator YHWH by the sacrificial lamb, the covering of the historical Jesus before entering St. Paul's Chapel.

After entering, I noticed a number of security guards keeping watch, and people from many different ethnic groups visiting with the guards, praying, and taking in the sights. We approached a woman who appeared to be on staff and asked if we could blow the shofar inside the chapel. She made it clear that would not be ok, so we decided to exit the rear door of the chapel and into a fenced in area that appeared to have several graves and markers scattered within the fence line.

We gathered in a circle, clasping hands, and prayed: *"Creator (Yod Hey Wav Hey) invoking the sacred name, we repent and ask for forgiveness for our sins, and we sound the alarm for prayer and repentance."* I raised the shofar to my lips in the bright New York sky, framed with beautiful white clouds, and gave one long blast, followed by three staccato tones, which spiritually sliced through the air of the enemy. Tina Cline began by praying in the Crow language and then in English. LoVina prayed next. Her prayers were in the language of the Colville Twelve Tribes and the Coeur d'Alene language. Daisy and NorthStar then offered their prayers, and I followed them with my own. As we were completing our prayers, I noticed that others had started to gather around. Our appearance hardly went unnoticed. A couple walked up to us and asked about the shofar and our regalia. After we explained that we were here to repent, and ask God for forgiveness on behalf of the nation, they thanked us, and confided that they agreed America has turned its back on God, and refused to repent.

We walked back into St. Paul's Chapel. I could see directly in front of me across the floor of the chapel, there was a small wooden gate. Beyond that, there was a wooden box, which stood before the giant statue of Mount Sinai with the Creator's original Hebrew name, *Yod Hey Wav Hey,* spelled out in large Hebrew letters at the top of the statue. We gathered around the wooden box. Inside the box was sand with a grey circular stone resting on top of the sand. This was the same grey stone in my vision dream! *Everything that I had experienced in the vision dream was materializing in the physical world before me.*

I removed the smudge, sweet grass, and tobacco sage from my medicine bag and placed them on top of the circular grey stone. We began to pray after I set the tobacco sage, smudge, and sweet grass a light, and the smoke drifted above. We began what became a two-hour prayer. We had a long list of sins[1] for which to repent, and this team of Native American warriors–male and female–all took turns as each person prayed to the Creator to forgive the Nation of the United States. We prayed for our elected leaders in the both the Democratic and Republican parties, and each of the sovereign Indian reservations that are scattered throughout the United States.

Before we even arrived in New York City for this pilgrimage, we all worked together to write down every sin that we could think of, and in particular, those sins from which the Creator had warned Israel and all nations to abstain. Among these many sins were murder, abortion, drugs, alcohol, jealousy, generational sin, corruption, greed, worshipping idols, and practicing false religions.

The smudge burned hot in the mixture of sweet grass and tobacco sage. The smoke began to fill the air as we voiced each sin through prayer and song. Our group asked the Creator to have pity on the United States of America and the Indian Reservations for our sin, and then we all sang the *Turn Around Song.*

I could see the security guards looking at us as we sung our prayers. They then returned their attention to other visitors in the chapel as if we were not even there. The chapel was not *that* busy with other visitors. We were left to sing our prayers for those full two hours–I *fully* expected them to escort us out at any moment, yet we remained undisturbed to repent on behalf of our nations.

Physically, we were all very exhausted from fasting before our arrival. The weight of the staff became unbearable after holding it high over our heads throughout the prayers. Our physical energy levels were depleted by this time, but I could feel the spiritual power of our prayers and songs more than ever before.

Tina was praying in Crow (*Apsaalooke*), sealing our prayers so the *Enemy* could not affect them in any way. My strength was gone, and I could feel the weight of the staff taking over my weakened physical state. Slowly the staff I held (the staff shown in my vision containing that famous Bible verse "*Your God the Almighty is One*") started to sink to the floor of St Paul's Chapel. Others in the group raised their hands to help keep the staff held high when they saw me struggling to hold it above our heads. The last words of our prayer echoed through the room.

We had driven across the country–from Idaho and Washington State to New York City. We came to pray for forgiveness on behalf of the United States and the many sovereign Indian nations. It was our mission to pray and ask the Creator to forgive us for many of the *same* sins for which God had judged ancient Israel. We had accomplished our mission, it seemed.

It could not have been more than a matter of seconds from the time we spoke our last words of prayer, until we heard the authoritative shout from the female security guard who had been looking at us all along for the past two hours. She watched in silence, as I set the smudge, sweet grass, and sage a light on the grey stone before the statue of Mount Sinai. Her comrades, equally alert and watching us, held their tongues as we prayed and sang at the altar of St Paul's Chapel–we were hard to miss even in New York City.

"Hey! What are you guys doing up there? You are not supposed to be there!" She was not waiting for an answer. I knew at that moment that God had placed a veil over her eyes and the eyes of the other security guards while we prayed for forgiveness. That veil lifted at the utterance of the last word. Before I could even respond, she was already on her radio, calling for backup as she marched up to the wooden gate and opened it. "Who *are* you guys? And who gave you permission to be inside the altar?" There was a glint of anger in her eyes as she glanced at the shofar, the staff I was holding in my hand, and the smoldering remains of smudge, sweet grass, and sage on the stone. "Are you a priest?"

"Hey, we mean no disrespect. We were not trying to offend anyone," I replied calmly. That was the first moment that I realized all of us could very well be in danger of incarceration while in New York. "This is a shofar," I explained as I showed her my medicine bag and its contents. "This is smudge, and in the Indian way, we offer tobacco, sweet grass, and sage to the Creator as we pray, asking for our prayers to rise up and be heard." The anger was dissipating from her eyes as I explained what we were here to accomplish.

"Ok. This is a restricted area of the chapel unless you have permission." I thanked her for her patience with us. Our group quickly walked through the wooden gate and made our way back to the entrance. For two hours, we had prayed, sang our songs, and burned smudge on the altar in a highly protected historical building in the very place America was founded in New York City. During that time, nobody accosted us or intervened in our mission. We knew that God had placed a veil over their eyes until we completed our prayers of repentance.

"Hello!" I heard a voice calling to us from behind as were leaving. We turned around to see a man and woman standing before us. "Where is your group from?" The woman asked.

"Coeur d'Alene, Idaho," I replied.

"Oh! So. . . What is that?" she asked, pointing in my general direction. I assumed she was asking about my prayer shawl.

"That is a prayer shawl," I replied.

"No, no, no—I *know* what a prayer shawl is," she responded. "I was asking about the staff and that very decorative shirt."

Taking the staff in my hand, I explained, "this is the modern, symbolic Staff of Moses. I saw this staff in a vision *before* a member of the Tribe of Judah presented it to me at a Sabbath gathering. The shirt was also presented to me after I had seen this in another vision several years ago." I explained to her and her husband how generations of Lakota people handed this shirt down, also known on the reservation as the "Crazy Horse Shirt." The Elders gave it to men of honor and strength, who serve the people. As I was explaining all this to the couple, I felt that familiar *nudge* from God, and a memory flashed through my mind.

Ezekiel chapter thirty-seven describes how the Tribe of Judah and the Lost Tribes of Ephraim would become one staff in His hand; hence the Staff of Israel. "You are Jewish, aren't you?" I asked.

"Why, yes we are! How did you know that?" she asked.

"We are of the Tribes of Ephraim and Native Americans!" I exclaimed. I felt like I experienced a reunion with family members after a long separation.

"See, honey?" she said to her husband. "I *told* you they were Ephraim! Only Ephraim would be so bold and daring to pray like *that*!"

10

After we all had a good laugh, we joined hands in a circle and prayed sealing the passage from Ezekiel thirty-seven while standing in the halls of St. Paul's Chapel!

It was about an hour later that we arrived at our hotel and checked in. We were all exhausted from the fasting, praying, and spiritual warfare. Not one to rest, NorthStar wanted to shoot a game of pool, so I went with her downstairs where we found an open table. We had barely made it halfway through the game, when Daisy Marie walked into the room.

She was unable to contain her excitement. "Dad, you *need* to come upstairs right *now*! You have a phone call!"

"What?" *I knew nobody in New York City.* She reiterated that I needed to follow her upstairs. *This phone call was important!* As I entered the hotel room, I could see my wife, LoVina sitting on the bed with a huge smile on her face. I glanced over at my adopted mom, Tina Cline, who was holding the phone and wearing an enormous grin. "Well? Who is it?" I asked them.

"Pick up the phone and find out!" Mom Tina replied. I grasped the phone from her and watched as she and LoVina continued to smile in excitement.

"Hello?" I spoke into the phone.

"Is this Duane?" there came a voice.

"Yes it is. How may I help you?"

"Duane, I have heard that you and a group of Native Americans drove all the way from Coeur d'Alene, Idaho to St. Paul's Chapel here in New York City to pray and repent on behalf of the United States of America. This is Rabbi Jonathan Cahn. May I ask you why you would travel all this way to do this?" The words were almost impossible for me to believe at first, but recently, *nothing* would really surprise me anymore.

"Well, Rabbi, it was your DVD, *The Harbinger*, which I watched with some close friends at a Sabbath gathering in CDA Idaho. Your teachings from Isaiah chapter nine about the warnings that God gave to the nation of Israel and how those same warnings and signs have been manifested here in the United States at ground zero." This had been on my mind that day when Ed and I watched the video by Rabbi Cahn.

I explained the vision that God gave to me, which clearly outlined the sacred mountain and the two houses–the Nation of Israel and the United States of America. I felt that the two houses represented the Christian Church (Ephraim) and the ten scattered tribes, and Judah, the two tribes of

Israel. In that vision, the spiritual urge I received compelled me to repent on behalf of our nation before more judgment and irreversible damage was delivered– just as it was when ancient Israel turned its back on God, and chose to rebuild bigger with hewn stone, and replaced the fallen sycamore trees with cedars. "We came here to pray, repent, and ask forgiveness and mercy, and for the smudge to carry our prayers on behalf of the United States and the sovereign Indian nations." As I spoke, I could hear the Rabbi draw a sharp breath.

"Are you First Nations Indian people?" he asked.

"Yes, Rabbi. Everyone in our group–five women and me."

"This is *incredible*!" he exclaimed. "I have a radio show on *right now* in New York with millions of listeners! Would you be willing to do a live interview with me on my show?"

"Yes, of course, Rabbi Cahn." I looked around the room at the faces of my entourage as they all glowed with excitement. After I received the remaining details about the interview, I hung up the phone. We all knew that our mission was complete, and that the coming live interview this evening only served as one of many more confirmations.

That evening, we told a live audience in New York City, with millions of listeners, how a small group of First Nations people came to New York to pray, repent, and ask for forgiveness from God. We prayed for God to forgive the United States of America and every sovereign Indian nation throughout the land to insure the safety and well- being of all people, and all races for generations to come.

Before we returned to the Coeur d'Alene Indian Reservation, we accepted an invitation to visit *Beth Israel/ The Jerusalem Center* in Wayne, New Jersey. Rabbi Jonathan Cahn's assistant, Ron Hazard took our group on a tour of this oasis of worship. Cars drove past, some slowed to watch us, and others focused on the distractions of their modern, busy lives. NorthStar glanced upward toward the front of *Beth Israel/ The Jerusalem Center*, as the rest of the world kept turning; she was carried to another realm. "NorthStar! Are you coming?" LoVina smiled as she waited for NorthStar to catch up to the rest of our group. Daisy Marie was already ahead of us, and looked back briefly to see why we were taking so long.

We walked past the front entrance and paused. A long, beautifully crafted hall stood before us. As we looked up, we could see the names and tribal banners of each of the twelve Hebrew tribes adorning the interior. Once inside the worship area of Beth Israel/ The Jerusalem Center, Tina drew a breath as she spied the Western Wall. Even though we understood we were in New Jersey, something spiritual tugged inside as we gazed at this replica of the Wailing Wall. Familiar Hebrew letters garnished the stage where the podium stood. A familiar feeling came over me. I felt as if I were whisked away to my childhood home, my spiritual home. I had seen numerous photos of the Western Wall from the Temple Mount, yet never felt this close to it. Of course, it was only a replica, but the backdrop lifted my spirits.

A man approached from across the room. Chairs surrounded the stage in a semicircular pattern, offering him a maze through which to navigate before he came close enough to shake my hand. "You must be Duane," he said as he extended his hand.

"Yes." I shook his hand.

"I'm Ron Hazard." I introduced him to each member of my family. "Rabbi Cahn is not here today, but he asked me to give you a tour." I thanked him, and he began with a history of the ministry as he walked us through the worship area.

At this place of worship, Jew and Gentile come together to worship God and give praise to Yahushua. The original Hebrew teachings, praise, and prophecies are given center-stage here, as people from all backgrounds celebrate the messianic path to salvation. I had to reflect on those moments back on the Coeur d'Alene Indian Reservation, when I knew that the Creator would provide the direction and purpose to our mission, even though I had absolutely no idea how. My vision dream had come to manifest in the physical world just as it had in the vision. I turned to the group–six beautiful Native American women, ranging from elder to small child in age.

"Watch what happens in America down the road–two, three, and even more than five years from now. What was accomplished here in the spirit today (2013) for Creator's purposes will now manifest in the physical. Throughout America, you are going to witness spiritual and physical battles as America, once again, returns to its foundations, and turns away from sin. Once again, America will turn toward Creator and the historical Jesus and a new period of spiritual blessings will spring forward." I said a silent prayer thanking God for each member of my family and for allowing us to share this adventure to New York together. Each of us knew that God had intervened on our behalf during our prayer for repentance.

13

As we returned to the front entrance, I thanked Ron again for his hospitability and said a silent prayer to the Creator, thanking Him for showing us the path that brought all of us to this far away destination.

Weeks earlier, I could never have predicted that I would be standing in front of the *Western Wall* in New Jersey, or that we would be on Rabbi Cahn's live radio show in New York City after watching his video, *The Harbinger* during our usual Sabbath gathering at Ed Casey's home.

Looking back on all the dark times in my life, wondering how it would all make sense one day, I could not have known that I would find myself at peace, and surrounded by loved ones. Like so many other Native brothers and sisters, I had struggled for many years to understand how my rich Native heritage on one side, and equally rich French- Irish heritage on the other, could come together in such unity. No person is half of anything. We are all full children of God, and through Yahushua, we will be together eternally with our brothers and sisters from every nation.

Chapter 2: My Task

"Teacher which is the greatest command in the Torah?"

And Yahushua, said to him. **"You Shall Love YHWH your God with all your heart, and with all you being, and with all your mind. This is the first and great command.**

"And the second is like it: '**You shall love your neighbor as yourself.' On these two commands hang all the Torah and the Prophets."**

– Mattithyahua (Matthew) 22:36-40

As I began to write the story of my life, it is fitting to note that the Creator, YHWH, or Yahweh, spoke to me in the bathroom! Our loving God desires a personal relationship with every one of his creations. In my case, the Creator had decided that the best place to get my attention was to give instruction while I was in the bathroom. Maybe it's because I was not fully awake, or had not had my AdvoCare Spark or coffee yet, but as they say in our social networking lingo, LOL!

I began the process of writing my story October 15, 2014–the very same time we began the celebration of one of Israel's fall feasts, the Feast of Sukkot or *Tabernacles*. Growing up in Marysville, Washington, I attended the Trinity Lutheran Church. I do not recall the pastor or anybody in the church leadership talking or teaching about God's feasts or holidays. In fact until I reached the age of forty-five, I have not heard any religious teacher–rabbi, pastor, or priest–ever speak or teach about the feasts of our Creator. I first learned of the feasts while studying the scriptures from the Institute of Scripture Research, using a bible that translates the text from first century Hebrew directly into English, bypassing the later translations.

In order to grasp the intended meaning of the text, it is critical to retain the original meanings of the Hebrew words. Hebrew letters can have as many as three different meanings, including a numerical value and a pictograph. Each letter of the Hebrew alphabet originally had a symbol attaching everyday meanings to the letter. For example, the pictograph assigned to the word, *"covenant"* is a picture of the "+" sign, which is very similar to Constantine's cross symbol. Yahushua died on this sign, a physical symbol of God's covenant, emphasizing the role He had in fulfilling the prophecy that God would provide a sacrificial lamb from the Tribe of Judah. Pastor John Hagee, a well-known Christian minister was the first pastor who I have heard teach the critical importance of Israel's feast days, as mandated by the Creator.

I have struggled to be accepted by both Caucasian and Native societies. Even though I am French and Irish, white society in the seventies and early eighties only recognized the fact that I was Indian. This recognition resulted in all the sly comments and epithets directed toward minorities from a certain element in American culture. One must remember, back in the 1970's and 1980's, being known as a Native American or Indian was not cool or trendy. Nobody lied about his or her ancestry in order to be cool. Some of my Native high school classmates and friends did not see me as their equal. I struggled with the same problem from some of my white classmates and friends.

Because I grew up in the white, non-tribal way, I almost had the feeling of being an outsider to my own people, most of whom were tribal members. I was laughed at and teased for being different. The mockery and hurtful comments came from both Caucasian and Native people.

Being a member of a *special* club carries a feeling of self-worth and belonging–it does not matter from which race or culture a person comes. Tribal membership carries as much–*or more*–feeling of belonging as others have about their nationality or family surname. Being a member of a tribe is formal membership in a *sovereign* nation; it is synonymous with citizenship in any country. There are many benefits associated with tribal membership, such as hunting rights, tribal voting privileges, per capita payments, and the ability to run for and serve one's people on Tribal Council. Tribal membership enables an individual to apply for and receive certain Government benefits, including financial aid and college assistance.

Tribal membership connects the current generation with previous generations that suffered innumerable tribulations at the hands of our enemies, whether they were rival tribes or the United States government in its policy to eradicate all Indian people who refused to relocate. It carries all the history and pride passed down through generations. No one can buy or sell tribal membership, and except for rare circumstances when a tribe awards an honorary membership, no individual can earn membership.

Those who are unfamiliar with the concept of tribal sovereignty might be surprised to learn that every federally recognized tribe has its own set of laws and by-laws, independent of any other government. The tribe–*and tribe alone*–determines the criteria for formal membership in its rolls. For some tribes, simply proving with birth certificates that a person has one or more ancestors in his or her genealogy is enough to grant enrollment.

For other tribes, it is not that simple; a prospective applicant for enrollment must prove a specific *blood quantum*, such as twenty-five percent ancestry from that specific tribe. Because of this, a person who is one hundred percent Native American, but descended from many different tribes, might not be eligible for membership in any of his ancestral tribes. Unless a prospective tribal member can verify that he or she has the minimum required ancestry in that specific tribe, the tribe to which a person is applying will not grant membership, depending on the tribe's enrollment laws. Each Tribe has its own treaty with the United States Government. These individual treaties contain certain rights and stipulations negotiated in exchange for millions of acres of land and resources, including gold, silver, timber, and other precious commodities.

After graduating from Marysville Pillchuck High School in 1985, I began to develop a very bad attitude. I was drinking more, fighting, and heading toward a path that would lead to nothing but trouble. After experiencing the heart-wrenching feeling of betrayal from a recent relationship, I changed my view of all women, and I began to see them as sexual objects. There were troubles in my family just as there are in any family, but looking back, I believe that my stepfather made choices that had a negative impact on all of us, particularly my sisters, Marie and Marcy.

I recently discovered that my biological father was almost full Lakota, including some heritage from the Colville, Chippewa Cree, and Assiniboine tribes. Like his father, Charlie Garvais Lawrence, he never enrolled in his ancestral tribes. My father was a very talented musician and athlete, but he also had a severe drinking problem that had a disastrous effect on his relationships, and ultimately, cut his talents and life short. I began to feel very angry at the world, and everyone in it, including family and friends.

Half Breed is the story of how the *Creator Yahweh* allowed the fires of life and lessons to burn, scar, and mold me into his desires, ways, and purposes. The intent of this story is to provide hope, inspiration, and guidance to the reader as we travel together from the past to the present. I have no need to sugar coat my failures and situations, as these very hardships were instrumental in shaping me into the person I am today.

I believe that God has tasked me with reaching out to all people, but particularly to my people, my Native American brothers and sisters. My goal is to teach and carry forward the original truths from our Creator. Generations of children endured involuntary removal from their families–forced into boarding schools, where they suffered physical, emotional, and sexual abuse. With Native children forced into boarding schools and physically separated from their parents, generations of children lost the influence and teachings from elders. This process, cultural genocide, almost wiped out the language and culture of Native Americans.

What is Life?

It is the flash of a firefly in the night. It is the breath of a buffalo in the wintertime, It is the little shadow which runs across the grass and loses itself in the sunset

– Crowfoot, Blackfoot Warrior and Orator, 1830-1890

Mary McDonald-Wenger looked down at her baby boy and cried. She felt helpless. *Why is this happening?* The winter of 1969 was particularly brutal on the Colville Indian Reservation. My mother barely had enough money to buy food for her two children, and with the subzero temperatures, there never seemed to be enough wood to heat the home. I had become ill a few days earlier with a respiratory infection that was causing me to grow weaker each day. My mother was doing everything she could with the resources she had; her limited income stretched even thinner with the seemingly endless need for more fuel. She had nowhere to turn for help.

Her husband, Kenneth Charles Garvais Lawrence, was a gifted musician who travelled with his band, *Red Cadillac*. Although they loved each other very much, their marriage suffered because of Kenneth's drinking and from his time away on the road.

She was so thankful for the young physician, Dr. Cowan, who had examined me the day earlier. He explained to my mother, "I don't have any real reason for this, other than a *gut feeling*. I am going to have your son stay overnight here in the hospital." Less than twenty-four hours later, I was fighting for every breath.

As she stood at my bedside, crying and praying for my recovery, the door opened and a Catholic priest entered the room. Mary acknowledged him as he approached, but she was unable to smile. He must have understood just how grave my condition was as he was unable to find any words of comfort for my mother. The priest appeared unsettled as he gazed at the little boy in front of him. Perhaps he noticed that I looked different from the Natives he knew in the surrounding area, and that I looked very different from most of the white residents in the county. *Hmmm, a halfbreed*, he thought. *Or, maybe he could even be a Hebrew halfbreed.* A frown formed on his face, betraying the irritation he felt. *Is he white,*

Indian, or Hebrew? Whatever this baby is, his life is going to be interesting–if he survives at all!

Standing at my bedside, the priest began the sacrament of last rite. He searched for words of comfort from the scriptures, but soon found himself with nothing to offer, and quietly made his way out of the room. Alone again with her dying child, Mary called out to God and her Indian ancestors, *what more can I do? Please help my baby boy breath and live!* She wondered how she would ever tell her daughter, Marie, that her little brother did not survive.

I often think about how alone and abandoned my mother must have felt at that moment. There can be nothing worse for a mother than to watch her child slip away as she looks on helplessly. My father had not arrived at the hospital yet, nor had he even called. My mother knew that it was possible he was in jail, or still partying. As she was thinking about Kenneth, she received a phone call. It was *Ken!*

After he hung up the phone, Kenneth thanked the Creator and Jesus for keeping his son alive. He offered to leave Wenatchee where his band was performing, and drive back to Omak to be with my mother during my recovery. He loved his children, and he loved his wife, Mary. Their relationship was fragile, even when they tried to work things out. Inevitably, they would begin the same cycle of fighting and separating all over again.

Kenneth did not blame Mary for wanting a divorce. Music had always been an important part of his life. It was in his blood; he could remember as a child watching his grandfather, Charlie Garvais Lawrence play his fiddle while his mother, Ellen Contway Garvais Lawrence played along with the guitar. This was part of the Lakota life. Music, like home, was comforting to Kenny. Kenny and his siblings, Elaine Garvais Lawrence, Darlene Garvais Lawrence, and Ron Garvais Lawrence Senior all spent countless hours singing and jamming with their parents.

He wondered if life would be better for Mary, Duane, and Marie if he retreated from the family, allowing my mother to find another man who might make her life better. The fighting, *at least*, would stop. As Kenneth hung up the phone, his attention returned to the pitcher of beer sitting on the table. He was reminded of how many times that scene had played out, how many times he saw the same people in the bar. The same kind of people returned night after night. *What brought them there? Were they looking for love? Were they trying to forget a bad situation, or were they simply addicted to alcohol?*

Kenny thought back to the first time he drank a beer with his friends at the Omak Stampede and World Famous Suicide race. As the alcohol made its way through his system, into his blood, he could feel its soothing presence invade every corner of his being and his spirit. Deep down, Kenny knew this was a *foreign* substance. He knew our people did not drink alcohol, choosing to live in harmony with Mother Earth, and with every drink, he created an ever-widening gap between himself and the Creator. With every swallow, he felt that *buzz* that so many of his friends had described. That first euphoria was especially elusive after that day–the young Lakota teen would seek that same initial intense buzz feeling for many years after, but *never* find it.

The sounds of laughter and music brought Ken back to the present. He poured himself another glass from the pitcher. He thought, *maybe one day I'll stop drinking.* He reflected about the good times he and Mary had, as he emptied his glass. No longer a teen, bonding with friends over their first experience, he was older and alcohol had taken his health, and robbed him of the gifts bestowed by the Creator.

Ken was a talented athlete–he won several Native American basketball championships, and earned the highly coveted leather jackets awarded to those who placed first. He went on to play basketball in the Air Force overseas in various teams. *Were the boys still running ball –as they say on the reservation? Foes like Willford "Deb" Louie, Dave Louie, Stan Timentwa, Soy Redthunder, Kenny Bourgau, and William "Willie" Wormer. Ken's brother, Ron Garvais Senior, and he battled the Nespelem teams, sometimes winning, sometimes drinking, and fighting.* No matter what the result–respect was *always* given and earned.

Basketball on the reservation had become the modern equivalent to the honor and status a young warrior would have earned in days long gone, achieving the same status by riding into battle against the enemy. To strike *Coup* upon the enemy was the greatest honor one could earn in battle. Ken recalled how his father passed down stories of these traditions, and how our line descended from Chief Crazy Horse.

Now there was a true leader, he thought. Riding into battle, he was *impervious* to incoming fire by the enemy, as long as he followed his vision, and put his tribe's well-being before his own he would remain unscathed in battle. *Staying true to his medicine, the small pebble suspended from one ear, and the Hawk circling around his head–just like in his vision.* As an elected *Shirt-Wearer* by the Chiefs, he had one purpose once he donned the garment–to serve the greater good and to lead by example. This would be the legacy and the tradition that Chief Crazy Horse would set–by his actions and by example. It would be a tradition of the Shirt Wearers passed down through the Chiefs to the people who displayed these traits.

Kenny thought about his mother, Ellen Garvais Lawrence who had taught him as a young child about another man who lead by example, and put his people's safety before his own. He remembered her telling him about the Chief Cornerstone, Yahushua, trying to help his twelve Hebrew tribes. Jesus walked on water, healed many people, and taught others using story telling–most of the time, in the wilderness near the water. There was an unmistakable resemblance between the manner of teaching by Jesus, and the manner of passing down stories and tradition by tribal ancestors.

Mary stood by my bedside, watching each rise and fall of my tiny chest, as I struggled to fill my lungs with air. She wondered how much longer I would last, how much strength I had in me to keep up this fight for my life. Mary was exhausted. Physically drained from lack of sleep, she had almost no reserve left in her. Her face bore the signs of one pushed to her limits. She felt stress–even before I fell ill. The merciless winter and limited resources were a cruel combination that was far too common for many people on the reservation. No parent should have to choose between feeding her child and heating her home. Sleep deprivation and emotional torment were affecting her very ability to think clearly.

Again, the door to the hospital room opened quietly. This time, it was no stranger standing in the threshold. Even with her thoughts jumbled from exhaustion, Mary recognized the striking natural beauty of the Lakota woman standing before her. Her long, silver hair, with streaks of brown, braided in two ponytails fell about her shoulders, and accentuated the sharp features that seemed to shout, *I am Indian!*

Mary wondered what Elaine was doing here. She approached my bedside, her heart aching as she watched me struggle to breathe. Elaine began to pray, *in Jesus name*, asking for strength and life for the baby boy. She acknowledged and called upon her Lakota ancestors to help.

As she completed her prayers, she returns her attention to Mary. She felt compassion as she watched Mary fight fatigue, struggling to keep her head up and eyes open a little longer. Elaine felt the presence of God, nudging her to help her brother's former wife. *How would Mary be able to cope if Duane did not survive?* Taking Mary's hand, Elaine whispered for her to go home. "Get some rest, I'll watch over Duane until you return."

The very idea of leaving the child's bedside disturbed Mary. She was exhausted but realized that Elaine was there to help. She agreed. Mary had done everything she could for the moment, and family had come to her side when she needed them the most. As Mary left the hospital, Elaine walked up to the payphone in the hallway. The unmistakable sound of quarters and dimes clunking their way into a payphone broke the cold silence of the hospital corridor. She placed a call to a little bar in Wenatchee, Washington.

Mary could barely remember driving home, or even walking into the house once she arrived. It took all her energy just to make it to her bed. She woke up in a panic. It was ten hours since she came home from the hospital with her former sister-in-law taking her place at Duane's bedside. *Is he still alive?* She grabbed her keys as her mind raced.

Unlike the drive home, her return to the hospital felt like it was in slow motion despite the accelerated speed. She could not drive fast enough. Her baby boy was clinging to life when she last saw him. It had been over ten hours, and she has heard nothing. She ran through the hallway of the hospital, the sound of her feet echoing off the walls.

Mary burst through the doorway. Elaine was standing at my bedside, where Mary had seen her when she left the room hours earlier. She felt instant relief to see that my chest was still rising and falling, still raspy and gasping for air. There was something different though.

She could not be sure. Mary came even closer and held her breath. Her heart was pounding so hard it hurt. She kept watching and listening. It was not her imagination. Her son's breathing had improved from when she was last here!

Mary began to thank God. She prayed even harder than before, praising Jesus and asking Him to give more strength to the child in front of her. She began to realize that Elaine had been doing the same. Together, they prayed. Elaine remembered the teaching she had learned long ago: *wherever two or more are gathered in My name, they will be heard.*

I gradually began to breathe easier. With each day, there were signs that I was growing stronger. The doctors were amazed. The priest returned for his visit, expecting to see the worst. He shook his head when he saw what Grandma and Grandpa Garvais Lawrence described as a *miracle*. My mother continued to pray for me and my recovery was complete within two weeks. I had lost a lot of weight and could not walk; in fact, this battle with sickness would require me to learn all the basic functions I had already learned all over again.

When it was time for her take me home from the hospital, she vowed she would never run out of wood again–not even if it meant cutting down a tree herself! She was thankful for the knowledge her father, Fred McDonald, had taught her while growing up on the family ranch in the Kartar Valley on the Colville Indian Reservation. She learned to grow large gardens of vegetables, called "*Depression Gardens*" because people were determined never to go hungry again after the Great Depression. She remembered watching her father, an enrolled member of the Colville Tribe, mount his horse, and sling his rifle, a Winchester two-forty-three, into the holster of his saddle. He would show her two bullets: one for dinner and one for protection. She would watch him ride away on his horse as he went hunting for elk or deer for his family in Kartar Valley on the Colville Indian Reservation.

Mary's mother, Mabel McDonald, taught her how to can the vegetables from the garden, clean the house, and care for the livestock. As Mary remembered all the valuable wisdom she learned from both her parents, she vowed at that moment that she would never allow her children to go without ever again.

Chapter 4: Childhood Memories

"Oh Great Spirit that made all races, look kindly at the whole human family and take away the arrogance and hatred which separates us from our brothers"
– Cherokee Chief Prayer

I grew up in the small town of Marysville, Washington–just off the Tulalip Indian Reservation and about thirty miles north of Seattle. It was the early seventies. For food and treats, *Mom's Hamburgers Drive-In, The Arctic Circle, Godfather's Pizza, Big Scoop and the Thunderbird Drive-In* were landmarks to everyone living in the community. There are so many happy memories when I think about stopping off at the small *Texaco Gas Station, the Sand Pits*, and of course, *Galaxy of Games* with my friends.

The Tulalip Indian Reservation was just a small tribe back then. The main hub of the reservation was in the old Administration building, a mere hundred yards from the crystal clear waters of the Ocean Mission Bay. The immense casino and resort, complete with destination hotel and open area shopping mall, had not yet been built. Where they stand now, thick vegetation and trees, so thick you could not see through them, lined the corridor of Interstate I-5. To access the Tulalip Indian Reservation, one needed to drive south on I-5 and take the exit marked by another landmark during that time, *Easterbrook's Gas Station*.

When we were up for a short drive, we would hop into our green Ford station wagon–much like the one made famous by *National Lampoon's Family Vacation*, and head into Everett, Washington to order a bag of cheeseburgers and fries, complete with their famous Fry Sauce at *Herfy's Drive In*. These burgers were unmatched in size and flavor, they brought a sense of small town goodness to the consumer, and the banter between the employees was refreshing and good medicine for the soul.

On the main road north, as you head out of Marysville, the road turned into a "Y." My friends and I used to ride our bicycles all the way from 2328 116th Street NE to the south end of the City of Marysville. Our usual route involved riding our bicycles along the dirt trails that ran parallel to the railroad tracks, then onto the sidewalks until we came to the *Seven-Eleven Food Store* located on the south end of Marysville, where we filled up on hot dogs–two for seventy-five cents! On our way back, we always stopped at a landmark mom 'n pop gas station and food mart–the *Texaco Gas Station Food Mart*, at the intersection of the "Y." This was the perfect place to stop for a real sugar Pepsi and the famous *Captain Crunch Ice Cream Bar*!

The Tulalip Indian Reservation was very small and secluded. I remember driving down our road, taking Interstate-5 South for about five miles, until we came to the exit where we could access the reservation. There were large trees on both the east and west lanes of I-5, where the Tulalip Tribes Casino Hotel and Resort now stands. Back then, road maintenance on that stretch was infrequent. The shoulders were narrow, resulting in numerous accidents over the years.

As a young boy, I was smaller in comparison to other children my age because of my close brush with death at an early age. I had to learn to eat, walk, and talk all over again. These early disadvantages lead to my having a speech problem and muscle weakness, requiring substantial time and energy to rehabilitate my strength and coordination. This was a huge obstacle to making friends as a young child.

One of my neighbors, Brett Berg, came from a Christian family, was taller than I was, spoke with confidence, and seemed to have all the best toys in the neighborhood. Brett and I soon became very close friends. We spent much of our time building tree houses and even our own tree house out of scrap lumber from the dump. Sometimes, Brett's father, Gene, would even donate extra lumber to the cause.

Gene was, in my opinion, the very best example of what a father should strive to be. I do not recall him ever yelling or using harsh language toward his son, or me for that matter, when we made the usual poor choices that all boys do at that age. The Berg family introduced my family to the Trinity Lutheran Church in Everett.

I remember sitting quietly with my older sister, Marie and little sister, Marcy in the pew every Sunday. Dressed in my best shirt, pants, and tie, I listened intently to Pastor John Greene preach about God's plan of forgiveness for mankind through His Son, Jesus. Once Pastor Greene finished his sermon, he excused the children from the service to attend Sunday school.

Attending church also had a social element; I quickly made several friends, including Sandy Greene, Bud, and Trisha Finley. Sandy was the Pastor's daughter, and a transparent, but unacknowledged, contest for her attention by my friends quickly ensued. I lacked the self-confidence at the time to compete with other boys my age. Maybe my cereal bowl haircut–an inspiration to Jim Carey's character in *Dumb and Dumber*–had something to do with it.

It was more common than not, in the seventies, for people to attend church. The Ten Commandments was a common sight in households. The economy was getting better, and people just seemed happier than they do today. The church was a place where we felt safe, a place where other adults felt like family, teaching, and protecting us as we participated in church activities and youth groups. I remember three men in particular to whom we were drawn. My friends and I referred to these three men as "Big Daddies," due to their height and weight, but also because each and every child attending the church felt safe around them. I remember running up to them on Sundays or after Sunday school and shouting "Big Daddy! Big Daddy!" then jumped up into the air and into their waiting arms, hugging and smiling. There, three Big Daddies always had a smile and time for every child. Every so often, we meet people who–for no *obvious* reason–cause us to retract; check our spirit because it is warning us. That feeling, I believe, is an innate spiritual defense that God gave to us when He created us in His image. That same spiritual barometer can tell us when we are in the presence of someone who has the light of God inside, and who is a comfort to be near.

Kids can sense weakness, or lack of confidence, in other kids and in adults. My family had limited resources, and we had to get by on what we had. My stature was somewhat small in comparison to other boys, causing me to lack confidence when they confronted me or assumed an aggressive posture. It was almost as if they could *sense* the fear, and like an animal, pounced on the kids who lacked the confidence to fight back.

School did not always feel as safe as Trinity Lutheran Church. Just purchasing lunch in the Pinewood Elementary cafeteria was a struggle. I reached into my Tuffskins pants pockets to feel the quarters and dimes my mother had given me for lunch. There had been days past when I went hungry because school bullies demanded my lunch money. That day, it looked as though I would go hungry again. I saw Mark, one of the bullies, coming toward me as I approached the lunchroom. I looked around for a teacher, but there were none in sight.

As I expected, he demanded my lunch money. I felt anger welling up inside, as I thought about having to choose between fighting a bully who was larger or going hungry for the remainder of the day. Before I had to surrender my meal, I heard a voice from behind, "Why don't you pick on someone your own size?" When I turned to look, I saw that it was Ron Hartman–whose confidence and posturing far exceeded any height superiority by the bully.

"This has *nothing* to do with *you*, Ron!" Mark responded angrily. I could tell that Mark was just as impressed with Ron's fearless confidence, and that this young kid had no intention of backing down. Mark became frustrated when he realized he had to back down–this would not end well for him if he persisted, and saving face became a more important consideration.

I extended my hand, "Thank you for doing that," I said.

"Are you the new kid who just moved into the house on Marshall Road?" he asked.

"Yes." I was surprised that he knew this about me.

"Well, that makes us neighbors! I live in the yellow house at the end of Marshall Road." This was the beginning of a lifelong friendship, and some of my best childhood memories.

Ron and I played together almost every chance we had. In the fall, we tried to catch as many falling leaves as we could as they fell from the big tree in my backyard. In the rainy season, the fields and woods behind my house would fill up with many ponds–both tiny and large, creating the perfect waterways for us to float homemade boats through the canals. Other times, we would pretend that we were hunting bad guys in the three acres behind my house, using pretend guns and knives. When we were not catching leaves or bad guys, we chased each other through the yard, tackling each other, and wrestling until one of us had the other pinned. The winner inevitably did the *typewriter* treatment on the loser's chest–an avalanche of concussive fingertips tapping out a make-believe letter on the loser's ribs. *Ouch.*

An older couple lived next door. Tom and Jan Ahern were good friends to my mother, and had a German Shepard named Tanya. The Ahern's shared a fence line with our yard, which gave me the opportunity to spend as much time with Tanya as I wanted. I spent hours throwing a ball or stick from my yard into the Ahern's yard for Tanya to fetch. She would bring the stick up to the property line, and try to press it against the fence until I could retrieve it. Whenever Ron or my other friends were unable to play, I spent my time with Tanya–bonding in the way only a boy and his dog can do.

One day, Jan Ahern and my mom were visiting in the kitchen while I played in the living room. I overheard Jan telling my mom that she and Tom were moving. I froze when I realized that, if they move, I would lose one of my closest friends. I slipped outside while Mom and Jan continued their conversation. A feeling of deep sadness came over me as I threw the ball again for Tanya to fetch. Just like every time before, she retrieved the ball and waited eagerly for me to take it from her. Her tail wagging wildly, Tanya readied herself for the next toss—she could not have known that my heart was in my stomach just thinking that these moments would soon end.

That inevitable day finally came. Tom and Jan came by the house to say goodbye. Tanya followed behind, her tail wagging, and carrying a ball in her mouth ready to play fetch at any moment. Jan and Mom were talking to each other while Tom and my stepfather, Steve were engaged in their own conversation. I threw the ball for Tanya while the adults continued their visit; this could be the last time I see Tanya. The very thought made my stomach twist in knots.

Jan walked up to me after a few minutes. "Duane," she began, "how would you feel about taking care of Tanya for us?" Her words dissipated somewhere in deep caverns of my mind. I cannot be sure how long it took me to realize what she had really asked, but I know now, looking back, that I was in shock. As her words began to make sense to me, my heart soared. The feeling of relief was so intense and entangled with feelings of excitement that I had to breathe before I thanked her.

Tanya seemed to understand that *something* was happening. The diversity of emotions that must have hung in the air would have been difficult for her to understand. Still, she seemed to get it as she buried her face in Jan's hand as if to say goodbye. Jan was fighting back tears as she caressed Tanya's neck and back. After she told Tanya she would stop by to see her from time to time and gave her one final hug, she handed Tanya's leash over to me and smiled. It did not feel real yet, but I did not waste any time—I lead Tanya out to the back yard to play fetch. *This* time, I was playing fetch with *my* dog!

Tanya and I played together every day. It is hard to imagine, but Tanya and I became even closer than ever. Ron had a collie named Nikki, who became good friends with Tanya. The four of us spent an immeasurable amount of time together, usually playing hide and seek. Ron and I would run and hide under the haystacks, on the roof of the house, or garage and see how long it would take the two dogs to find us. The fun was in watching the dogs run all over the place trying to pick up our scent. The longest time we were able to remain hidden was about thirty minutes, when we hid up in an apple tree located in my front yard. Tanya would come close, then stop and look around. Unable to find us, she would circle close by, and then come back to the base of the tree where she was closest to us. Finally, she figured it out, and looked straight at us–barking to let us know that she won the round. That was when I realized just how intelligent she was!

When I was fourteen years old, I took over the paper route from my older sister, Marie. Every day, including weekends, I delivered the *Everett Herald* to each customer on the route. I also had to collect monthly fees from the customers, which included a percentage for my service. Back then, I earned a lot of money for a kid my age, sometimes as much as fifty to seventy-five dollars a month. As I learned the route, I met each of the customers and quickly became familiar with which houses had unfriendly dogs. Most of the time, I was able to avoid them, but there were a few close calls in which I had to kick my way to safety. I decided to take Tanya with me on the route, since she would love the activity–but really, I knew I would be safer with my loyal German Shepard at my side. Tanya trotted alongside me carrying a ball in her mouth, while I rode my bike with the newspapers balanced on my lap. We approached one of the most dreaded houses on the route–the home of the Doberman. This dog was big and mean; when he bared his teeth and curled his lips it was a terrifying sight. Tanya did not hesitate to return the message, teeth appearing behind her snarled lips like a theater curtain drawing to display the actors on stage. *The show was on.* Looking up at me, Tanya waited for my direction, her eyes searching my face. "Sic 'em!" I yelled, and watched as Tanya raced up, catching the Doberman off guard, and knocked him down with her powerful strength. The Doberman struggled to regain footing as Tanya continued to circle back for more, her mouth curled back snarling, and barking as only a German Shepard can. By that time, the Doberman Pincer wanted nothing more to do with my German Shepard or me, turned and retreated to his yard.

Tanya became my paper route partner, accompanying me on my daily route and sometimes, having to keep the peace in the canine world. After a few days of that, every dog–with the exception of Nikki–knew and respected Tanya as the new boss on the block. Some of my fondest memories were created when I collected the monthly fees associated with

30

delivering the *Everett Herald Newspaper*. With Tanya at my side, and no newspapers weighing me down, I would set off on my bike to knock on each customer's door. As I stood just inside the doorways of the customers houses, I would more often than not see a picture of the Historical Jesus or the 10 Commandments on the wall. My customers would offer me a cookie or a cup of hot chocolate while I waited.

One couple always stood out with acts of kindness and blessings. Harold and Bridget Wilkins lived on the south side of Marshall Hill, about three quarters the way up. Harold and Bridget were well known for their support and donations to local youth sporting programs, to the City of Marysville, and to various scholarship programs and they could frequently be seen at local sports games. Every year at Christmastime, Harold and Bridget would give an extra tip of twenty-five dollars during collections in the month of December. Back in the early 80's this was considered a huge amount of money especially to a young boy! These times were special in a young boy's life.

My sister, Marcy Hodgson Petzold is an inspiration to me. Born with a seizure disorder, she has battled the devastating symptoms and life-threatening seizures throughout her life. I first witnessed her seizure when she was about nine years old. I stood by, helplessly, as the convulsions worked their way through her spirit. Marcy has not allowed this to hold her back. She has a beautiful family–a husband, two children, Michelle and Brandon, and now, two beautiful grandchildren as well.

I have so many fond memories of our time together as children. We used to play football in the big field next to our house at 2328 116th Street Northeast in Marysville, Washington. I was *Jim Zorn* and Marcy played the part of *Steve Largent*. We spent endless hours practicing routes–running over and over until the pass and catch was made. Other kids teased Marcy when she attended public schools. In fact, this had a lasting impact on me. I remember watching her cry when she stepped of the bus. This really pissed me off. I become incensed when I witness someone deliberately inflicting cruel treatment toward another just for the satisfaction of being a bully. That day, I boarded the bus–much to the shock of the school bus driver! I had just seen my little sister step off the bus in tears–hurt by the unnecessary cruelty of her peers.

Once on board, I scanned the faces of each kid on the bus, making eye contact with each one. I issued a warning to everyone on the bus, that if I ever found out that anybody ever made fun of my sister–or anyone else for that matter–I was going to kick somebody's ass. From that day on, my little sister, Marcy never had another problem with those kids.

Growing up with a sibling who had to battle harder than most others her age made me reflect on the plight of others. I developed compassion and empathy for those who had to fight harder to achieve their goals. I had a friend who lived on Marshall Road by the name of Johnny Ray. There were a number of times I noticed others making disparaging comments about his intelligence or appearance. I intervened when possible. One time, in particular, when I was home on leave from the Marines, Johnny arrived at my house to show me his new car. I listened as Johnny described his new car, his love, and joy. Even though this car was older and in rough condition, he was proud of it. We talked for about an hour. The next day, my mother, Mary McDonald Wenger told me that the time I spent with Johnny made an enormous difference in his esteem.

Another friend and classmate of mine, Bud Trubshaw also had a soft spot in his heart for those who lived with unique challenges and disabilities. Bud joined me in volunteering our time with the Special Olympics taking place in our area. Once again, Creator was allowing me to experience and learn the beauty and good medicine of helping others. Sometimes, making even the slightest effort to help someone out can make an immense difference in his or her life. For Johnny, all somebody had to do to make his day was to *listen* to him.

Back at home, a friend by the name of John "Chico" Moss came by for a visit. Chico had a gift for installing tape decks, speakers, and car stereos of any kind. The *Bump-Bump* of his speakers pounded the walls of our house from a quarter mile away signaling his impending arrival. When he pulled into my driveway, Tanya looked at me with eyes that seemed to ask, "Who is *that*?" Before Chico could get out of his car, I told Tanya to *"Sic the car!"*

The sight of my German Shepard terrified Chico, as he remained paralyzed in the car. Tanya sprang into action; growling, barking, and baring her teeth– jumping up to the window as if she was trying to bite through the glass and steel.

I told Tanya to "Heel!" and she trotted back to my side as if nothing had happened. I told Chico it was ok to exit the car, but he shook his head, "No!" and stared at me. After a few minutes of this, he slowly opened his door, and walked up to my front door–keeping his eyes fixed on Tanya as he walked.

As I grew into my teens, I began to notice a grey coloration forming around Tanya's mouth. One day, I threw the ball as I had done so many times before. There was something different this time. Tanya's hind legs were not moving quite the same as they had. It must have been a subtle progression, because I had not noticed her having discomfort or difficulty before. Over the next year and a half, her legs gradually deteriorated; clearly causing her difficulty from moving even a short distance, and I could tell that she was in pain when she walked. She continued to greet me when I stepped off the school bus, doing everything in her power to run to me with a ball in her mouth–ready to start playing our favorite game together as soon as I came home. The sight of her struggling in pain broke my heart every time I saw her.

I knew I had to make an unavoidable decision. I included Tanya in my prayers and asked for guidance about making the most humane choice. Wincing in pain as she tried to walk from room to room, soon caused a sadness to come over her eyes. She was a highly intelligent dog; there was no question that she knew her condition. My best friend, my playmate and protector was tired and her spirit was ready to make the journey.

Tanya rested her head on my lap as I drove her to the Veterinarian's office. I stroked her head and neck and told her how much I loved her, how much I appreciated her loyalty and friendship. She seemed calm and ready to make her journey. I remember looking into her eyes and seeing peace, as if she knew it was her time to go. This was the peaceful confirmation my mother my sister and I were looking for. After she passed, I carried her body home for burial in the backfield where we had played fetch and many other games so many countless times. I made a small white cross–painted white to mark her grave.

For the next few years, I found myself looking for Tanya to greet me right on schedule. Every time I saw a ball or the right kind of stick in the yard, I would look for Tanya–waiting to see her bright smile and wagging tail.

I developed a number of other interests to help me in the grieving process upon losing my best friend. Ron and I got together and made rubber band guns, played tag, and rode our bicycles down to the sand pits where we would collect beer bottles and cans for recycling. Later, after we had filled the gunnysacks we carried, we rode several miles into the town of Marysville. We waited anxiously for the old man at the recycling center to weigh our bounty–as he muttered incoherently throughout the entire process. It was all worth it. Several dollars for our time meant that we could ride our bikes to *Galaxy of Games Video Arcade*. It was easy to get lost in those good old games, like *Pole Position, Pac Man, Defender, Wreck it Ralph*, and of course, *Asteroids.*

My sister, Marie and I each had a pony that our mother had bought for us. I remember training and walking *Cinnamon* while Marie did the same with *Sugar,* her pony. Cinnamon was considerably more excitable than Sugar; he often bucked and tried to avoid me when I was trying to train him.

One rainy day, I prepared to take Cinnamon for a ride–a *chill* hung in the air as I checked the saddle. I had come to expect a certain amount of defiance from Cinnamon; such was his temperament. That day; however, Cinnamon regarded me with flash of recalcitrance that should have been enough for me to reconsider my plans. Just as I have learned–with people–to *check my spirit* when I am in the presence of an aura that exudes darkness of any kind, I should have done the same with Cinnamon when her uneasiness became evident.

I swung my leg up and over, landing in the saddle as usual. Cinnamon reacted wildly, running in circles and bucking until I landed with tremendous force, face down in the mud and dirt below. *How could he do this to me?*

After I pulled myself up and wiped the mud from my face and mouth, I realized this was *not* going to work out. About a month later, both Marie and I sold our ponies. Even though we missed them, Marie and I agreed that we had done the right thing. My friend, Brett Berg had horses, which afforded me the opportunity to continue riding horses as often as I wanted, and Marie's friend, Julie Earnest shared her horse when she and my sister were together.

Brett and I rode together in the heavily wooded acres of his and my family's property. Often fighting imaginary wars against our enemies, we became legends and heroes in our own minds. Our imagination was as much a playground as the lush green woods through which we galloped. Common sense would *not* inhibit our creativity, and our newly invented game, *Crazy Rider* was the product of our mutual talent.

If the name does not speak for itself, maybe a brief review of the rules and strategy will offer some perspective. Crazy Rider required a horse, saddle, and several acres of heavily wooded land. One of us–usually me–reached down to loosen the belt on the horse, which kept the saddle and riders in place. Then, with both of us on the back of his horse, we started with a brisk trot toward the woods. As we got closer, we began to gallop, barely avoiding the trees as we weaved our way through the midst of them. At this point, all that jostling began to loosen the saddle–often causing me to lose my grip as I rode perpendicular to Brett and the horse. If that was not exciting enough, watching a solid tree trunk approach at lightning speed got my heart pumping. Luckily, no such disasters ever transpired in our game. Without fail, one or *both* of us would fly off the horse and land in the brush below. The harsh landing was painful enough. Our rib-splitting laughter almost seemed worth all the bruises and scrapes.

Those memories of my German Shepard, Tanya and my good friends, Ron and Brett were good. Even though our family did not always have a surplus of cash for luxuries that other kids enjoyed, my mother strived hard to teach me the values of work, respecting authority, and treating others in the same manner that I wished to be treated. I realize now just how blessed I am to have been raised by a mother who loved me enough to equip me with the ethics and values that would help me overcome numerous obstacles ahead.

Chapter 5: Ross Lake

Somewhere there's a person who lost a mother
Lost a son, lost a friend, lost a brother
Way back, they had a fight. Never spoke hardly
Now they'll never get the chance to say I'm sorry
– SupaMan, "Somewhere"

As a teenager growing up in the late seventies and early eighties, I spent most of my spare time outdoors. Even though we had to cut some financial corners–haircuts and *Toughskin Jeans* come to mind–I felt blessed in so many other ways. Our house stood on a heavily wooded tract of acreage, complete with deep ditches that carried the heavy rainfall away, and offered perfect canals for floating little wooden boots on rainy days. It was located only about three miles from *Ross Lake*–nature's *Disneyland* to surrounding communities.

We often went on long walks, starting from our house–located on Marshall Road–and followed the two-mile loop around Marshall Hill. Armed with triple-decker peanut butter sandwiches, Capri Sun, and a variety of fruit, we had the proper supplies for our adventures. Traffic back then was minimal; there were a few cars travelling to work in the morning, and returning home around five o'clock. Between those times, though, we would lie down in the middle of the freshly paved asphalt and talk about what we planned to do that day, soaking up the energy and heat from the asphalt. If we got thirsty under the hot sun, we would simply cup our hands under one of the many natural, clear springs that hid in the rocks of Marshall Hill, bubbled out, and seemed to speak to us.

When it rained, spending time outside was a less attractive option. I soon discovered the imaginative world of J.R.R. Tolkien's books, *The Hobbit*, and *The Lord of the Rings Trilogy*. Lying on my bed as the rain pelted the roof above; the adventures of Bilbo and Gandalf enraptured me as they battled the forces of evil. Our close proximity to the coast invited long stretches of rain. Lavish vegetation on the forest floor and thick canopy overhead gave my imagination a vivid point of reference. Middle Earth, in my mind, appeared very similar to the Pacific Northwest.

I remember my first adventure to Ross Lake, and how the long journey with my sister, Marie Hodgson Garvais Lawrence, Ron and Dan

Hartman, reminded me of Frodo, Aragorn, and Gandalf traversing the treacherous landscape, *orcs and wraiths* hunting them as they went. We packed a brown bag lunch for each, and walked to the top of Marshall Hill on the south side, winding about two miles. We continued our trek up the next incline, a mile long dirt hill, until we arrived at the three big sand hills–so incredibly steep and sandy that there was no way a bicycle would make it–heck, a motorcycle could not even reach the top– the only way was to *walk* to the top. As we trudged through the sand up the steep hills, then back down, we knew the last mile to Ross Lake would be much easier. It was also the most enjoyable part of the journey.

The four of us ambled beneath the overhanging canopy, the smell of the trees and the clean air mixed by a slight breeze, and followed the narrow logging trail. Old trees lined the path on both sides, like venerated elders guiding our way. When unpredictable weather chose to challenge our plans, the protective canopy shielded us from the sudden onslaught of rain.

Life was abundant everywhere I looked. Old stumps scattered through the foliage. Even these remnants, now only a small fraction of their original size, sprouted new life. Wild Huckleberry and Blackberry bushes were sufficiently abundant to offer a savory treat along the hike–these were *not* the large seedy kind. *These* berries were smaller and sweeter; a natural trail mix, and perfect for snacking on or making homemade blackberry pies,

The journey to Ross Lake was *almost* as much fun as the time we spent there. We all heard the rumors that bears, packs of wild dogs, and wolves made their homes in the woods and in the land surrounding the lake. This only added an element of danger to our adventure. That last stretch before we arrived seemed to change more and more as we drew closer to the lake. The air seemed fresher and cleaner; new varieties of trees and shrubs appeared in greater frequency.

My first view of Ross Lake was exhilarating–the bright surface glistened in the sunlight, framed by trees as far as I could see. The lake was about half a mile long and half a mile wide. Trails spotted the area around the lake, inviting us to explore the lake. We eventually found one trail, winding around the left side of the lake, which became our favorite. The trail snaked back and forth, and over large tree roots in a zigzag pattern, up and down, that challenged the walker or runner to finish the course. There were many small roots of the various tress exposed on the trial, which required the runner to quickly adjust and jump at a moment's notice or risk tripping on them. We followed this path for about a quarter of mile until we came to a small clearing, leading to the water's edge.

We were staring in awe, as we took in the gleaming jewel, when our wonderment soon transformed into an entirely new level of excitement–there were two large docks tied to a large tree, partially extending over the water. Suspended directly over the water, a rope swing (like the rope swing from the movie, *Grown Ups*) hung from the larger branch of the tree. Ron, being the most adventurous member of our party, waited for *no one*. He scurried up high up into the tree, holding the swing in one hand, and gave a shout before launching himself from the branch. We stood below transfixed by the sight of Ron flying above us. Ron let go when he reached the apex of the arc, sending him flying–*arms and legs flailing wildly*–through the cool air. Then at the last possible moment, Ron gathered himself and dived, knifing into and disappearing, beneath the clean clear water and disappearing beneath the clear water.

The swing returned to the dock as Ron emerged from beneath the surface. At that point, it was game on! All of us scurried up the tree and followed Ron's lead, laughing, flying, and disappearing into the waters of Ross Lake. Several hours later, we lay on the docks after consuming our food supply and soaked up the sunshine, marveling at the new playground we just discovered.

The four of us had so much fun that first trip to Ross Lake, that we spent the night up there any chance we could. Never a shortage of imaginary *bad guys* to chase, we somehow found time to cut down branches from which we fashioned fishing poles. Freshly caught trout was our primary source of protein on our overnight excursions–cooked to perfection over the campfire. Those nights spent at Ross Lake were magical; the sky opened up a vast canopy of stars and planets before us. Our group would lie on our backs and count the satellites traveling across the sky, which resembled moving stars. Ringing across the still water, one of us would shout to let us know he or she just spied a new shooting star.

One day while digging around the dump for materials to patch up our tree house, we came across a large electric fan that was in good working condition, minus the nicks and bad paint. It was not an easy task getting that thing up to Ross Lake, but as it turned out, it was well worth the effort. After mounting the fan securely to one of the docks, we found an old car battery back at the house that, once charged, still worked just fine. With the battery connected to the fan, and the fan secured to the dock, we were ready to navigate the furthest boundaries of Ross Lake.

From the shore, we saw a floating object in the middle of the lake. We speculated many times wondering what the floating object was; it appeared to be a series of docks formed in a huge square. Now, with our motorized dock, we decided to find out what this mysterious object really was. Once we drew closer, we discovered that this large floating object was really *four docks*–tied together forming a square. In the center, we could see nets in the water with hundreds, if not thousands, of tiny fish swimming frantically., we had come across a small salmon hatchery–owned and maintained by the Tulalip Tribe of Indians. Just as he had shown with the rope swing, Ron lived in the moment; he had donned his goggles and snorkel just before jumping in to join the numerous tiny fish. Even the tiny salmon wasted no time joining the fun, and seemed to be dancing around Ron as he felt them surround him from every conceivable direction. Unable to contain ourselves *any* longer, we soon found ourselves joining Ron and the salmon. The bright reflective surface of the tiny fish sparkled in the sunlight through the translucent water. The sight was like *nothing* I had ever seen before, and the experience was even more extraordinary. As we swam in this huge secondary square lake within Ross Lake, the tiny salmon swam with us creating a fluid outline of us as we explored the depths of the hatchery the salmon and the lake.

During one of our first overnight visits to Ross Lake, we devised a new game that was perfect for such a clean lake. Much like the game, *Follow the Leader* that many children play with their friends at the park or playground, we appointed a leader who dove deep to the bottom, where there were numerous fallen trees, branches, and other debris. The others tailed close behind under these logs and branches, becoming bolder with each dive. Soon, we discovered that if we submerged large empty garbage cans (*upside down*) under the dock or large trees, we could significantly extend our diving time by swimming to an underwater can of air where we could breathe the trapped air. This allowed us to extend our time under water in our game. Several times, two or more of us would be inside the submerged garbage can laughing, talking, and sharing thoughts that only boys of that age knew and did.

Using nearby stones, we built a fire pit on the dock. This was the perfect headlight (and heater) for our electric fan-powered dock. Our trips around the lake under the night sky were easily visible from anyone on shore, especially once we figured out how to keep a fire going on our fan-powered dock. That must have made quite a sight by anybody from shore, a dock slowly cruising around the lake, a fire burning to provide heat and light, and the unmistakable sounds of teenage boys discussing the mysterious of life, girls, girls and girls.

From an early age, I have felt the protective hand of the Creator watching over me, protecting me and keeping me safe from danger. The dangers from which I required rescue were not always the malicious villains or sworn enemies that one might imagine. Most often, the Creator simply rescued me from the consequences of my own actions. One hot, summer night, at the age of fifteen, while spending an overnight campout with my friends up at Ross Lake, the beer flowed faster than my tolerance could handle. I was good for about four beers before I felt the familiar buzz take over. By that point, I could feel the euphoria cloud my senses. Thoughts flowed freely and a sense of warmth came over me, taking my judgment with it.

I cracked fifth beer, and took a drink. Beads of sweat formed on my forehead, and I could feel the gentle warm breeze across my back, where the humidity and perspiration drenched my t-shirt. AC/DC and Def Leppard rocked the portable cassette player–a good supply of D cell batteries could keep a party going most of the night.

I am still not certain to this day, and might never know, why I decided to go into the lake that night, but I do know that I thought nothing of it at the time. I did not question the potential hazard, or think that I was a mere mortal capable of succumbing to any number of unpleasant outcomes. I had removed my t-shirt a few minutes earlier. It was clinging to my skin in the humid night air.

The moon was full and lit up the lake like a jewel. My mind was following the beat of the music, the feverish guitar riff by *Def Leppard's,* Steve Clark, and the hypnotic image of the moon reflecting its image back to me from the lake. I watched the reflection as I walked up to the edge of the water, not paying attention or caring if my feet got wet. I could feel my body fall into the rhythm of the music as the alcohol emptied me of all inhibition.

That image of the full moon on the water was within arm's reach by now. All I had to do was reach forward and I could touch it. As I reached for the flickering image, I could tell that my fingertips were only a few inches to short. The music sounded muffled for some reason, but I paid it no attention. I felt good. My friends were here with me and we were having the time of our lives.

I never did take another sip from that beer. I was not even sure where I had set it down, but it was out of sight and I gave it no more consideration. The feelings and thoughts that ran through my mind seemed to have more clarity, no distractions from the bustle of modern life. No drama to distract me from reaching a little farther for the moon. I reached out again. I extended my hand toward the glowing orb as it shone and flickered *above* the water.

The time from when I was standing at the shore, watching the reflection of the moon on the surface of the water, and until that time, when I was below the surface reaching up to the moon in the sky had vanished. I had no recollection of wading into the water, and no memory as to why I would do that in the first place. Now that I was beneath the surface, I felt peace and serenity.

A hand forced its way through the water, startling me. It grasped me by my hair and pulled me upward, tugging my limp body toward the surface. Shouts from my sister and friends penetrated the hazy dream-like trance I had entered. Once lying on the shore, I looked up at the faces of my friends and my sister. They were still shouting, but now, it was more a matter of chewing me out for scaring them.

Of course, they demanded an explanation, for which I had none, but they were right to be concerned. I had walked out of sight for a few minutes to gaze at the lake. For all they knew, I was peeing. I could have easily drowned and it would have been awhile before they would have even thought to search for me.

The experiences I had growing up with Ross Lake–virtually in my backyard–had a profound impact on my childhood. It was the perfect place to learn about the outdoors and to experience what mother earth has to offer if we simply take the time to listen, observe, and grow.

Chapter 6: Marysville Pillchuck High School and Partying

And I pray for wisdom and I prayer for power
　　And I pray for being ready in the final hour
　　And I pray for those who keep judging men in the streets
　　And I pray for my friends and my enemies
　　– SupaMan, "Prayer Loop"

It was May 18, 1980, and I was fourteen years old. As an active member of the youth group in Trinity Lutheran Church in Everett, Washington. I was excited to attend a summer retreat in the San Juan Islands. Our group was blessed to have a fairly large cruise boat named *The Christian*. That day, we were out on the beautiful clear waters of the San Juan Islands, enjoying the sun and a faint breeze, which carried the refreshing ocean scent across our deck, where I stood talking with several other members of the youth group. Everyone wore a smile. Around us, we could hear the laughter of other friends as they joked around. A few members of the group were standing near the edge, pointing at dolphin or whale sightings. All that peace and calm came to an abrupt end with the sound of an enormous *BOOM*!

It was similar to the sonic boom of jet breaking the sound barrier, but *much* louder. Shock waves shot through our bones, giving the impression we could feel the blast as much as we could hear it. In my spirit, I knew that something big had happened, and it was something different from anything else I or anyone else on that boat had ever experienced. The Captain of *The Christian* also knew something had occurred–something unusual. I watched, as he returned with a radio and set it up where we could all listen. The radio crackled to life, with static hissing until he adjusted the tuning to the right frequency.

"*...Mount St. Helens has just erupted!*" exclaimed the announcer, panic evident in his voice. "*I say again–Mount St. Helens has just erupted, spewing a huge towering cloud of ash into the atmosphere!*" We listened to the radio for the remainder of the day, checking for updates, and praying for those who lost their lives in the eruption. After we returned to shore, and all the youth returned to their homes, I sat glued in front of the television, as reports came in describing the impact and devastation of the eruption.

It was thirty-seven years ago when Mount St. Helens erupted in Skamania County, State of Washington. Approximately fifty-seven people died in the eruption, and there was about 1.1 billion dollars in property damage. The eruption caused a partial collapse of the volcano's flank, and deposited ash in eleven states and five Canadian provinces.

I did not feel like I fit in with the rest of my classmates at Marysville Middle School. I was shy. At that awkward age, it seems like kids can find any reason to feel inadequate in some way. I was no different in that respect. I had a diverse range of interests. I loved music and sports–two talents that were prevalent in the paternal side of my family. As depicted in many popular movies from the eighties, such as *The Breakfast Club, St. Elmo's Fire,* and *Weird Science* kids from middle school through high school form cliques and see one another in these, often cruel, stereotypes without ever trying to know the individual. Maybe I could have made life easier on myself by surrendering to the pressure, accepting the stereotype assigned by my peers. It was not that easy. I was Native, and white, a musician, and an athlete. In time, I would even feel at home in the partying club.

I started playing the clarinet in middle school. Music came easy; in fact, it seemed to run in the family. My father, Kenny and his siblings, Elaine, Darlene, and Ron sang and played guitar with Grandpa Charlie on the fiddle and Grandma Ellen on the guitar. Everybody sang along. It was not long before I became just as hooked on playing an instrument as my family was.

Having played for several years in AAU Soccer (Amateur Athletic Union), I understood the concept of teamwork. We had a local youth soccer team comprised of young boys from the city of Marysville. Soccer practice was fun and something I looked forward to as a youth. Andy Boursaw's dad was our coach and we were blessed to have him coaching our team.

Over the next several years, our team would learn quickly the many complex concepts of the game. We began to win more than we lost, which resulted in our team moving up into a stronger bracket, where we met the *Everett Strikers*–our archrival. No matter what we did, we always lost to the Strikers, a team of select soccer players. We did not give up–we kept practicing and improving each year. Players came and left as we grew older, but the core of the team remained intact–including Rich Hansen, Mark Zanoni, Ron and Dan Hartman, Kurt Liefer, Todd Cort, Fred Stevens, Shawn Ledford, Russ Boulding, Chris Castle, and Andy Boursaw.

Our perseverance finally paid off with a resounding victory over our hated rivals, the Strikers, on their home field. Our players jumped in excitement as we finally realized as a team when we finally defeated the Strikers five to three!

I can still remember the Snow Game at the soccer fields in Monroe Washington. Fred Stevens had recently moved up from California and joined our team. He proved to be an important missing link for our defense as a very good middle fullback. Mark aka *the Z Man* became a superb goal tender, with Ron Hartman and I rounding out the defense.

Our other good friend, Rich Hansen was a very capable striker with a nose for scoring goals, and Chris Castle, a select soccer player himself began playing at a very high level as our mid fielder. That game was a once-in- a-lifetime game, as the snow started to fall right at kickoff. By halftime, the entire field was covered in pure white snow making conditions perfect for some great slide kicks, traps, and other basic moves associated with the game of soccer. We went on to win this game in overtime with Rich Hansen scoring the game-winning goal on a break away! This pattern would repeat itself in High School, as our Soccer team would go on to pose a serious challenge to Cascade Soccer team who had won the WESCO Soccer title the last 10 years.

My friends from the neighborhood, Ron Hartman in particular, often invited me to shoot baskets in their driveway. Starting as a very casual pastime, I grew to love the sport. I decided when I reached the seventh grade that I would try out for the team. That first day of tryouts did not turn out well. I had *no* idea how to run basic drills, like the three-man weave, two-on-one drill, or even the left-handed layup. When the coach cut me from the team, I was neither surprised nor devastated. By that time, it did not matter–I had the basketball bug and there was no stopping me.

I returned my eighth grade year to try out again. This time, I felt proud to show how much I had learned, how my skills had developed since that disastrous first day of tryouts in seventh grade. Still, the coaching staff cut me from the team. The kids, with whom I was competing, had been playing basketball together as long as they were old enough to run and carry a basketball. Just as I had been practicing soccer from a young age, these kids had a substantial advantage over me, and I was not about to allow this to discourage me.

Ninth grade tryouts came around before I knew it. I was determined to make the team, working on agility, aim, and handling the ball. Soccer had prepared me in ways that no other sport could. I was more coordinated in my footwork than anyone else; my speed was unmatched, especially the lung crushing sprints from one end of the field to the other. The progress I had made from the last two annual tryouts won the attention of the coaches. I made it through the first day of tryouts, an astounding feat in itself, but once again, they cut me from the team. This time, at least, I made it to the last day of tryouts and the feedback on my improvement was encouraging.

Between my eighth and ninth grade tryouts, while I was working so hard at refining my basketball skills, I continued to cultivate my interest in music. Starting with clarinet, I soon expanded my proficiency to alto clarinet, the bass clarinet, and the contra bass clarinet. Music came easy to me, and learning a new instrument seemed like an almost effortless endeavor.

Toward the end of my eighth grade year, I discovered a new genre of music. Jazz captivated me with its tempo, creativity, and rhythm. I knew—when I first heard the school jazz band playing that I would be trying out for a chair. Much like basketball, Jazz Band would be an accomplishment I earned through a great deal of effort. When I expressed interest in auditioning for the clarinet section, the band teacher explained that jazz band did not have a clarinet section. Again, like basketball, I knew I would need to try harder and work harder to counterbalance the odds against me.

I borrowed a second hand alto saxophone and practiced all summer. I was up for the challenge—not only did I have to learn a completely different instrument, but I knew I would have to compete against other saxophone players who had the advantage of playing three or four years longer than I had. I was no stranger to playing an instrument, and clarinet, like the alto saxophone, is in the woodwind family. I knew that the only equalizer between the more experienced saxophone players and me would be the quality and quantity of practice I completed over the summer.

When I returned for my freshman year at Marysville Pilchuck High School, I won Third Chair in the *three-person* alto saxophone section! I was acquiring new skills, gaining confidence in my abilities, and learning that sufficient determination could push life's obstructions to the side where they belong. In those years of my life, I was too close to the situation to see the lessons I was being taught

A new nemesis was on the horizon. It would deplete my spirit and impede my relationship with God. Clutched in its talons from eighth grade until the age of thirty-seven, alcohol had the sinister ability to remedy any number of serious problems, while gradually becoming a more serious problem. It was the perfect remedy for the crippling effects of shyness. As the warmth began to spread through my body and the buzz came on with each sip, I could feel all the tension and worries slipping away. No longer afraid that, when initiating conversation with one of my peers, I might say the wrong thing or say it the wrong way, I now had all the poise I needed to get through an otherwise frightening experience.

My good friend Jodi McCory and I were attending classes at Marysville Junior High School one particularly sunny day. The lunch bell rang, and we joined our classmates in the stampede. Jodi and I were walking past our lockers when we heard our names called out from the midst of the crowd, *"Duane! Jodi!"* I heard two distinct voices calling us, and I recognized them immediately. It was my sister, Marie, and Jodi's sister, Heidi, walking toward us. Laughing and talking as they came closer, I could see that they each held an *Arctic Circle* soft drink in their hand. Marie handed me her soft drink and Heidi offered hers to Jodi. "We're taking you two off campus for lunch today!" Marie explained. *How cool!* I thought.

Jodi and I followed them through the hallways and out to the parking lot where I spotted Marie's red and white Pinto. After Jodi and I climbed in back, we took a sip from the Arctic Circle cup and discovered it was *Boons Farm Strawberry Wine!* We pulled out of the parking lot with *Prince* booming from the car stereo. Over the next fifteen to twenty minutes, Jodi and I managed to finish most of our wine before we returned to class. Exiting Marie's Pinto, we realized that, if anyone discovered our secret, we were in serious trouble. We walked through the hallway, laughing and stumbling occasionally, on our way to our next class. I became more aware that it would not be easy to conceal the smell of alcohol even if we could act sober. I broke out the very best defense I had against alcohol breath–*Hubba Bubba* bubble gum. Chewing furiously, we managed to make it to our next class without drawing too much attention to ourselves. As I entered the classroom, I sauntered past several of my classmates, who had been chatting in a small cluster near the door. One classmate extracted his attention away from the dialogue and focused on *me. Maybe I looked remarkably handsome that day–or maybe my cereal bowl haircut was finally getting the attention it deserved. Not likely.*

I carried myself in a fashion that was alien to my usual introverted manner. No longer shy and self-doubting, I discovered a more deliberate, assertive stride; I sustained eye contact instead of allowing my gaze to retreat downward. Even the witty aspect of my personality emerged once the wine liberated me from the shackles of timidity.

If one–*or more*–classmates discovered I was drunk from that brief encounter, it would not be long before the teacher came to the same conclusion. I wasted no time finding my desk and settling in. I had no experience pretending to be sober. As I sat through class, I deliberated on my best course of action. *I can't look at Jodi–we'll both crack up*, I thought. As if the effects of alcohol were not enough to contend with, trying to keep a straight face is nearly impossible when *forbidden* from laughing. It is, in fact, a certainty that hysterical laughter will ensue when there is a great deal of effort invested in preventing it.

To my horror, I suddenly realized that I was still holding my cup of Boon's Berry Wine! I glanced over at Jodi, and saw that she also held her cup of wine in her hand. Seeing no other option, we quickly finished off the wine in class. We made it through the remainder of the class without raising the suspicion of the teacher. It remains a mystery how we avoided detection that afternoon. It could have been so easy for a classmate to give us away or for a teacher to detect that slight unsteadiness in our gait.

I was terrified to start high school, and rightly so. In the early to middle 1980's, incoming freshman were considered *free game.* Apprehension by an upper classman could result in being duct-taped to the flagpole in your underwear, or having the displeasure of *Swampmore* for a disparaging new title. There were several irrigation ditches to catch the heavy rainfall, which occurred about three hundred twenty-four days of the year. The classical introduction ceremony for freshmen and sophomores commenced with participating seniors gathering at the bus stop, ready to capture the unfortunate student stepping off the bus. Seniors took their captive to the irrigation ditch and tossed him into the filthy water. Emerging from the swift current, with some effort, the Swampmore could look forward to calling home for a change of clothes.

The prospect of having to endure humiliation at the flagpole was unthinkable. Ron, being a year older than I was, had already faced that terrible first day one year earlier. At least I was lucky to have the benefit of knowing what the inevitable first day would bring. Ron was *not* duct-taped to the flagpole in his underwear for everyone to see. Ron simply refused to appease the seniors' appetite for revenge. For his size, he was amazingly strong and fast; Ron could out-run good athletes without showing signs of exhaustion. His reputation among seniors only made him the perfect target for the Swampmore ritual, and they were more than happy to tell him they would be waiting for him. It was not completely clear why they felt so compelled to teach him a lesson, but more than likely, it all began when he failed to show any sign of fear or respect. If anything, he taunted them with his cavalier response to their attempted intimidation tactics. Nothing worked. The more threats they issued, the wider Ron's smile became.

That rainy first day of school finally arrived, and Ron seemed completely unaffected by the group of seniors waiting for him. He smiled as he exited the bus. Then, without warning, he took off in a sprint, catching them by surprise. The chase was on, as the bus driver and other kids looked on. Ron jumped back and forth, crossing the swamp unpredictably, and avoiding the clutches of his pursuers with each move. I have to believe that Ron had this all planned the way it finally went down; it was too perfect and he was too confident in the outcome. A senior reached out to grab Ron when it seemed he was perfectly within reach. He missed by a narrow margin when Ron suddenly changed direction, catching him off guard and throwing him off balance. Waving his arms wildly to regain his balance, but to no avail, the senior knew for those last few seconds what would happen no matter how hard he tried. He fell backward into the irrigation ditch, while Ron smiled and waved *goodbye* to him, now thrashing to escape the cold, murky waters.

It was one year later, and my turn had finally come. Thanks to Ron's advice, I knew better than to take my chances as he had. I worried about how I would deal with this day for an entire year. The solution was so simple; I am surprised I had not thought of this earlier.

Just before that first day of high school, my sister, Marie surprised me with a trip to the Everett Mall, where she took me shopping for an entire wardrobe upgrade. In 1982, *Hash*, *Star*, and *Lawmen Jeans* were the symbol of prestige; they were the pass you needed to move in the *popular* circles. I had been wearing a particularly unattractive pair of glasses that year–dark, plastic, and thick. The optometrist fitted me with my first pair of contact lenses. Switching out the glasses for contacts made such a profound change in my appearance, I almost did not recognize myself in the mirror.

There are many terrifying thoughts that run through a kid's mind his first day of high school It was never easy to fit in under the best of circumstances, so when I no longer had to worry about wearing "*birth control glasses*" and outdated clothing, I had such a wave of relief come over me. When I arrived at school, and stepped off the school bus, I would have a pack of seniors waiting to pounce. Before I could come up with a plan, Marie took care of it. "Nobody's gonna mess with my *Bro Wa!*" She said and offered me a ride to school. That would do it. I would avoid the entire bus ride and take away their opportunity–some other unsuspecting freshman would have to take my place.

Marie was a senior when I was a freshman. She had a very gracious group of friends, including Heidi who was Jodi's sister. Marie, Heidi, and her friends often invited Jodi and me to hang out, which gave us instant access to the best keggers, senior parties on Friday nights, and cruising Colby Avenue on Saturday nights. Jodi had a number of friends, some of whom I considered friends of mine as well. One such friend was a girl with striking red hair and a gift for music.

I have many fond memories of watching Jodi and Patti stroll around the school campus cracking their famous one-liners at every opportunity. Often, Patti and Jodi would meander their way to my direction, as I shot the breeze with my group of friends. Jodi's friend, Patti, had a nickname that caught on very quickly. If you have ever watched any of the *Peanuts* cartoons, featuring Charlie Brown, Lucy, Snoopy, Linus, and Beethoven, then you might remember Lucy's sidekick, *Peppermint Patty*. The *Peanuts* character was cool, had her best friend's back in all situations, and referred to her friend, Marcie as "Sir." Patty Schemel embraced the nickname given by her best friend, Jodi.

Patty's gift of music became well known in high school. She was known as the second-best drummer in our high school–second only to the legendary Chris Kutz! Chris and Patty were close friends and they helped each other become even better musicians. At our ten-year class reunion, most of my class did not even recognize me. Many of my classmates thought that I was the husband to one of our female classmates! (Remember, at graduation I stood 5 foot 9 inches and weighed only 155 pounds. I was not known for causing a scene or drawing attention to myself–I was just that guy who was *around*.)

At our ten year reunion, I stood between 5 foot 11 inches and 6 foot tall and weighed about one-hundred-ninety-five pounds of lean muscle, sported a goatee and long hair. My appearance was the result of the time I had been working in the North Central Washington Drug Task Force. I carried a chip on my shoulder, so to speak, and I was not taking any crap from anyone at that time in my life! Back in high school, I was known as one of the partiers, but I did not drink at my Senior Party, or at my 10, 20, and 30-year reunions. By the time I had reached the age of thirty-seven, I had quit drinking completely.

As the night progressed at our ten-year reunion, my classmates began to loosen up considerably with all the alcohol that was flowing. The buzz that made its way from one circle of friends to another was that Patty Schemel was the most famous person from our graduating class. *Peppermint Patty* was now the drummer for Courtney Love's all-girl rocker band, *Hole*! Patty was close to the late Kurt Cobain, the "Godfather of Grunge" and who also originated from Seattle, Washington. Patty's music career has been a tremendous success. Just to mention a few projects, she joined Hole (1992-1998), Courtney Love (solo), Juliette and the Licks, Upset (2013), and has formed her own band.

After the night ended at our ten-year reunion, I returned home to my residence in Okanogan County at 779 1st Avenue South. A few days later, I was washing the dishes in the big old sink common to older houses. The television was on in the next room, tuned to MTV. When I heard that a segment featuring the new album by the *Red Hot Chili Peppers* was coming on in the next hour, it caught my attention. I stepped into the room just in time to hear the DJ from MTV introduce the new song from Hole. To my delight, I watched my old friend from the class of 1985, Patty Schemel drumming for the band, *Hole!*

I have not spoken to her since high school, but I will always consider her a great friend. One of the best memories I have from high school is watching her and Jodi walking around the campus, and often frequenting the area that my friends and I hung out. I loved hearing Jodi and Patty crack their one-liners about anything, including me, as I seemed to be an easy target! I value those jokes and the laughter–they were good medicine for all of us. Once we boarded the big yellow school bus, Patty would predictably pull out her drumsticks and hone her craft on the back of the seat in front of her, using the leather as a drum set until we arrived at our destination.

Mr. Bowen coached the soccer team at MPHS. He had a love for soccer, but his first love was track and field. As a result, the soccer team was in great shape, but lacked the technical skills to advance to a higher level. That year, we won four out of fifteen possible games.

One of my good friends, Rich Hansen, split time between varsity and junior varsity. Ron Hartman was the star of the varsity team. He was exceptionally fast, and had made a name for himself in the game. Known as "The Sweeper," Ron was selected WESCO First Team Defender twice while in high school.

When soccer season ended, basketball began. I continued to practice hard during the summer. Those two consecutive years of not making the team were crushing, but I did not allow them to discourage me. That first year, I did not even know what a three-man weave was. The next year, I showed enough improvement to make it to the last day of tryouts before the coaching staff cut me. I was determined not to allow that to happen one more year. I played on the MJAA basketball team under Coach Darrel Enick. He was the first coach to show confidence in my abilities. At the MJAA level first draft, all the players practiced drills for several days while the coaches observed and took notes. Coach Enick drafted me for his squad, along with others I had played ball with over the summer: John Green, Jr Lukes, Chuck Calk Looking, Junior Jones, and others. We played a different brand of basketball, known as *Rez Ball* back in those days. While other teams were using a more structured offense, we were *running and gunning*. Our tempo, unlike theirs, was much faster and the tactic was as simple as it was effective–we drove hard and took our shots often. Coach Enick encouraged us to play in the style that worked best for us. When I missed a shot, I expected Coach to sub me out, as was customary in school basketball. Coach Enick built up our confidence, and inspired us to work harder. He never yelled at us. One time, during a time-out, his only comment to me was, "Duane, shoot the ball!"

As the season progressed, we played more as a unit than we had before. We did not win every game, but we earned the respect from some of the other teams and coaches. We heard compliments about the progress we were making as individual players and as a team. Coach Enick granted us the freedom to play without fearing every misstep, which in turn, gave us greater opportunities to learn from our mistakes.

With another year of practice and a new level of confidence while training under Coach Enick, I was ready for basketball tryouts on the high school team. I had learned the art of defense under Coach Enick, how to use my speed above-average foot dexterity to lock down and cut off an offensive player. The game itself seemed to have decelerated for me; I understood the basic concepts in my subconscious, and no longer had to think through every move. I could anticipate the moves of my opponents, using my agility and speed to my advantage. I was not on par with the elite players in my grade, but I was gaining ground fast. Between drills, I would admire the skill of the juniors and seniors during their practice.

In my sophomore year, the varsity team was very successful and rated nationally. All my time and effort paid off that year. I made it through tryouts and the coach gave me a place on the team as a defensive player. I loved every minute of the practice and games. I had become a considerable force as a defensive player, and enjoyed the challenge of shutting down every offensive player with whom they paired me. As a part time starter, the coach usually paired me with his nephew, Darwin Enick. (Darwin and I would meet again in our adult life, but on opposing sides.)

We complemented each other well. We were both Native Americans; he was a very polished shooter, and I was becoming a solid defense player. At the end of the season, the coaches called each player in to a closed-door meeting to review the player's progress, and provide suggestions on areas that needed improvement. They told each player at that time where they stood and what they could expect the following year.

As I entered the room, I saw three coaches sitting at the table: Mike Lowery, the varsity coach, Brad Stokes, the junior varsity coach, and Andy Delagons, my sophomore coach. I sat down at the table and listened as coach Lowery expressed his thanks for all my effort and dedication. Each coach took turns offering a compliment on my defense, my commitment to improving my skills, and sticking with the game after enduring a string of disappointments. Then the conversation shifted to their plans for next year, and where I fit in, given the information they had at that time. Coach Lowery explained that next year was going to be very competitive; a group of very talented freshmen was coming up, players like Kurt Sunitch, Sean Phillips, and Chad Laughlin. The coach continued, "We want you to try out, and make it, but we can't guarantee you a spot on the team with what we know." I was in shock at hearing this. I could feel anger boiling up inside. *What a thing for a coach to tell a young man!* I thought. I said the only thing I could think of at the time.

"What do I need to work on?" The words came out of my mouth before I knew I was even speaking. Coach Stokes seemed surprised, but pleased, at my response. Coach Lowery was clearly taking the lead in leveling the hammer.

"Well, ball handling for one thing, "said Coach Lowery. " You need to make better decisions on the court, when to pass, and when *not* to. . ." I was listening and taking mental notes. Part of me felt like the room was getting darker, and the voices were fading out as all I could think about were countless days and hours practicing to catch up to my peers who had started earlier than I had. "Your place on the JV team isn't guaranteed because you had a late start. This goes for your senior year as well. We'll place you based on how you perform in tryouts, but that's all we know right now."

"Thank you for meeting with me," I said, managing to contain the demoralizing feeling that had come crushing down on me. The four of us stood and shook hands. "And I appreciate your honesty–I know what I need to work on."

As I was walking out, I felt let down, unappreciated, and that much of what was said came with a very condescending tone. I *had* to eat it. To argue or protest would get me nowhere. Worse yet, I would look like I lacked the professionalism to take critique in a constructive manner. Again, I would take a hit. I did the only thing I could do–I pushed those painful emotions deep down, and asked for more. What they said was true–I started basketball later than the others had, but I worked very hard to catch up to them, finally made the team, and gave everything I had. *How could they tell me this now after all that?*

The game of life was testing me. I thought to myself, *who are they to tell me this? I will show them!* This was my first critical crossroad in my young life. I had a choice to make–I could accept what the coaches said. I put up a good fight. I achieved far more than anyone could have imagined. That was the safe choice. On the other hand, I could continue to practice hard over the summer and force myself to beat the competition, even those who were taller and had been playing longer. The odds were not in my favor, but I was developing a character trait that would follow me to the Marine Corps, Bureau of Indian Affairs as a federal agent, in law enforcement as Chief of Police, and finally, into ministry where I now tell my Christian brothers and sisters the original message, the original covenants taught by the historical Jesus. When I was eventually prosecuted for crimes I did not commit, which slandered my reputation and my family name, I faced the same kind of choice as I did that day sitting before the coaches in that room, but on a *much* grander scale.

I decided at that moment, that no person or coach would tell me I would fail, or that I could not perform a job. That summer I worked even harder at handling the ball, playing with other kids in the neighborhood every chance I had–keeping in mind that I needed to make a noticeable change in passing and shooting to teammates, and knowing the right times to take the shot. More than that, I got serious. I hit the library and checked out autobiographies by famous athletes, such as Willie Mays, OJ Simpson, Hank Aaron, and Jerry West. I read technical books on the sport, specifically looking for tips on improving my decision-making skills. I began to recognize a common thread within their stories–they had a tremendous amount of determination and they all used negative, critical comments to fuel their success.

When I arrived my junior year for tryouts, I watched the sophomores warming up. Every one of them was taller, faster, and seemed far more confident than I was. I decided at that moment to fight for every ball and to give my best effort in every drill, especially running the baselines. My accuracy had improved significantly; I made enough shots to make it on the junior varsity team.

Junior varsity coach, Scott Stokes had a compassionate and supportive personality. He always seemed to have a smile on his face. Coach Lowery seemed to like a certain type of player, and standing at five-nine, I was not the dream player he had in mind. I lacked the self-confidence in jump shots and running offense to stand out among the taller, younger players.

At the start of the season, I could see that my time on the court would be limited. In fact, all the underclassmen were ahead of me. All the effort I invested in making the team was starting to seem like a lost cause, which did nothing to help my self-confidence. All that would soon change, as my breakout game was just on the horizon.

The varsity squad made the playoffs that year in 1984. The team was hot–lead by the guard combination of Keith Brashler and Clark Easterbrook. Clark was a junior and this was his second year playing on the varsity team. He was, by far, the best guard to emerge in the MPHS system in recent years. Since the varsity squad made the playoffs, the junior varsity team was able to play additional games. Then, flu had struck a number of players on our team, and the coaching staff asked several members of the junior varsity team to suit up for the playoffs. In those next few games, I played a substantially larger proportion of the game than any time before.

Marysville was playing at the rival team's gym, and the junior varsity team was up first. There are certain moments in life that, looking back, had a lasting and profound impact on my future. One of these moments came in the last few minutes of this game. During the first three quarters, my performance was unexceptional but adequate. I looked up into the bleachers, where I could see the varsity team with Coach Lowery watching the game. I was on the bench when another player fouled out.

Coach Stokes called my number and I went into the game.

With 20 seconds left in the game, we scored a basket and the opposing team scored immediately after. We fouled, putting the other team on the foul line. Our center, Lane Shinnick, was intense and said to block out and get the rebound. I heard someone else say that we had no more time-outs left. *If he makes the shot, it won't matter anyway*, I thought. *They'll be up three points, and there's no way we'll have enough time to score twice.* In 1984, there was no three-point line. Lane, looking at me, said, "Duane, be ready!"

I nodded affirmatively, but thinking his statement was odd. I looked at my teammates, seeing the same intensity on their faces. The opposing player stepped up to the free throw line, and making two deliberate bounces, raised the ball over his head. Letting it fly in a perfect arc, it swished through the net. Lane grabbed the ball under the net, and stepped behind the baseline. Looking at me before the pass, he yelled, "Go!" At that moment, everything seemed to happen in slow motion. As the ball came toward me, and I stretched out my hands to catch, I remember seeing Lane sprint past me shouting, something to our teammates. I turned with the ball and began dribbling. As I approached the half court line, I thought about all the people watching, especially the varsity team and Coach Lowery. It seemed certain we were going to lose anyway, so I decided to have some fun. An opposing player raced toward me. This seemed like the perfect time to try the unexpected. I reverted to my days playing Rez Ball. I dribbled the ball around my back, and with my right hand, pushed the ball through my legs, deliberately exposing the ball to the oncoming player. His face lit up. It must have seemed certain, in his mind, that because of my carelessness with the ball, that he would steal with minimal effort.

At the last moment, just before he could lay hands on the ball, I reached out with my left hand and made a hard cut with the ball to my left, leaving him behind me as I moved even closer to the basket. I could hear the crowd yelling frantically at me, but I was unable to make out anything. Everything seemed to move in slow motion. My mind was racing; processing every possible combination of moves from my current position to being able to sink a shot.

Another player came at me, and as I came out of a spin, I lost yet another defensive player behind me. This player, a particularly tall African American, had the ability to jump higher than anyone I had ever seen. His feet seemed to float so far off the court with no visible effort. I dribbled to the right side of the basket, as he followed me to the hoop. *There's no way I'm gonna let this guy block me*, I thought. I could see Lane Shinnick and my other teammates yelling at me. I vaulted into the air, watching as the tall defense player I had left behind, followed my jump, intent on blocking my shot. In these split seconds, I thought to myself, *what would Michael Jordan do?* As I tried to maintain control of my body midair, I double-pumped the ball. All of this happened in a matter of seconds, but my perception was much different. Holding the ball close to my chest until my opponent attempted to block and floated past me. He missed his opportunity to sweep the ball out of my hand. I was still in the air, but most definitely past the apex of my jump. Just as I was about to descend, I took my only opportunity and pumped the ball back up in the ready position. With no one left to stop me, I focused on the rim, and released the ball. Split seconds passed more like minutes as I watched the ball, rotating like a planet in slow motion. I could still see the familiar black lines of the basketball, as it arched up and drifted above the hoop. It descended with a swish through the net as I landed steadily on my feet.

Well that was fun, I thought as I walked off the court. I knew the coaches would not be happy with my taking so many liberties at the end. I made the decision to be creative with the ball, but as I saw it, we were not going to win no matter *what* we did. As I continued off the court, I heard the thunder of everyone yelling and stomping their feet on the bleachers.

Before I could even turn around, my teammates knocked me to the floor. All that yelling and excitement was starting to make sense. I looked up at the scoreboard and realized that I just tied the game with my shot. We returned to the bench. The game was now in overtime. Coach Stokes looked at me and smiled. Gary Rumbaugh, one of my teammates, looked at me with a huge smile and said, "Duane, your shot is *on*!" Gary and I would often stay after practice to work on shooting. There were times that I would make several shots in a row, all *net* shots. Gary, too, would have those moments when he was hot, and every shot seemed to be dead on. We often remarked, during these streaks of unbreakable accuracy, that his shot or my shot *was dead on*!

Coach Stokes told us to run the offense. "Set it up and look for layups. Each possession is *critical*!" We returned to the court.

I looked at Gary and said, "I'm shooting the ball. Set up a screen for me when I call out the motion offense, roll to the basket and I'm gonna let it fly." We won the tip off. With the ball in my hands, I dribbled across the half court.

"Motion!" Coach Stokes called out, as the opposing team moved into position, ready to defend the basket. I called the play, motion number one. Gary moved from his position to set up the screen. I came around, feeling confident and in control, and watched Gary closely, waiting for him to roll to the basket. If he could get open, I would pass the ball to him. If he were not, I would dribble back around and pass the ball to the off guard. Instead, without even looking at Gary, I stopped on the high side of the screen and released the ball. As the ball left my hand, I could hear the coaches screaming, "What are you doing?" The ball swished through the net and we retreated to play defense.

One of my teammates told Coach Stokes, "Don't worry, Duane is on!" My teammates could feel impending victory, and began setting up screens that were not in the offense. I dribbled around the screen and shot the ball. Every shot was a swish! That day, the *underdogs* won the game by eight to ten points. I still remember the varsity players yelling and cheering us on. It was a big victory, boosting our confidence for the upcoming senior year.

At the end of my junior year, the coaches had their annual meeting with each player to talk about his progress and to offer insight to what next year might look like. I could tell that Coach Stokes liked me. Coach Mike Lowery had his own idea as to what a varsity basketball player should look like. Based on last year's meeting, and from every interaction I had with him, I could tell that he was not in the market for a five-nine, half Native, aspiring basketball player. This year, just as before, he said there would be some competitive new players coming up, and that he could not guarantee a place for me next year on the team. I asked the same question that year as I had the year before, "What do I need to work on?"

"Offense, scoring baskets, making jump shots." Coach Lowery offered up another obvious list of skills that typically contribute to winning a basketball game. To be fair, he feigned no interest in having me on the team, whether I improved or not. The point that I was *supposed* to get from his advice was that he was looking for somebody else. *Anybody* else.

At that time, my older sister, Marie, had an African American boyfriend. John was easy to talk to, and took the time to hang out with me. He also happened to be a very talented basketball player. It was not long before I told him how I was trying make it through senior tryouts, and how I had been forced to fight for every minute I got on the court. He agreed to teach me how to improve my jump shots, including a number of techniques that would make a big difference on the court. We spent the entire summer playing basketball pickup games at the Boeing Field Basketball Gymnasium. I learned how to read a defensive opponent, shoot a mid-range jump shot, drive to the basket and score over opponents with pump fakes, and reverse lay-ups.

During this time, I experienced a second brush with death. On our way back from Boeing Field one cloudy day, John, Marie, and I were on the highway that eventually turned into Interstate 5. The speed limit back then was fifty-five miles per hour. John was driving his car and Marie was in the passenger seat. She was not wearing a seat belt, even though John told both of us to put it on. I was in the back seat, exhausted after playing so many games, just trying to relax. I looked through the windshield, and could see that we were approaching the intersection just before the onramp to I-5. The light was green. I felt something stirring inside me, like something was wrong, but I had no idea what it could be. Then I looked out the window to my right. I felt my heart sink to my stomach as I saw a car enter the intersection and speed directly toward us. Everything seemed to slow down, as if in slow motion as it had on the court when I tied the game. I noticed Marie was not wearing her seatbelt, so I leaned forward and wrapped my arms around the seat, holding Marie as tightly as I could. The incoming car struck the right fender and hood area. All I could think at the time was, *hang on to Marie!* John's car spun around several times until we came to a stop on shoulder of the other side of the intersection.

John looked visibly shaken. I hit my head hard on the seat in front of me. I could feel my heart pounding through my chest. Marie hit her head hard on the glove compartment. I could hear her crying and screaming. *Praise God* we had no serious injuries. The driver of the other car was not seriously injured, but like us, very shaken up. Even though I did not recognize or acknowledge it at the time, God was working in my life, keeping me safe to complete His plans for me.

As the beginning of my senior year approached, I continued to run ball at Boeing gym. I played in a number of Indian Basketball tournaments that summer, running ball with Junior Jones, B.J. Jones, J.R. Lukes, Mike Maltos, and others. We played teams from Seattle, featuring "White Boy Roy" and Vernon Diggs, and sometimes teams from the Swimmish Tribe and Lummi Nation. My friend, Mark Fry, had a girlfriend who was from Lummi, so he would occasionally jump ship and join them.

When basketball tryouts arrived my senior year, I was nervous but confident. I was unprepared for the high turnout of players who were also competing with me for a place on the team. There were over one hundred who showed up for the first night of tryouts. One of the new faces was a young sophomore with whom I had played in tournaments that summer. Mark Fry would go on to be one of the finest Native American basketball players and win almost every major Native American basketball tournament for the next ten to fifteen years. On the very first day of tryouts, the coaches had everyone line up on the baseline. They cut over sixty players that night. Mark and I both made it to the second round.

Mark was a completely different brand of player. His talent for the game was unmatched by anyone playing varsity ahead of me, or for that matter, that I had ever watched. During the second round of tryouts, Mark was effortlessly dominating the court. Players who had been the sparkle in Coach Lowery's eye were looking like amateurs next to Mark. They had to run faster, work harder, and their fatigue was showing. Meanwhile, Mark was taking the game at his own pace. He never broke a sweat, and never looked concerned. Mark always had the ball in his hand, and when he did not, he found a way to reach out and take it before anyone even knew what happened. Mark could easily have been the meal ticket for Marysville Pilchuck varsity, but he–like me– was *still* nowhere close to the archetype of Coach Lowery's ideal player. In the past, I knew being five-nine had to be a factor in Lowery's distaste for me. How could he possibly have a problem with Mark? Height certainly was not a factor. Talent was, without question, not a factor. I have never been one to hide behind racism as an explanation for every ugly behavior, no matter how obvious it seems. There comes a time, though, when the unavoidable truth needs to be acknowledged.

Despite all my progress, and no matter how much respect I showed him, I knew that Coach Lowery had no love for me. I rationalized it as having to do with my late start in the game and being five-nine, even though I knew better. Mark was a little more direct than I was. Like me, he felt the undeniable vibe that the coach had an instant dislike for him. It happened the moment Coach set eyes on him. Mark lost his respect for Coach Lowery once he realized what was causing this reaction. He had seen it many times before. This was an unveiled disdain devoid of any unpleasant prior interactions. Mark had not acted disrespectfully toward Coach Lowery to deserve this reaction. Had this been an isolated circumstance, I might dismiss it as a misunderstanding, but I knew from my own experience that Lowery's clear dislike for both of us fit a pattern that I would recognize years later in the Marine Corps and in my first job as a police officer. It was hurtful because *I liked* the coach, and he had many good qualities as a human being and an educator.

During the second round of tryouts, Mark was giving the elite varsity players a workout. All their training and techniques counted for *nothing* as Mark stole the ball, scored repeatedly, and blocked every shot and pass. The MPHS varsity team ran a complex Motion offense, drilled repeatedly by Coach Lowery. Whether Mark had some prior knowledge of this offense was not clear, but he anticipated every move and seemed to play above it. If Mark could do this, what was stopping an opposing team from doing the same? Mark had potential to be the team's secret weapon. Not only would Mark dominate the opposing team as he did with ours, but he could be an invaluable training tool for our elite players, teaching them to anticipate moves as he was doing that day. It should have been obvious to anyone watching, that this player was gold. I will probably never know if Coach Lowery recognized the value of having Mark on the team. If he did, then his feelings about race were more sinister than I had imagined. For every pass that Mark intercepted, and every shot he blocked, Coach Lowery became more visibly angry. What should have been delight, quickly turned into rage, as Mark exhausted his opponents physically and emotionally. What, exactly, did he want from Mark? Play slower? Miss the basket? Look a little *less* Native.

Our six foot seven center, Lane Shinnick–who would eventually go on to make all conference in 1985–was backpedaling to get into position, trying to block Mark's path to the basket. Lane was unable to establish the position he needed, and Mark seized the opportunity to go straight to the basket. With just as little effort he slam-dunked the ball. I gave a shout to Mark, feeling so proud to see another Native rise above the gold standard of Lowery's world of high school basketball. Coach Lowery wasted no time blowing the whistle and yelling some indistinct criticism at Mark. It was not so much a critique or correction, as it was an assault. It was a personal attack against Mark for forcing Coach Lowery to watch his worldview collapse in front of him. An unknown Native who learned his craft on the Rez just dominated the court and made Lowery's elite squad of handpicked players look *inferior*. These players all started at the *correct age*, learned all the right techniques according to Lowery's playbook, and more critical than everything else, they fit the stereotype he was seeking in a varsity player.

Mark lost his respect for Coach Lowery early in tryouts. I never did see what led to this bad start, but if it was anything similar to my experience, Mark knew exactly where this feeling came from. When Coach had a glow in his eyes while making eye contact with another person, then shifted his gaze to me, his smile instantly dropped to a frown. The glow changed to a glare, and if he even made an effort to utter a word, it was forced and insincere. I knew the feeling, and I too, had lost respect for the man who had the power to make or break my high school basketball experience.

Anger boiled up inside Mark as Coach continued to berate him. He picked up the basketball from where it had settled, and after squeezing it between his hands a few seconds, recoiled and threw the ball at Lowery. Watching Lowery cower as the ball sped toward him was worth any consequence they could have imposed, but Mark just laughed and walked out of the gym. He never returned.

That was one of my first memories of prejudice toward Native Americans, and it happens almost every day. Mark was from a good family on the Tulalip Indian Reservation. I am sure he has made his share of mistakes like everyone else, but Coach Lowery certainly was not privy to that information. He knew nothing about Mark, except that he was the best basketball player to try out for the Marysville Pilchuck varsity team and that he was Native. Everything about Mark proved Lowery's worldview to be factually incorrect–a Native who learned to play on the reservation *really can* run circles around Lowery's cookie cutter system of discernment. Had Lowery set aside his prejudices, he could have had the player who went on to be inducted into the NAIA Hall of Fame and as an adult, served his people later in Law Enforcement and as a Tribal Council member. Mark became one of my good friends throughout high school, and remains so to this day. Coach Lowery, could not allow Mark to play ball on his team. Had he done so, he would have had to reconcile his prejudiced beliefs. Coach Lowery was probably a very nice man; I did not have any serious issues with him on a personal level, and he was an excellent basketball coach. He certainly was not the only one at that time who exuded that vibe. I felt unfairly judged as someone not worthy of the team based exclusively on my ancestry more than my ability or my dedication to the sport.

Racism goes far deeper than rude behavior; it is not only hurtful on a personal level, but there is Biblical evidence that racism was a tool used by Satan to eradicate God's chosen people. Anti-Semitism is almost as old as the covenant God made with Abraham, and the Enemy's strategic response to the many messianic prophesies clearly stating that the Messiah would come from Israel. The battle plan for the side of evil is to attack God's plan of redemption for mankind. For centuries, those who have taken the side of darkness have joined forces to eradicate God's chosen people. It is a dangerous position to take, as Genesis 12:3 (KJV) warns. *"And I will bless them that bless thee, and curse him that curseth thee: and in thee shall all families of the earth be blessed."*

On the second night of tryouts, we ran a number of drills. I knew I would have to show the coaches something new and bold. In the past, I had often deferred to other players, clearing the path for them to take a clear shot. I decided that if I had any chance at all of making the team, I would have to show the coaching staff how I could shoot. That is exactly what I did for the rest for of the drill.

Every chance I got, I took the shot. When I would have passed to another player, I took the jump shot. When I saw a clear path to the hoop, I made the lay-up. I took shots that, today, would have been three-pointers, and swished. My confidence began to soar, as every shot sunk through the net with predictable accuracy.

I started to feel noticed. The coaches were watching me closely, as I sunk each shot. Other players were looking at me in a completely different way, and it became clear, that their respect for me had changed dramatically. During drills, instead of me passing to them, they passed to me. When I was not in view, they were looking for me.

I continued to play defense, which was a clear strength that I had proven over time. I hustled to the baseline drills, and kept a positive attitude at all times. I got word that they were going to keep no more than fifteen players on the varsity squad that year. The coaches would choose fifteen players from over one hundred twenty prospective players who turned out for the 1985 tryouts. When it was finally over, I had to look forward to waiting through the weekend to find out who would make the team.

The weekend seemed to drag on forever. I pulled up in the student parking lot at MPHS in my 1971 Chevrolet Monte Carlo. There were so many conflicting emotions that it was hard to know how I felt, as I walked through campus. I was on my way to the window where they posted the list of the fifteen players. I felt nervous, yet excited beyond my capacity to contain the enthusiasm, and I almost had a sense of preemptive disappointment–just in case I was one of the one hundred five players who were not on the list. I was completely unaware of my surroundings as I strolled past other students in the hallway.

Before I knew it, I was standing in front of the window. Nervously, I began reading down the list, looking for my name anywhere among the fifteen names. I almost ignored the first ten names, as I knew it would be the usual people: Clark Easterbrook, Jim Fraunholtz, Lane Shinnick, Dan Rauch, Sean Phillips, Kurt Sunitch, Jeff Hilton, Chad Laughlin, then skipping to the bottom, I saw it–at number fifteen, Duane Hodgson! I felt a sense of paralysis come over me. I could not speak, and with some effort, I moved out of the way, and made my way to my first class with an overwhelming feeling of accomplishment, excitement, and satisfaction. I felt like the "Indian Rudy" of basketball!

I and four other players who comprised the last five names on the list had a name all our own. Coach Lowery called us the *Kamikaze Squad*. It was our job, when we entered the game, to execute a full court press and to make hustle plays against our opponent. Even though we did not receive a lot of time on the court, we did get a chance to play. When we did play, we got results.

There was one game in particular, in which our first and second-string players were both out of sorts. They missed the easy shots; in fact, they were having trouble scoring under every circumstance. I sat on the end of the bench, watching the coaches as they became more frustrated with each failed play. Tied for first place in our league, every game was critical. It was difficult to hear what the coaches were saying, but I caught enough to know they were debating a plan that would shake things up a little, and that it involved the Kamikaze Squad. Coach Lowery had his head in his hands, staring at us at the end of the bench, and it was obvious that he was struggling with a decision he had to make soon. At that moment, the opposing team just scored another basket, putting us twenty-five points down with three minutes to go in the third quarter. I held my breath as I watched Coach finally make peace with his choices.

"Call time out," I heard him say. "Kamikaze Squad, check in!" We jumped off the bench and gathered around him in a semicircle. "You have two minutes full court press. I want to see bodies on the floor, diving for loose balls, rebounds, everything you see!" With stress hanging heavy on him, Coach returned to his seat, still standing, unable to relax enough to sit.

We jogged onto the court and took our respective positions. Each member of the third, or Kamikaze Squad had been waiting intently for a chance to get on the court and make things right. After three quarters of feeling helpless while the opposing team dominated our first and second squads, each teammate was hungry for the ball. That enthusiasm was tangible.

I was all over the court–diving for loose balls, playing defense hard, and passing the ball to open players. Every player on my squad was doing the same: diving for the ball, stealing, and scoring. I could hardly contain myself as I confused and frustrated our opponent. Tyler McCoy hit his mid-range jump shots; Jeff Hilton drove hard, scoring baskets with Gary Rumbaugh and Mike Simonsen. We cut into the lead, reducing it to a five-point lead in only three minutes. As we lived up to our name, the Kamikaze Squad turned the game around. The first and second squad players cheered with enthusiasm every time we intercepted, stole, and launched the ball spinning through the net. When the first and second squad checked back into the game, they continued what we started, and won the game by a comfortable margin.

Our high school was very competitive. So many talented athletes came out of Marysville Pilchuck High School, such as Rich Magnesium, Clark Easterbrook, Lane Shinnick, Kurt Halverson, Marvin Torie, William Olsen, David Shoup, Tim Brennick, Scott Manipon, Jim Frauholtz, Dan Rauch, Kurt Sunitch, Rod Vesenmeyer, Ron Hartman, Rich Hansen, Mark

(Z-Man) Zanoni, Joel Nations, Keith Brashler, Jeff Hilton, Phil Staley, Jeff Riley, Jeff Essers, and many more.

I lettered in football, basketball, and soccer during my senior year, known as a "three sport letterman." Marysville Pilchuck was a good school, but like any school, we had our share of problems. In 1985, students had no confusion as to their social class in the school. There were three distinct classes: the popular class, the middle class, and the *other* class. My intent is not to offend anyone reading this, especially since I would be one of the first to admit that I acted horribly and inappropriately during many situations during my high school years.

I fit neatly into the middle class, but I was friends with many students who belonged in the popular class and the other class. As I think back to these years, I understand better how any number of actions or decisions early in life can generate lasting consequences and memories. I remember one of these moments very clearly. I had recently become a three-sport letterman, and I was walking near the forum wearing my letterman jacket. I saw a cheerleader walking toward me as I walked. I thought nothing of it, since most cheerleaders had never said so much as a word to me in the past. As I passed her, she said "Hi Duane." I was so surprised to hear her speak to me, and even more surprised that she even knew my name. I do not recall responding since I was in shock.

Later that night I reflected on what had happened earlier. Never before, had that cheerleader or any other, said hello or even hinted that she knew my name. The only difference was what I was wearing, the three-sport letterman jacket. As I ruminated more, I became increasingly more incensed that we consider ourselves superior to others because God blessed some with the gift of athletic ability, beauty, or wealth. I thought about my own actions, mean actions that I had done to others. I felt ashamed as I remembered giving my heart to Jesus at a church when I was about ten or eleven years old. *What was I becoming?* I was going to parties and keggers on the weekends, directly in conflict with the teachings I had learned in church and Sunday school.

In fact, I was drinking more and more between the various sports seasons–basketball, football, and soccer. Deep down, I knew I was on the wrong spiritual path. Drinking was slowly killing me, and making me numb to the poor choices I was making.

My girlfriend and I were becoming very close. I was becoming more possessive of her and gradually, I began to walk away from God in the process. Ultimately, this all lead to a wakeup call, when I learned that my girlfriend got back together with her previous boyfriend while we were still together.

I was furious. I had invested everything in this relationship. I trusted her and told her secrets that I had never disclosed to my best friend, Ron Hartman. Then, there was the issue of pride. Her decision to choose her previous boyfriend over me made me look bad. What were other kids saying? When my friends found out, they were stunned and very upset at the betrayal of their friend. I had a sinking feeling in the pit of my stomach–that was hurt and betrayal. That emotion soon gave way to a profound feeling of rage. All I could think to do was to find this *boy* and fight.

Back in those days, if there was going to be a fight, word spread rapidly among the students. The students understood that every fight took place at the big tree near the high school, but just off campus so that no one got in trouble, and always, it took place on a Friday. When I arrived at school that morning, all I could think about was getting John Tully to meet me at the big tree after school on Friday to duke it out.

Kids can be cruel to each other. For some, anything to provoke others to turn on one another was its own brand of amusement. As the lunch period grew near, I could sense many of my classmates smirking–some were more forthright in taking pleasure at the obvious hurt I was feeling from my girlfriend's betrayal. Between classes, I saw John briefly in the hallway. As he passed me in the hall, there was a brief moment of eye contact, paired with an unmistakable sneer. It just kept getting better and better. At that moment, I resolved that I would fight John Tully at the big tree on Friday after school.

When the lunch bell rang, and I entered the cafeteria, I was wearing my letterman jacket. It reminded me about one very important detail. I thought, *how smart of me to fight Tully at the big tree–I can defend my honor while completely staying off campus where I will avoid jeopardizing my place on the basketball team.* After filling my tray with FDA-approved soybean hamburger and fries, I walked with one of my friends to our table. As we walked through the maze of tables, we passed the table where John was sitting with his friends. Again, he took the opportunity to smirk at me, knowing very well how I felt about my former girlfriend. Anger stirred inside, and my heart was pounding so hard I could feel my hands move with every beat. I walked up to John in front of all his friends and said,

"Friday–at the big tree. You and I are going to fight and you better be there!" The anger had consumed me. I barely remember what he replied, or if he even said anything at all. I walked through the doors of the cafeteria and over to the forum.

The MPHS Forum is large square, made completely out of concrete, with a series of steps around the perimeter and leading to a smaller square where a person could address or perform in front of a crowd. Students regularly brought their lunches out there in the eighties, where they would gather with friends to eat, talk, and relax before the afternoon commenced. As I began to step up and onto the forum, I heard a voice behind me say, "Why not now? Let's fight *now*–I'm ready." I turned around and saw John Tully standing there. *This was my enemy–the kid who got together with my girlfriend behind my back at a beer kegger.* I remember partying with John and his brother, Matt Tully several times over the past two years, but things were different. I was a three-sport letterman, a senior on the varsity basketball team. John was what we considered a partying dude–someone who smoked, drank, and attended rock concerts routinely. In fact, John outweighed me by at least five to ten pounds. I was a whopping one hundred fifty-five pounds, and stood five feet nine inches tall. I could see the other kids gathering, telling other kids what was about to go down. That ageless phenomenon–whether a conflict is about to happen in the fifties or eighties–it is always the same with kids–Fight, *fight, fight!*

As I sized up John Tully, I realized I was not in a good position. That day was cloudy and it had rained most of the morning, making the forum half-wet and half-dry. Thinking fast, I told Tully I would fight him on Friday at the big tree after school. John again said, "No–let's fight *now!*
"

By then, the crowd had completely encircled us; their chanting grew even louder, "Fight! Fight! Fight!" I made a critical mistake that almost cost me my honor, my pride, and my status. I started to take off my letterman jacket, and with both arms tied up behind me in the sleeves, John seized the opportunity and hit me with his best shot. He punched me square in the chin, knocking me back several steps until I fell to the ground. I was in serious trouble. Just like in the basketball game, and the car accident, everything slowed down. I could hear the kids yelling and shouting. Even the voices were in slow motion. I struggled to my knee in a half-crouched position, trying to clear my head. Glancing at the crowd could see a familiar face, my best friend Ron Hartman. As I looked at Ron, I could feel the anger return, rising up inside. He was shouting, "Duane! Get up, Duane!"

I was back on my feet. The next few moments are, to this day, difficult to describe. I looked at John, as he was standing there with his fists up. I locked onto his left eye and began moving toward him, the anger bubbling to a dangerous level as I thought of being hit first by the kid who went behind my back with my girlfriend, and now, forcing me to fight on school property. They could kick me off the team for that. All that emotion came together in less than a second as it manifested in one very solid punch. The feeling of flesh cracking and popping as my right fist struck John's left eye is something I will never forget. John crumpled to the ground. Ron told me later, that if I had simply walked up to him where he lay on the ground, and put my hand under his chin I could have knocked him out. I had never been in a fight before, and I knew nothing about it. My punch was off balance, and still being groggy from taking that first punch, the momentum of my punch carried me forward. I slipped on the wet surface and fell a second time.

This gave Tully the time he needed to recover from my blow. He rushed me as I was getting to my feet. He picked me up off my feet, clearly trying to slam me back down on the concrete. I was able to get my hand out behind me to cushion the blow, but it still hurt when I landed. He grabbed me in a front wrestling hold, and all I could think of was punching him again. I reached to the back of his head, pulling it back by his hair, and began striking him repeatedly in that same eye. The crowd, like spectators in the Coliseum, were yelling, shouting, and cheering at a deafening roar.

John and I continued to fight. He kept hitting me in the ribs, punching me several times with a few solid hits. I noticed that his breath was short and heavy. *Tully's getting winded!* I struggled to get him off me, to break his hold, and I could sense victory as I slowly pushed his arms off me. I reached back with my fist balled up once again and was just about to commence a series of final blows, when John and I both felt the firm grip of a giant, lifting us off the ground. It was Mr. Ken Collins, former NFL linebacker for the New England Patriots. Sometimes walking, occasionally dangling midair, we must have looked like broken puppets dragged off the stage.

As I sat in the office, tending to my swollen lip and very relieved that my teeth were all present and accounted for, I considered the lesson for the day–never, *ever* take your coat off just before engaging in a fight. John Tully had a solid punch, and he tagged me good that day. The door opened,

69

and standing there before me, I saw Mr. DeGross, our Vice Principal. In order to understand the full ramifications of Mr. DeGross being involved in any part of this mess, one must know that I spent the better part of my junior and senior years torturing the poor man. There was little need for me to hear what he had to say–I already knew the score. My place on the team was as good as gone. My mother would surely kill me; resurrect me, only to kill me again. Still, I had the feeling of satisfaction from defending my honor, and I made a good show.

The door leading to the hallway opened, and there she was. My former girlfriend, for whom I had to suffer the humiliation among my classmates, walked through and looked at John. Then, to my surprise, she walked over to me, reached up to my face, and said, "I can't believe you *fought* for *me!*" That just pissed me off. It did not take me long to cast a corrective shadow over her rays of glory.

"I fought for *my* name. I fought for *me, my* family name, *not* you!" I said abruptly. Not waiting to see her reaction, I left the office. On my way out, I could see that John's eye was almost completely swollen shut. *Good!* I thought. *He deserves it!* But did he really? My mom arrived to pick me up, and as we were walking to the locker bays, I saw Matt Tully, John's older brother and my classmate, standing with some of his friends. Matt started yelling at me, telling me that it was messed up I had beaten up his brother. That provoked the last reserve of anger I had left. I started toward him with every intention of fighting him and his friends, when my mother and a teacher intervened. The drive home was silent. I went straight to my room and waited to hear from my mother what punishment was waiting for me.

I was physically and emotionally sick for the next twenty-four hours. How could my girlfriend, *whom I loved and trusted*, do that to me? I had done nothing to her, except to try my best to treat her in the best way I knew how. We had spent many hours together–most of it at her parents' house after school, football, and basketball practices, not to mention the weekends. I tried to understand. *Was it something I did?* I will probably never know her reasons for going out on me.

As I deliberated on the injustice of it all, I thought back to the first day I met her, how I felt, and then two days before the day we became emotionally involved. I asked myself, *what was I doing? Was I happy spending my time with my friends and my family?* The answer, of course, was *yes!* I was breathing, I was happy, and enjoying life before I made the decision to enter a committed relationship with my high school girlfriend.

I returned to school and basketball practice–even though I had to sit out the first practice until my injuries could heal. John Tully packed a very powerful punch! My classmates started calling me Rocky, and word got around school that this was one of the better fights of 1985. Even better, there was an overwhelming consensus that I was the victor in that match, mostly due to the swollen state of John's eye. After seeing his eye when I returned to school, I felt bad. A part of me felt that I needed to apologize, but as a senior and a three-sport letterman, that was not going to happen. Pride and public opinion drove my thoughts and my actions. I spent the better part of my life fighting to live, fighting to be accepted, fighting to keep my milk money, and now, fighting to protect my family name and my reputation.

This experience had a profound impact on how I viewed the world and the people around me. I became colder, numb to emotions. Instead of looking at girls as people with feelings, dreams, and goals as I had done in the past, I began to see them more as sexual objects whom I could no longer trust. With each new girlfriend, I doubted their sincerity and wondered if they were lying. *How many others had they been with before me?*

I was sick of being the object of ridicule. My anger was no longer a fleeting reaction, but came to be a constant companion. I was operating more and more on the emotions of anger and distrust. Before another woman could hurt me, I fought back. I became a womanizer, jumping from one relationship to another, always thinking that this one would go behind my back, hurt me in some way. I started drinking more, not caring whom I was with, but seeing if I could conquer the challenge of life. This pattern continued until the age of thirty-seven, when I met my best friend and wife, LoVina Louie–former 1990 Miss Indian World. This also happened to be the age when I rededicated my life to the Chief Cornerstone, more accurately, Yahushua of Nazareth, or, as most people know him, *Jesus.*

As we journey through life, we meet people and become friends with many. We keep some friends for life, some for a time, others are intended to be in our lives during high school, only to fade out like a beautiful sunset at Kayak Point.

One of my very close friends was Dan Furiack. Every one of us has those friends who seem to carry *crazy* with them everywhere they go. These friends have an almost *supernatural* ability to make crazy situations and events just appear without any apparent effort. My partner in crime was Dan, and I met him at a house party, featuring beer on tap.

He was brash, cocky, and witty. He had an aura about him that demanded fun times. Dan transferred to MPHS from our rival, Cascade High School. He quickly made many friends, as he had a great sense of humor and talent for making friends.

One evening, Dan called me at home. He told me to pick him up at his house when it got dark so we could check out the scene that Friday night. Dan instructed me to kill the motor and turn off my lights when I approached his house. I had a blue 1971 Chevy Monte Carlo–three-fifty, four-speed with a big cam and dual exhaust. This beast announced its presence on approach, so I understood that if silence was necessary, I needed to kill the engine. I did not understand, however, *why* I needed to suppress the engine and conceal my presence near his home.

As I coasted to a stop and killed the engine and lights, I could see a line of bed sheets descending from the second story bedroom of Dan's house. Baffled, I watched as Dan slid effortlessly down the makeshift rope–as if he had done this many times before. He landed on the lawn and ran to my car, opened the door and said, "Let's *go!*" It all seemed to be so second nature, as if he had walked out the front door of his house, maybe waving goodbye to his parents on the way out. No, it was nothing like that at all. As we drove off, I realized that we had *no beer*! As usual, Dan had a plan. He instructed me to drive to Super One Foods Market located across the street from Godfather's Pizza on the north end of Marysville.

As I pulled up and parked, I was curious about Dan's plan. He jumped out and I found my favorite cassette tape of *AC/DC, Back in Black*. I listened to Brian Johnson scream out the vocals as I watched Dan enter the store. I could see him through the glass. He was spending an awful lot of time in there–talking and laughing with the female checkers, then talking to the store manager. *Just Dan being Dan*, I thought. I wondered after this continued, *what is he doing in there?* He finally went to a cashier, paid for an unknown item, and started to walk toward the glass doors. I watched as Dan paused just short of the doors, bent down, picked up a large item, and exited the store.

The passenger door of my Monte Carlo opened, and Dan put a whole case of *Rainier Beer Bottles* in my back seat. He looked at me calmly and said, "Let's go." With *AC/DC* at mind-numbing decibels, we drove out of the parking lot and headed to the north end of town to see where the house parties were going to be. It finally dawned on me–neither Dan nor I were twenty-one.

"Hey, can I see your fake ID?" I asked. I was curious to see just how genuine it looked.

"*What* card?" he asked. "I don't have one." At that point, my blood ran cold as I realized that Dan must have stolen the beer.

"Dan, did you steal that beer?" I asked looking out my rear view mirror to see if the police were tailing me.

"Yep," he replied. " *Don't worry*. It's all handled!" This was no act–he had total confidence in the power of his persona. I was freaking out inside. Society was a little different back in the eighties. If the police caught us, I knew I would spend some time in jail. If you have ever seen the movies, *Weird Science*, or *Pretty in Pink,* you might be familiar with the characters portrayed by Michael Anthony Hall. Not only did Dan look *exactly* like him–including the braces–but he also carried the same humor and brazen manner.

The faculty at MPHS had finally figured out that many of us were leaving school early and driving to Ross Lake or Twin Lakes to take advantage of the sun. If you have ever lived in the Pacific Northwest, you know exactly what I am talking about; when the sun comes out, people lose their minds in their pursuit for every ray of sun. Dan and I sat on the forum between classes one sunny day, brainstorming on how we could get my car out of the parking lot without the teachers catching on. We were desperate to enjoy this rare sunny day, and the perfect way to do that was a trip to Twin Lakes–with strawberry wine coolers packed on ice. There were so many different options, but none panned out after thinking them through. The last, and more brilliant plan, was to drive my car across the green grass field up to the paved back road of the student parking lot, then off we go.

The only drawback was that first stretch across the grass, where we would be driving right in front of my classroom. The teacher's desk sat in front of the windows and facing the class. If the teacher sat at her desk, she would not see us. If she happened to be walking in the aisle facing away from the window, she would not see us. Unfortunately, we had no way of knowing where she would be at the exact moment we were making our break across the field. I remember the initial fear as I started the Monte Carlo, and the voice of reason telling me to think this over one more time. Dan's voice always overpowered that internal warning, and before I

73

changed my mind, I pressed the clutch, put the car in first, jumped the curb, and started across the field.

As we grew near to the classroom window, I realized the obvious flaw in our plan. Our plan, no matter how carefully we thought it through, really came down to *luck*. I cranked up the stereo–AC/DC just seemed perfect for the occasion. Dan rocked his head to the beat of the tunes, an enormous grin on his face as if he feared nothing. We were now in position to put our plan to the test. I could see the door to the classroom, and imagined I would be seeing the teacher sitting at her desk with her back to us. I decided at that moment, I would wave to my classmates as we passed by the window–but only if our plan worked the way we imagined.

Sweat was beading up on my hands as I gripped the wheel. My heart pounded in my chest. This was the decisive moment; our plan would work perfectly or we would soon feel the wrath of MPHS administration. All of their frustration with other students who had skipped to do exactly what we were doing right then, would come raining down hard on us– as an example to all. I could see some of my classmates by then. Some of them saw us and began to laugh uncontrollably. Others, though, were not amused and appeared genuinely pissed off. I wasted no time looking for the teacher, while doing everything possible to maintain an even speed so as not to cause additional noise.

I saw the teacher. She was walking down the aisle with her *back* to us! Dan gave me the *high five*, and we broke out into laughter. As I continued to watch my classmates, I waited until we were in the clear. As I promised myself, both Dan and I began to wave at our classmates as we left the view of the window. As soon as we reached the back road, I sped up and made our escape to the lake.

My group of friends, Dan Furiack, Z Man, Rich Hansen, Scott and Joe Leffler, and I discovered the unforgettable club, *Buzzy's on Broadway* in Everett. The club was equipped with a state-of-the-art sound and light system, and a large dance floor with no shortage of beautiful women! We typically hit the club before eight in the evening, and then later, from eleven to closing.

As a matter of routine, we went to the local mini-market on Broadway just prior to showing up at Buzzy's. The mini-market was owned by an older Chinese couple, who were very friendly and, more than likely, they did not realize we were under age. All I knew at the time was that–if we needed strawberry wine coolers–that was the place to go. My group of friends and I would slam a big wine cooler, pop some gum for our breath, and enter the club immediately after. By slamming the cooler just before entering, we avoided all the telltale signs of intoxication, as the alcohol would not have time to hit us until a few minutes later. Once we were inside, the alcohol would begin taking effect, and we were ready to have some fun.

Between the hours of eight and eleven, we hit the after-hours scene using all the same tactics. The police busted many of our friends–usually because of noise complaints. They never did raid our spot, though. We always drove to the same place, a place that Dan picked, even though my initial reaction was that of serious reservation. We partied in front of the *Everett Police Station*! During the year and a half that we frequented that same location, the police never noticed.

For the most part, I only had one particularly unpleasant experience at Buzzy's. Dan, my girlfriend, and I arrived at the club, wine coolers in our system and ready to have some fun. Dan was flirting with every girl he saw. I was on the dance floor, when everyone's favorite tune started over the speakers. People packed the dance floor as soon as everyone heard those famous lyrics, "*The roof, the roof is on fire!*" Dan was dancing with a girl who happened to be dating Pete Raney at the time. Pete was a year older than Dan and I were, and he ran with his own group of friends. I did not know him well, but Dan hung out with him occasionally. I remember thinking, *Dan better quit dancing with Pete's girlfriend, or he's gonna be pissed when he arrives.*

When the song started, and everyone rushed the dance floor, Dan started dancing with Zanette Giesler, with whom I was dancing, and I found myself dancing across from Pete's girlfriend, Penny. Without warning, Pete ran up and hit me with a combination punch, which threw me back onto my butt and I slid across the floor, disappearing into the crowd of people. The dance floor was in chaos. Everyone started shouting. Everything seemed to slow down around me, as I rose to my feet. Penny was crying as she ran up to me, asking me if I knew why Pete hit me. I had an idea, but I told her I did not know.

I felt a rage come over me, and I asked the people around me if they knew where Pete Raney was. One girl told me that she saw him run outside, so I followed, holding my jaw, which was in excruciating pain by that time. Once I was out the door, I heard a voice calling to me. It was my childhood friend, Ron Hartman. I asked if he had seen Pete and if he was the one who hit me. He told me that Pete threw the punch, and was just getting into his car. I ran around the building, down the alley, and into the parking lot. I could see Pete sitting behind the wheel in his car, and was about to drive off. I ran up to the car, and with my fist, hit his window, yelling at him to get out of his car. He drove off, leaving me standing there holding my jaw and very pissed off. I was still trying to understand what had just happened.

My jaw swelled up even worse, and the pain became unbearable. I do not remember the drive back to the Cedar Street Apartments in Marysville where I lived. Once I entered the apartment, I reclined in my chair and started to suspect that my jaw was broken. A short time later, I heard yelling outside my door. Ron answered the door for me, and I could hear Pete Raney screaming for me to come outside and fight him. I was in no condition to fight. I could barely stand, and my swollen jaw made swallowing very difficult. Ron told Pete to leave or he would have to deal with him. Pete and his crew left after hearing their options. For the next two weeks, I had to drink out of a straw until my jaw healed.

Dan apologized repeatedly for what happened. I eventually had to tell him not to worry, but please, *stop talking about it*! I had plans for Pete Raney when my jaw healed completely. When that time came, I looked for Pete everywhere, but I never did find him. I picked up where I left off–partying with my friends, dating one girl after another–not considering if I hurt them in the process. In fact, I lost five girlfriends in one day during a party at the Cedar Apartments.

I arrived home from my job at Skipper's in Marysville. Irritated at seeing my parking spot taken, I fumed into my apartment, while thinking that I was going to crash someone's party. With so many cars, *someone* was having a party. I was not expecting to walk into a wall-to-wall party in *my* cramped apartment. There had to be at least fifty people or more, standing room only.

Dan, of course, was standing there laughing. After telling him how surprised I was to walk into a party, he gestured for me to follow him. He had another surprise for me. That was an understatement as I walked around the corner of my living room and saw all five of my girlfriends sitting at my kitchen table. As I came around the corner, everyone stopped talking. They hurled Rainier bottles, wine coolers, a fork, plate, and even a shoe as soon as they saw me. I had to leave my own party for safety reasons.

One of these girlfriends eventually got pregnant. I remember asking if she was on birth control, and she assured me she was. As it turned out, she was not. We had to make some choices, and I made a bad decision. She was eighteen years old, I did not want the constraints of raising a child, and I did not want to get married. I agreed to pay for the abortion.

It was wrong, and it was a sin. I thought about how this unborn child would tie me down and affect my plans. If I could change any decision, that would be it. Knowing what I know now, I realize that this gift of life can never return to this world. Everyone has their own opinion about abortion. The law created by man says that this is a woman's choice. I do not agree with this ruling. The gift of life is the Creator's choice, a blessing, a gift, and a treasure. Many will disagree, cite rulings, ideas inspired by man, but my response will always be the same—what did our Creator say?

If nine men in black robes make a ruling for all people that are contrary to the Bible, I for one will not acknowledge their law. I do not fear man, but I do fear the Creator, Yod Hey Vah Hey. I will have to stand before the Creator one day and answer for every one of my choices. I feel better knowing that, by accepting the blood sacrifice of Yahusua of Nazareth as my sacrificial lamb, that I am forgiven.

My eyes water up as I think about this little one. I think about how my selfish decision affected his or her chance of life. There are other decisions I have made in my life, especially in my younger years, fifteen to thirty-seven that hurt many people, caused a lot of pain, and divided people against one another. For all this, I ask your forgiveness, I pray for honor and blessings to be restored to each of you one hundred times over–just as the Father YHVH has forgiven me through and by the blood and name of the Chief Cornerstone–I humbly ask for each of you to forgive me.

For all those young women at Marysville Pilchuck High School, all the women I knew while in the United States Marine Corps and while in various law enforcement positions up to the age of thirty-seven, this poem and apology is for you!

"You are a Beautiful Flower"
A women is to be treasured, even above oneself, selfish is a cancer, like lust, not trust

As men, we are the spiritually leaders of our house, to cover, take care, provide for our spouse

One of the greatest of all gifts, is the ability to bring into this world,
life

Becoming one together is the beautiful mystery of life

Yahweh Creator God provided the covenant of marriage for man
and his wife

When the relationship is based on Creator, there is little strife, all
the women, I used for physical pleasure in my younger years

I am sorry for my selfish behavior under the influence of beer

I humbly ask for your forgiveness as I can't take past actions back,
please accept my apology, and know I have your spiritual backs.

May your lives, families and friends be blessed this prayer is for all
of you by the blood of the Chief Cornerstone Yahusua/Jesus in the name
of Yod Hey Vah Hey (Yahweh)

Chapter 7: United States Marine Corps

This is my rifle. There are many like it, but this one is mine. My rifle is my best friend. It is my life. I must master my life. Without me, my rifle is useless. Without my rifle, I am useless. I must fire my rifle true. I must shoot straighter than my enemy who is trying to kill me. I must shoot him before he shoots me, I will. My rifle and I know what counts is not the rounds we fire, the noise of our burst, nor the smoke we make. We know it is the hits that count. We will hit. My rifle is human, even as I, because it is my life. Thus, I will learn it as a brother, I will learn its weaknesses, its strength, its parts, its accessories, its sights and its barrel, I will keep my rifle clean and ready. We will become part of each other. We will. Before God, I swear this creed. My rifle and I are defenders of my country. We are masters of our enemy. We are the saviors of my life. So be it until victory is America's and there is no enemy, but peace!

– Marine Corps Rifleman's Creed

I stepped out of the shower just after eleven on that cold January morning. The hot shower felt good. My sister, Marie had been bugging me to join her in the living room, so I put a rush on my routine.

"Hurry up Duane–you're going to miss it!" Marie was in the living room, watching television. She had been glued to the set all morning, waiting for liftoff. It was an exciting day for the nation, as the Space Shuttle crew prepared for the big moment.

"Ok, I'm hurrying!" Looking up in the bathroom mirror as I brushed my teeth, I realized I had forgotten a critical step. My hair hung lifelessly down without the magical stroke of the brush. *Duane! That was a close one!* I feathered my hair back, as any stylish young man would have done in 1986. *Yep, that's more like it!* My attention to detail had nothing to do with vanity, and everything to do with not looking like a *dweeb* in front of my friends. Fitting in was hard enough for me already.

I opened the bathroom door, now that I was dressed. I figured I could at least listen to the live coverage as I got ready. "Hey, Bro Wa, they're lifting off. You know you want to see this!"

"Be right there!" I hung up my towel, and cleaned up my mess before I left the bathroom. As I shut the light off, I heard my sister gasp.

"Duane!" My sister screamed at me from the living room. "Come here! Come here!" This was not her usual prodding. She was in distress. Something was very wrong. I whipped around the corner, still holding my clothes. I found my sister standing in the middle of the living room, her hand over her mouth, eyes wide, and pointing at the television. I looked at the screen, unsure if what I saw was real. This was live coverage of the Challenger Space Shuttle launch.

A huge cloud of smoke hung in the air, the trail leading off in at least two different directions. One expects to see a giant trail of smoke during a launch, but this was very different, and clearly, a tragic accident had taken place. My thoughts raced–what about the *crew*? This was not an ordinary shuttle launch. The crew of this mission included the Commander; Francis R. Scobee, Pilot, Michael J. Smith; Mission Specialist, Ronald McNair; Mission Specialist, Ellison Onizuka; Gregory Jarvis, Civilian; and Christa McAuliffe, Civilian and first school teacher to go to space. Christa's students watched the entire tragedy unfold right before their eyes in real time over the live feed. The entire crew perished in the accident. Marie and I looked at each other in shock.

Debris was everywhere. The huge billowing cloud of smoke hung in the air, as bits and pieces of flaming debris scattered here and there, and others fell to the ocean below. The television announcer was in shock. He struggled to find the right words, trying to conceal his own emotions, as he searched for a way to comfort the nation watching these horrific events. A generation of children had waited eagerly for the first schoolteacher go to space with the crew. This was important and exciting, because it brought the world of science fiction that much closer to reality–a time when ordinary people could go to space.

President Ronald Reagan appointed the Rogers Commission to investigate the accident, which discovered that NASA's organizational culture and decision-making process had been contributing factors to the accident. The agency violated its own safety rules. NASA's managers had known since 1977 that contractor, Morton Thiokol's design of the solid rocket booster (SRB) contained a potentially catastrophic flaw in the O Rings, but they failed to address this problem properly. The O Ring was not designed for the cold temperatures present during a January launch, and as a result, it failed to seal the joint properly. Ultimately, hot gases under high pressure made contact with an external fuel tank. This tragedy could have been prevented.

Everything was closing in around me. It had only been one year since I graduated from Marysville Pilchuck High School. I had hit the local clubs, like Buzzy's on Broadway, sometimes going as far as Seattle to party when I was not drinking beer with my friends around town or on the Tulalip Indian Reservation.

I was a proud graduate of the class of '85, and as I thought back to all the accomplishments I made in the face of adversity, this routine I found myself in was beneath me. I made a commitment to make the basketball team, and finally, after having every door slammed in my face, I made the team in my junior and senior years. They told me I could not play clarinet in jazz band, so I learned to play alto saxophone over the summer and successfully made third chair. In fact, I was not supposed to live past the age of two due to a severe respiratory infection, but because God answered my mother's prayers, I am here today. The effort it took for me to achieve all these accomplishments was staggering, as I thought more about it. Even more important, though, were the people who encouraged me, defended me when bullies tried to extort lunch money, and gave me a break when I needed it the most.

I would not have graduated on time were it not for my favorite teacher, Mr. Linden. Had he not passed me with an "A," I would have had to come back the next year and repeat my senior year. I remember that day. I walked into the physical education classroom–grade slip in hand. J.L Linden was sitting behind his desk, in his usual attire, cotton dress shirt and sweat pants. Mr. Linden was a former football player for the University of Oregon and stood six feet four inches tall. His eyes narrowed as he recognized me over his reading glasses. "What do you want, *riff raff*?" He barked. I handed the grading slip to him. Looking at it, he chuckled under his breath. "Ok, what do you need to pass this year?"

"An A," I replied. He shook his head slightly. "Or I will be back next year to see you every day." I smiled as I watched him mull over this thought.

"Done!" He marked the grade sheet with an A and handed it back to me. "You owe me some *Henry's Doughnuts* you knucklehead." Another term of endearment so common from Mr. Linden.   His smile dissipated slightly.

I will always remember his words that day. "You know Duane; you are better than this. You have some gifts others don't have–perseverance, strong will, character, and a never-give-up attitude. These things could carry you a very long way in life, *if* you embrace and use them."

As I stepped out of his office, I thought about what he said. He was right, that much I knew. I refused to back down when the coaching staff told me there was no place on the team for me. Those were just the situations that Mr. Linden knew about. He did not know that I survived an abusive childhood or that I struggled for acceptance in both white and Indian cultures. After that day, Mr. Linden's words stuck with me, even if I *did* push them to a dark corner of my consciousness during that next year of partying.

One year from graduation and I was lying on my bed contemplating my future. I did not know what I wanted to do specifically, but I did know that I was looking for something bigger and more exciting than staying around Marysville, going to college, and settling in to a job for the next few decades. I had been releasing a lot of pent up energy this past year, which might have been therapeutic and necessary, but I have seen others who find themselves caught in this trap. One year leads to another. They party, work, and repeat the process only to wake up many years later and realize that they have done nothing to fulfill their dreams.

Much of my turmoil was rooted in my insecure feelings about being both European and Native American. From what I know today, I might not have had the same problems were I born a few years later, when being Native American was a good thing, even a trendy thing for some. I was not a tribal member, and I was fair-skinned enough that–because of my appearance–other Natives made inquiries about my ancestry out of curiosity.

I wondered for many years how much Indian ancestry I had. When I looked at pictures of my dad, I noticed how much he looked like an *Indian*. My Aunt Elaine Moomaw, Uncle Rich Moomaw, Alan, Jay, Julie, and Tom Moomaw all had very dark complexions. When I looked in the mirror, I could see that I had their facial features, but my skin was much lighter. Yet, when I was with white people, there always seemed to be someone who would stare at me or make a remark about my skin tone. Then when I was with my people, an Indian–usually a dark-complected Indian–would make remarks about my light skin tone. I realized that I was a half-breed, but would the rest of my life be like this? Having to deal with both sides, and *neither* fully accepting me. Why had the Creator God made me like this? Why could I not be all white or all Indian?

I knew I could not change who I was, and even if I could somehow do the impossible, I did not really know if I would *want* to change who I was and how I looked. I lacked role models who were like me, and there was no community of biracial (Native and white) people like there was in Indian and white societies. If I wanted to lead a European-American lifestyle, I could settle into a white community, and if I wanted to lead a Native American lifestyle, I could do that simply by living in a predominantly Native American community. There is no such thing for biracial people; we have to choose, split our time between the two different worlds, or mingle only with people who are equally comfortable in both worlds–which can be difficult to find. Most people simply spend their time around people with whom they are comfortable–race and culture are hardly a conscious part of that choice. As long as I interacted with society to any degree, I would not be able to avoid dealing with who I was and how other people related to me.

A local community college awarded me with a partial scholarship for soccer. Our first game was against Skagit Community College. I was playing the right wing defender position, but the Skagit starting forward was sick and their backup forward was injured. That meant I was playing against the third string forward.

It was a sunny day, and I was feeling very confident knowing that my opponent was neither a first nor a second-string player. The ball was in play, and launched into the air toward my side, called a "through ball." The forward, normally would run toward the ball, trying to beat the defender there, then try to make a goal or pass to a teammate for him to take a shot. The ball was in the air and the race was on between their third string forward and me. I have always been one of the fastest players on the field. The opposing team's forward beat me to the ball by about two feet, which stunned me. I was not expecting a third string player to be that fast! That moment also made me realize that, if this was the *third* string player, I could only imagine what the first and second string forwards would be like.

A few days later, I had to appear in front of the local judge for a traffic infraction. I had parked on the hill near Buzzy's on Broadway–the starter in my 1971 Monte Carlo was going out, and a hill could be helpful if I had to pop it into gear to start the car. At the time, I moved the barricade temporarily until I could use the hill to compression start my car, and then after it started, I put it back. As I was putting the barricade back where I found it, a police officer approached, and informed me he was going to

83

have to give me a ticket for moving the barricade. Despite the problems with the starter, my Monte Carlo had a Muncie four-speed manual transmission, dual chrome exhaust, a huge cam, and leather interior. I bought it from Kevin Peralia for three thousand back in the summer of 1984, just before my senior year. This car was my accomplice in my campaign of nonstop irritation to local police departments, including the Snohomish County Sheriff, Washington State Patrol, Everett Police Department, and Marysville Police Department. The barricade ticket, although not that serious, was the sign I needed to wake up and realize I was not growing or moving forward with my life.

Another ticket in Marysville, I thought. It was difficult for me to get a date in this small community. I thought about my options at that point. I was not mature enough for college; in fact, I had little interest in attending. I had concerns that what we were learning in college was politically motivated. Most colleges shamelessly pushed the liberal agenda and anti-Christian attitude on students who paid good money to attend.

Military recruiters were a common sight on the campus of MPHS. I knew very little about any of the branches. My stepdad, Steve Hodgson, was partial to the Air Force because he served for a brief time. Most of my knowledge involved the uniforms they wore. Navy uniforms were, by far, the most amusing–and not in a good way. I was young and looking *cool* mattered. The Marines easily had the coolest uniforms of all the branches. I decided that I would give each branch a chance and visit each of the recruiters.

I walked into the recruiting office of the United States Navy. The first thing I noticed was the mustard stain on the front of the recruiter's shirt. He was overweight and appeared unkempt. After talking for a short time, I had made up my mind that there was no way I was going to enlist in the Navy. My next stop was the United States Army.

As I entered the office, I could already tell that the Army recruiter was in better shape. He stood and shook my hand when I entered. The overall presentation was more appealing compared to my previous encounter. He talked about the mission, slogan, and history of the Army. He described the Army's mindset and direction for the future. I was impressed with the recruiter and his message, but I was determined to listen to each recruiter before making up my mind.

I met with the recruiter for United States Air Force. One of the first things I noticed was how clean and basic the uniforms were. I also noticed that the recruiter was somewhat small in stature, but very intelligent. He conducted a very persuasive presentation about the history and mission of the Air Force, how it differed from the other branches and prioritized education and housing for its service members. I liked what I was hearing, except that it started to sound a lot like college, and I was not interested in anything resembling college.

Within the next few days, I had taken the required tests for entrance into the United States Air Force, finished the interview, and began working on the medical history and background forms. A short time later, the recruiter called back to tell me that my scores came back. I cringed. My high school grades were average mostly due to lack of effort. As I listened, the recruiter told me that I *passed* all the required tests for entrance into the Air Force. I thought about the opportunities that I would have to see the world and meet new people. *Any* field of study or occupation was instantly available, and tuition expenses were no longer a concern.

My excitement was short lived. The next day, I received a second call from the recruiter. This time, he told me that my eye exam had returned *below* the acceptable limits. Just like that, I was on to the next branch.

I thought about the Navy recruiter with the mustard stain on his uniform. *Maybe, I should look into the Army*, I thought. I was more disappointed than I would have expected. My good friends, Rich Hansen and Mark Zanoni had enlisted in the Army, both stationed in Germany. If necessary, I could return to the Army recruiting office to find out if their medical standards were different from the Air Force.

I remembered seeing a commercial for the United States Marine Corps. Whether it was true or just the impression I got from movies and commercials, Marines were the most *exclusive* branch of the military, and not everyone should apply. They were meaner, tougher, and had uniforms that rocked.

When I walked into the recruiting office for the United States Marine Corps, I noticed a young man sitting behind a desk. Immediately, I could sense something different about this office. The young man's uniform, posture, and presence conveyed no question about his confidence. He was in shape and disciplined–a polished product of the United States Marine Corps and *I* could be *him* if I just signed on the line. I walked to the back of the office, and another Marine, Gunnery Sergeant Burdett stood as soon as he saw me.

"Jump up, and show me how many pull-ups you can do," he said, gesturing to the pull-up bar. I grasped the bar, and with a little effort, I pumped out twelve pull-ups. I landed on my feet and it was on to sit-ups. Gunnery Sergeant Burdett held my feet as I cranked out eighty sit-ups in less than two minutes. He smiled and asked, "How fast can you run the mile?" Thinking back to physical education class, I remembered doing a mile in about six minutes. Both Marines were smiling at each other when I told them this. I felt compelled to inform them about my failed vision exam with the Air Force recruiter, but they did not seem to care about that.

I returned home to await the results of my entrance and medical exams. When Burdett called to tell me that he was "pleased to announce [my] enlistment in the United States Marine Corps," I was surprised that I had passed all the tests, including the vision exam. I would be entering the most disciplined branch of the military in a very short time. That summer of 1986 was memorable.

The departure date for boot camp was fast approaching–I would be flying out of Seattle for California in about a week, and I would spend the three hottest months of summer in boot camp, with August slated for graduation. My friend, Ron Hartman, decided we needed to party one more time before I departed for boot camp. That was a mistake.

Ron and I drove to Everett to cruise Colby Avenue one last time before I left Marysville for the Marine Corps. Everything went smooth, at first. I was in my element, flirting with attractive women, revving up my engine and racing a few cars we met while cranking out *Twisted Sister*, *Quiet Riot*, *Aerosmith*, and *AC/DC* on my stereo. As the evening progressed, I became more intoxicated even though Ron did his best to slow me down. I was having *no* part of that. With every Rainier beer I pounded, the more courageous I became. Waiting for the light to change, I started revving up my engine. When the light turned from red to green, I popped my clutch, my tires smoking as I took off.

Then it happened. Blue and red flashing lights accompanied by that familiar siren came from nowhere, and were now engulfing the space around me. My head was swimming. The buzz complemented all the fun we were having before that moment. Now, it was just a haze hanging over my head–causing confusion and hampering my ability to process thoughts rationally. I pulled over to the side of the road. I knew how much I had been drinking and that now, I was going to pay for it. I remembered that it was three days before I flew out to boot camp, and that a driving while intoxicated ticket could do unspeakable damage to my plans. I said a quick prayer to God, pleading for His help.

The officer approached my window, asking for my driver's license, insurance, and registration. I realized that I was in trouble. A number of tragic accidents had made the news, and there was pressure everywhere to keep people from drinking and driving. Public service commercials about drunk driving were running every time I turned on the television. The newly created activist group, MADD (Mothers Against Drunk Driving) were working with politicians who jumped on the bandwagon with their campaign promises to tighten the punishment for offenders. Ron seemed relaxed and hardly affected by the alcohol, even though he had as much as I did. This was nothing new, really. I always seemed to become intoxicated before my friends did, and in the right time and place, that was a good thing—this time, it was bad medicine.

The Washington State Trooper returned to my window. I can only imagine what he was thinking. The trooper asked me to exit my car. I failed every field sobriety test before the trooper gave up and put me in the back of the patrol car. Tussling with the handcuffs, I thought, *there goes the Marine Corps*. I looked on as the Trooper talked to Ron, then searched my car for about ten minutes. The trooper and Ron resumed conversation, and then Ron walked over to the driver's side of my car, opened the door, and got in. The trooper was on his way back. My future was about to go down the toilet unless I could think of something fast. Anything.

The trooper got back in the car. "What is your name?"

"Duane Hodgson," I replied. He knew that.

"What are you planning on doing with your life?" he asked. There was a subtle smile forming, but from my experience with law enforcement, not every smile was friendly.

"I just enlisted with the Marine Corps. I fly out in three days for boot camp. Well, that was the plan before tonight. I don't know how this'll play out, sir." It was too late to play sober, but still, I was trying everything I could and my destination still looked to be the county jail. The trooper nodded as he buckled himself in. That was the end of the conversation, and my chances of talking my way out of this.

The trooper pulled out and I caught a glimpse of his face through the rear view mirror. He was smiling. *Could be worse*, I thought—*but kinda weird*. I was not finding humor in my situation, but something struck *him* funny. He even chuckled quietly to himself when he glanced back at me. I tried to get some slack in the handcuffs, but they just tightened even more with every tug. I looked over my shoulder–I could see Ron driving my Monte Carlo behind the patrol car. I was surprised that Ron got away without suspicion, *but good for him*, I thought–*no need for both of us to go down*. I was worried that another officer might pull him over for driving under the influence.

The drive took forever. It gave me time to worry. *What would I tell my mother? How would I explain this to Gunnery Sergeant Burdett?* All these possible scenarios swam around my head, but no matter what happened, it would not be a positive ending. Then the trooper took my exit on the Interstate-5 and headed down the residential street where I lived. A minute or two later, he pulled into the driveway and Ron pulled up next to him. I had no idea what to make of any of this. I watched as Ron followed the trooper up to the front door of my house and knocked on the door.

My mother emerged from the doorway, looking at Ron and the state trooper with a very concerned look that only a mother can wear. The three were talking by the front door for a few short minutes, but it seemed like an eternity as I sat in the back seat of the patrol car, handcuffed, and waiting to be booked into jail. This stop along the way just confused me even more. The three of them walked toward the patrol car, with the trooper in the lead. He opened my door, and I expected Mom to start yelling at me as soon as she made eye contact. She was calm. "So, I hear you are going into the Marine Corps?" He asked leaning his arm on the car door with the famous Washington State Patrol Smokey Bear hat slightly tipped back.

"Yeah. That's right," I answered. I felt a little annoyed with him. I did not know why he was taking this detour on his way to jail, and I was convinced this was a deliberate jab. I looked over at Ron, who was standing off to the side with a grin on his face. The trooper nodded and helped me up and out of the car.

"Turn around." He motioned with his hand. I turned around and leaned into the patrol car for balance. I could feel him unlock the handcuffs, which surprised me even more. I turned around to face him after he had removed both cuffs. He had my attention. I filled my lungs with air, and released it slowly to calm my mind. He locked eyes on me, piercing as if to say, *I should listen to him.*

"Duane, there's no amount of punishment *I* can give you … no amount of *physical and emotional stress* that'll come even close to the *hell* you're going to experience in the Marine Corps." I expected to hear a mind-numbing lecture, and even though I did not comprehend the prophetic nature of his statement at that moment, in a matter of days I would experience that 'physical and emotional stress.'

I nodded, "Yes, sir." I found out later that he had served his country in the Marine Corps before starting a career in law enforcement.

"If I find out that you do not report for duty, if you miss your flight, I *will* come back. And when I *do* come back, I'm going to *arrest* you, and *charge* you with a DUI. You aren't going to make me do that, I hope?" His stone cold glare softened. I could detect a faint smile.

"No, sir, I'll definitely report for duty. Three days I'll be there." I was sobered up artificially fast due to adrenaline, but as I spoke, I struggled to enunciate every syllable. The trooper nodded and smiled.

"Good and I wish you luck, you're gonna need it!" He said. I thanked him again before heading into the house and going straight to my room, except for the kitchen stop for a couple sandwiches on the way.

I woke up with a massive hangover the next morning. Splashing water on my face and running a brush through my hair, I caught a glimpse of my reflection in the mirror. No white in my eyes, everything was red and swollen. The throbbing was unbearable in my temple and back of my head. I could almost *see* the headache in my reflection and the nausea had not even begun yet. I brushed my teeth like that was going to get rid of the alcohol–old alcohol from the night before. That was when the nausea started in full force.

I had no energy, as I sauntered into the living room where my mother was sitting. She did not look happy. "Duane, do you know how lucky you were that God was watchin' over you? How many times have you been in a jam and God helped you?" She was right, but I did not fully appreciate her words at that time. I certainly did not heed or learn from them, as there were many more times in the Marines, working in law enforcement, or everyday life that I avoided jail and even death. I would eventually learn to appreciate God's interventions in my life, but at that time, I had a long way to go.

Ron's plan to celebrate before my departure did not turn out exactly how we thought it might, but it gave me some memories nonetheless. I spent the next two days taking care of all the necessary errands before I left town, and said my farewells to friends and family members.

Gunnery Sergeant Burdett was on his way to my house. It was a little after five in the morning, and everyone in the house was up. My sisters were upset as I prepared for the trip. When my mother was not crying, she was trying to fight back tears. My sisters watched through the front window as Gunnery Sergeant pulled up in the driveway and walked briskly up to the front door. I hugged and kissed both my sisters goodbye, then gave my mother a hug and kiss and told her I loved her. I looked back up at the house as I shut Gunny's door behind me. This would be the last time I saw my house for the next three months. Gunny backed out of the driveway, took the exit onto the I-5 toward Seattle.

I was feeling a little down, already missing my family. Gunny cheered me up with some fresh coffee and kept the conversation on a more positive track. It was reassuring to hear advice from another Marine who had the experience of being through boot camp himself.

We arrived at the Military Entrance Processing Station (MEPS) in Seattle and walked toward the area where they swear in new recruits to the Marine Corps. I thought about all the contradictions in what I was about to do. I was a half-breed, not one to respect authority, or take orders. I was enlisting in the hardest and most demanding branch of the military. As our footsteps echoed off in the long hallway, I heard a voice shout "Duane I have great news!" Pausing we turned around and I saw the Air Force recruiter walking toward us. Maybe he did not realize the situation, or maybe he thought I would decide to enlist with the Air Force. Whatever the case, it did not turn out well for him. "Great news, Duane. The eye test results somehow were mixed up, our test is fine and you are eligible to join the United States Air Force!" he exclaimed with a huge grin.

Gunnery Sergeant Burdett's response was swift, intense, and fierce. "Get the hell away from my recruit you piece of *shit* before I gouge out your eyeballs and skull-fuck you!" The Air Force recruiter was appalled and probably a little scared, as he stammered a few incomprehensible comments, and stumbled backward from the onslaught of the Marine Corps Gunnery Sergeant. Laughing, as the Air Force recruiter retreated, Gunny turned, looked at me and said, "Problem Solved–let's go!" Right then and there, I knew the Marine Corps was the right path for me–just what I needed at that time in my young life.

I was ready to take the oath. I raised my right hand and repeated the oath of office, enlisting for four years to serve my country in the United States Marine Corps, and prepared to go to war if needed. When it was over, Gunny and I continued to a number of smaller stations, filling out paperwork, signing forms, and verifying flight arrangements. Two hours later, I was sitting in a window seat of a jet airliner. I had never been on a jet before, and I had never been outside the State of Washington without my parents. The roar of the jet turbines kicked in and I was on my way to boot camp in California. I could see the city of Seattle grow smaller and smaller as we climbed. Everything would be different when I landed. I had no idea exactly what was in store for me, but I considered the dreadful possibility that, for the next three months, I might have to go without coffee! As if gorging on it during the flight would somehow help, I downed as many cups as they could refill.

After landing, we boarded a bus, which took us to the receiving area. If you saw the movie, *Full Metal Jacket*, you might remember the new recruits arriving at basic training in the receiving area. Art imitates life, and my experience could not have been any closer to that scene. As soon as the bus came to a stop, the doors opened, and no less than twenty drill instructors stormed the bus screaming profanity, insults, and confusing orders.

"Get the *hell* off my bus!" screamed one DI to the first victim he saw. Everyone was on his feet, scrambling in a chaotic fashion to follow the contradictory impossible orders as they were hollered an inch from our faces.

"What the hell are you doing you *piece of shit*?" With no time for a reply, the drill instructor screamed back, "Don't look at me, *boy!* Get the hell off my bus *now!*" I saw yellow footprints in front of the bus where we were to line up. I tried to keep my focus amid the screaming and jostling of everyone in that cramped space. Everyone was trying to make it to the front door of the bus before he could draw the attention of a DI and become the next target of a profanity-laced tirade, sometimes accented with a punch, slap, or shove just to make the point even clearer. We found the footprints, and did everything in our power to remain at attention and in place. With all the drill instructors screaming at us from the side, from the back, the front, we all struggled to focus on that one simple task. It was not that simple. I found my place and stood on the yellow footprints. Before I could even gain my balance, I felt the jarring assault of a DI screaming in my right ear from behind me.

Then a push from the left by another, and I was off balance. "What the hell are you doing? Get back you scumbag!" screamed the DI from behind me.

Every one of these drill instructors was a trained killer. Each had a presence about him that said as much, and if that nuance was lost on anyone, the bulging muscles, veins popping out of their foreheads and arms should have been enough to send that message. Some recruits were lucky and only had to deal with the yelling and personal insults. Others, like me, were on the ground doing pushups–*Marine Corps pushups*.

There is a difference. While in the pushup position, the Marine lowers his body to the ground, then up, then back to the ground, and then back up with arms locked–for *only one* pushup! I lost track of how many pushups I did that day. I was in great shape and managed to score a perfect three hundred on the physical fitness test before entering the Marines. In order to achieve a perfect score, I had to run three miles in under eighteen minutes, crank out eighty sit-ups in less than two minutes, and be able to do twenty pull-ups–my weak link. I was able to do twenty-one pull-ups in the test, and was getting stronger every day.

The drill instructors kept us awake for seventy-two hours straight. During this time, we removed all our civilian clothes, received our "high and tight" haircuts, and reported to the barracks. These living quarters would be my home for the next three months. Looking in the mirror after the haircut, with my *Revenge of the Nerds* black-rimmed glasses–complete with tape in the middle–I knew that my girlfriend would leave me if she could see me at that moment.

After the seventy-two hours passed, they allowed us to sleep for six hours. I was so mentally and physically exhausted that it seemed as if only a few minutes had passed before the drill instructors returned, yelling, throwing things around, and screaming at us to get out of bed. I stumbled to the front of my metal rack bed, still asleep and wishing to God that I had not enlisted in the Marine Corps! No coffee!

Sipping on a fresh cup of coffee in the morning at my kitchen table, waiting for the caffeine to ready my brain for the day was now just a memory and a fantasy that no longer seemed real. Verbal and physical abuse was the new stimulant. It was effective, but intolerable. Some of my fellow recruits were the recipients of the *Pyle treatment*–if you recall the scene from *Full Metal Jacket*. The drill instructor placed both hands in a choking position in front of the recruit and ordered him to *choke himself* on the DI's hands. It happened to several of my friends, but somehow, I escaped that one particularly sadistic experience.

Everything they ordered us to do involved some new form of degradation and humiliation. Our routine vaccinations were no different. I stood in line with the other one hundred or more recruits waiting my turn to receive a shot. When it was my turn, I walked down a hallway, and then to my right I saw a doorway. Someone–I could not see who told me, said to walk into the room. I saw a booth and a white blanket hanging. When I heard them give me the word, I walked through the blanket and, to my surprise, I saw a very attractive blonde woman sitting on a stool. Just when I started to think there might be a bright moment in my day, I noticed she was wearing a nasty scowl on her face. "*Drop your shorts!*" she barked. I hesitated. Noticing my hesitation, she repeated her order with an even meaner tone. "I'm only going to ask you *one* more time, now *DROP YOUR DAMN SHORTS!*" she screamed. I pulled down my shorts, and she motioned for me to come closer. I stepped toward her, not sure what to feel or expect. I watched in horror as she cupped my testicles and told me to "*Cough.*" Then, in a very matter-of-fact tone, she said, "Next!" She motioned for me to proceed to the next doorway.

Feeling violated and somewhat amused, I walked to the next doorway. My face was burning from embarrassment. In the next room, just like the last one, I saw another beautiful woman waiting. *What the hell is going on?* I thought. *Are the drill instructors getting a kick out of this?* She motioned for me to walk toward her. Reluctantly, I did so, and I heard that same command, "Drop your shorts!" After I lowered my shorts, she said, "Bend over, and *don't* move!" I turned my head slightly as I followed her order, only to see a long needle plunge into my buttocks. I pulled my shorts back up and went around another corner to stand in line again with my fellow Marines while we waited for the others to go through the process.

Marine Corps boot camp was the most challenging experience I have ever attempted and accomplished. The mental component of basic training back in 1986 exceeded every expectation–the movies did not prepare me for reality. Drill instructors yelled at us, mocked our mothers, sisters, and our personal appearance. Any possible insecurity was a target for the worst emotional abuse a person could dream up. For recruits who were Black or Native, we heard every racial slur imaginable, including a few epithets I had not heard before. They woke us at five-thirty in the morning, sharp. We had exactly two minutes to make our bed, get dressed, and be standing at attention for inspection by the DI. One minute, I was in a dead sleep–happy and cozy under the covers. No one yelled at me or made me drop and do push-ups. Two minutes later, I was standing in front of my bed at attention, fully dressed, and my bed made with a perfect forty-five-degree angle tuck on the flat sheet. The only certainty I could count on, was that my worst moments during the day could always get worse. More often than not, our platoon would run 3 to 5 miles in combat boots before breakfast! That old saying *"We do more before 0930 than most people do in a day"* is right on the money.

Later in the evening, my turn came for fire watch. During fire watch, each recruit in the platoon has to pull a one-hour shift guarding your fellow platoon members, the base camp, and he would sound the alarm in the event of enemy attack on the base. The guard previously on duty, woke me, handed me the flashlight, and briefed me on the status before he went back to sleep.

I walked up and down the aisles, checking both the top and bottom bunks to see that a recruit occupied each bed. There were about one hundred of us that first week. I approached the last four rows and began scanning the racks to see that everyone was present.

When I came to the second to last rack, I scanned the area with my flashlight. Something looked very wrong. My blood ran cold before I was conscious of what I perceived. A darkened, irregular circle formed under the bed; more drops descended as I watched. It was *blood*!

After pulling back the covers, I could see that it was the recruit known as "Kurser." He held a small knife in his hand as he sawed frantically at his wrist. Looking into his eyes, I saw *nothing*. His eyes were dead, like the eyes of a shark–but not the kind of dead that suggests a psychopathic killer lurks within. If eyes are the window to the soul, as we commonly hear, then what do we see when we look through the window and there is no soul? If the soul has given up and hidden itself from contact, we have *these* eyes.

I ran to the Sergeant's room. All military protocol escaped me at that moment. I banged on the door with my fist and yelled, "YO! Kurser is cutting his wrist!" The door swung open, slamming into the wall.

"What did you say?" He asked grabbing me by my shirt and pulling me forward. I repeated myself and explained what I saw while on night watch. The drill instructor and I ran to Kurser's rack and the drill instructor applied direct pressure on his wrist then escorted him out of the squad bay. We never saw him again.

In fact, we lost many recruits–some after drug testing, others from physical fitness problems, and some for firearm violations. There were those who simply quit because they could no longer tolerate the verbal and emotional abuse coupled with the physical demands that separated the wheat from the chaff. Every recruit felt the brutality of the testing process. This design strengthened those who made it through basic training, while eliminating those who should never have been there in the beginning. Out of more than one hundred recruits who showed up that first day, only sixty-five graduated boot camp.

The first physical fitness test was approaching soon, but I was not concerned. I had confidence in my physical abilities, and since my arrival, I had been sizing up every recruit–only Private Curry looked to be a serious contender. The fitness test included all the usual components–sit-ups, pull-ups, and the dreaded three-mile run.

The day finally came for the test, and I watched as my fellow Marines gave everything they had on the pull-up and sit-up testing. I scored a perfect one hundred points on both, and my level of confidence grew even more. Private Curry also scored a perfect 200 points. Instead of individually timed runs, or having the platoon run together as a group, I would be testing with the entire battalion of five hundred to eight hundred Marines running together on a hot August day in California.

When I stood at the starting line, there were so many Marines that I had to adjust my strategy. Crowds are fluid. They form bottlenecks, affecting the flow, and the speed. They also coagulate like a gel, restricting movement, and keeping one from moving as fast as he normally could. I decided to start at a much faster pace and take the risk that I might expend too much energy.

The gun fired. I sprinted to the front of the pack. Private Curry was in front of me, and a tall, African-American recruit was in front of him. Our pace was brisk that first half-mile, at which point it was the tall recruit in the lead, then Private Curry, then me in third. At the one-mile mark, we were still running at a rapid pace–too fast for me to avoid exhaustion if this were to continue. I dropped back and watched the two in front continue ahead.

At the halfway mark, I could see that Private Curry also had dropped back, and the tall recruit was a tiny figure in the distance ahead. I pushed ahead with no intention of trying to catch up. I focused on my breathing and my pace. Looking around, there were no other recruits anywhere close, and the finish line was just ahead. When the finish line came into view, I started to sprint. As soon as I crossed the finish line, I started throwing up. Dry heave after dry heave. I saw the tall recruit standing to the side–sweating but not showing any serious signs of exhaustion. Private Curry was standing close to him and he looked like he had just thrown up before I started. I heard the time shouted at me as I crossed the line. It was my personal best at sixteen minutes and twenty seconds. Private Curry came in ahead at sixteen minutes five seconds, and the tall recruit finished at fifteen minutes fifty seconds! I earned a perfect score of three hundred on the fitness test–one of *twelve* perfect physical fitness scores I would achieve during my four years as a Marine.

I arrived at boot camp weighing one hundred fifty-five pounds, carrying a very bad attitude toward authority, and suppressing my anger with a lot of drinking. Basic training was tough. Nobody could do anything right the first three weeks. I started to understand that this was all part of the plan–to tear down the undisciplined old self so they could rebuild us as trained killers, ready to dispatch the enemy at a moment's notice. It was at this moment that the Creator allowed me to experience and develop the "never-give-up-attitude" that would serve me well later in life, as I battled drug dealers as a law enforcement officer. That same attitude kept me going to clear my family name and restore my honor through my epic seven-year court battle against the Federal Government for corruption. When I left basic training, I weighed one hundred seventy-five pounds and, if I did not know better, I would have thought I had grown from five-nine to five-eleven.

I had never fired a rifle before in my life. When they introduced me to the rifle range, I had no bad habits to break–I was the perfect blank slate they needed to teach me the correct way to handle a firearm. The drill instructors provided each of us with everything we needed to master the M-16A2 assault rifle. This weapon became our best friend.

We carried it *everywhere* during the rifle phase of Marine Corps training. My rifle was next to me as I slept, and accompanied me to every activity when I woke up. I learned how to disassemble and reassemble my rifle–sometimes while blindfolded. Everything we did during those weeks prepared us to fight, win, and succeed in war and peace. I became qualified as a rifle expert, hitting the bullseye target at one thousand yards in the prone position and I retained that status throughout my military career.

Our platoon had to pull a week of kitchen duty, known as "KP," and the platoon that previously held that duty trained us on every aspect before we took over. I learned that my duty would be to keep the freezer stocked, clean, and tidy. While looking over the freezer contents, I heard a familiar voice, "What's going on, brother?" I looked up and saw Jeff Hill from the Tulalip Indian Reservation. It felt so good to see a familiar face! Jeff explained, after looking over his shoulders quickly, that if we worked as a team, one of us could get twenty-five minutes of sleep by getting into one of the freezers while the other Marine kept watch. It might not sound like much, but twenty-five minutes of sleep in Marine Corps boot camp was like a million dollar check when you were not expecting it. My partner and I used this tactic during the entire two weeks of kitchen duty, taking turns, and then passed this information on to the next platoon. To this day, I do not know if platoons have continued the tradition of passing this secret treasure on from one platoon to the next.

The heat could be intense at the rifle range. Before we even started target practice, we had to check each of the wooden crates we used for support, and check for scorpions and poisonous spiders. Our focus had to be clear, with thoughts about scorching heat and venomous critters, neatly tucked away from conscious thought. We used open sights and learned the concepts of proper breathing, pulling up the slack on the trigger until the round went off.

At the end of rifle training, we faced a new challenge, affectionately referred to by everyone as *Mount Mother Fucker*." Each recruit was required to trek up this intimidating mountain or risk discharge from the Corps. We heard the stories from others who had made the climb before us. This would be a real test of physical fitness, mental focus, and pain tolerance. On the day of the climb, our platoon was both excited and nervous. I wasted no time thinking about my strategy–I would need to focus, and force myself to continue ahead regardless of pain and exhaustion. It was not so much a strategy as it was a pep talk. The stakes were high, but I knew that if others had done this before me, I would succeed.

We were off. Each of us had to carry a backpack–fully packed, and our rifle. With the weight of the extra payload, and the summer sun beating down on us as we fought gravity up this merciless climb, the signs of exhaustion were more evident all around me. Beads of sweat pooled on the faces of Marines walking next to me, and I could feel the quickening of my breath as I struggled to fill my lungs. *One step at a time. Climbing. One step in front of the other. More climbing.*

I was getting closer to the summit. My forehead was soaked in sweat and streamed down my face, into my eyes, and soaked my green t-shirt and my hair. It was difficult, to say the least, but I was not falling behind. Private Richard Curry, who had come in second in the three-mile run, was keeping pace with me as was the African American Marine who finished first in the run. Just before we crested, gravity took its last swing at us, straining my leg and back muscles particularly hard, and forcing me to breathe faster and deeper than at any other part of the climb. Then it suddenly got lighter, easier, and I was on top.

Private Curry and I wiped the sweat from our foreheads and tried to catch our breath. Then we heard a drill sergeant say, "Hey *boy*! What are you fucking looking at? You made it to *Bitch Ridge, boy*!" I looked up in disbelief.

When I saw that I was not done, and what I had to climb ahead, I muttered to myself, "*Mother effer*!" Private Curry and I looked at each other, knowing we were going to be the first to grapple with this steep mountain. We realized the race was on! It was up to us to make a good showing for Platoon 1042 and our company. I decided at that moment that I would not look up again until I reached the top of this enormous mountain.

There was a small group of Marines in front of Private Curry, and he was no more than five feet in front of me. We continued our climb in the California sun, our packs growing heavier with each step and our clothes were drenched in sweat. I thought back to the three-mile run–how he finished ahead of me and the African-American recruit finished ahead of him. I was very competitive. Looking to my right, I could see that same, tall Marine who finished first in the three mile was just slightly behind me. That competitive drive was all I needed to lighten my steps. I found a rhythm, and focused on moving forward at a steady pace.

I was even with Private Curry. He glanced up and acknowledged me as I passed him. Drops of sweat fell steadily like drizzling rain. It became pointless to wipe it away–it just kept pouring as I forced myself forward. I caught up to the small group of Marines who were ahead of me. I heard a voice from the group say, "Who the hell is that?"

"Private Hodgson Garvais Lawrence, sir," I replied as I passed them.

"Fuck you," was the reply.

I thought the end would never come. Just after sunset, I arrived at the top. I was breathing hard, my heart was pounding rapidly, and sweat had drenched my hair and shirt. "What's your name, recruit?" I heard a voice ask. There was an air of authority in his voice, or maybe even some inherent command for respect. Turning slightly toward the voice, I saw the sun reflect off the stars neatly pinned on his collar. Immediately, I snapped to attention and saluted.

"Good evening, sir!" He returned the salute.

"At ease." That was a relief. Even holding my frame upright seemed impossible after the tortuous climb. "What's your name?"

"Private Duane Hodgson Garvais Lawrence," I replied.

"Where are you from?"

"Seattle, Washington, sir." To my surprise, this general of the United States Marine Corps was very cordial and seemed to take a genuine interest in our conversation.

"You do realize that you are the first one to the top of Mount Mother Fucker out of the entire battalion, right?" He asked.

"Yes, sir." We made small talk about the weather, mostly, before the drill instructors crested the top of the hill. They paused to catch their breath and glared at me when they were not wiping away the sweat.

"It was a pleasure talking to you, recruit, but now; I must be on my way." I snapped to attention and saluted him.

After he walked away, the drill instructors encircled me. All of them were screaming at me simultaneously. I felt their eyes attacking me the moment they arrived and saw me talking to the General. It was a matter of timing–they were too cowardly to make a move while in view of the General, who *clearly* liked me. They *had* to notice that, and it did not ultimately help my cause.

"Who the *hell* do you think you are? Who gave *you* permission to pass *us*?" Their rant was nothing less than an assault, coming at me from every side. Until the rest of the battalion reached the top, I had to do push-ups, sit-ups, run in place, and bend-and-thrusts. This was a long wait, so I paced myself as best I could.

When the rest reached the top, some were throwing up and all of them were gasping for air. Staff Sergeant Clark was among those who surrounded me and hurled insults for making it to the top first. Drill instructors do not like anyone, at least, that is the impression they try very hard to make. Staff Sergeant Clark was different from the other drill instructors, in that he seemed to have a very personal dislike for me as soon as he set eyes on me.

Marine Corps recruiters and drill instructors told us early on *"Color does not exist in the Marine Corps."* At first, I thought it was just the drill instructor routine, and I tried not to take it personally. I noticed over time, though, that SSGT Clark singled out recruits of color, predictably, to take the brunt of his hostility. Spiritually, a person can tell if another person does not like you. In his case, he did not like *anyone* of color. I realized early on that he was prejudiced. The signs were everywhere in his pattern for which recruits received the most sadistic punishment or degrading epithets. I knew he had a problem with me when he whispered in my ear, "What's your problem, *buffalo nigger*?" During my senior year in high school, I had a serious anger problem toward others who picked on the weaker kids. Seeing that always provoked a physical revulsion, and usually, I was not able to stop myself from physically intervening. I never would have imagined that I could keep my cool through this kind of test. It took everything I had to restrain my temper when Staff Sergeant Clark slithered up to me in line and addressed me as *"half-breed"* in his usual, *cowardly* manner–whispered in my ear so only I could hear him. Every time he started his racist tirade, I could feel my blood boil, a slight tremor in my hands as I tried to calm my blood pressure.

I was squad leader on the parade deck when we were practicing our marching maneuvers. Staff Sergeant Clark called out the cadence, but for some reason, I did not hear his command, "Column half right, march!" I continued marching straight with my squad behind me, when I should have marched right. Clark ran up to me, screamed at the top of his lungs, and pushed me hard enough that I had to take three or four steps back. Feeling enraged, I shoved him back. Much to his surprise, he stumbled back as the force of my M-16 A2 rifle butt stock hit him directly in the chest. I had had enough and lost all military bearing. My squad was in shock. The other drill instructors ran to our positions, some stepping in front of Staff Sergeant Clark and the others in front of me. I received the worst end of that deal as I was thrashed right there on the burning hot asphalt for my actions. Looking back now, I can once again see how the Creator was protecting me as I did not receive office hours or sent to the BRIG.

That oversight led to my demotion as squad leader, which directly affected my chance for promotion to Private First Class upon graduation.

I found out later, though, that the Marine Corps demoted Staff Sergeant Clark to the rank of Sergeant for hitting recruits of color over an extended period. At graduation, we were able to shake hands with all our drill instructors.

When I approached Staff Sergeant Clark, I could feel that familiar tightening around the corner of my mouth–a sign that I was ready to *fight*. I extended my hand to shake, maintaining piercing eye contact with him. He appeared agitated as soon as I entered his field of vision. I was not about to waste this opportunity.

"Staff Sergeant Clark, I want to *thank* you for all your hard work during our time here at Marine Corps boot camp." As I tightened my grip on his hand, I continued, "And Staff Sergeant Clark, if I ever see you in the Fleet Marine Corps, *I'm gonna kick your ass*!" He was not pleased, but somehow, he knew that his response had to be *nothing*, or maybe he was just at a loss for words–not like him at all. I made my point very clear, from the expression on his face, and I moved on, quickly.

There were no avenues for lodging a complaint against a drill instructor because his choice of words were unsavory, because he picked on one person a little more, or even when they got physically mean. Even if those channels existed on paper, they were not to be used. Case in point–in 1986, President Ronald Reagan issued an order prohibiting drill instructors from physically assaulting recruits during training. The newspaper came out with an article on his new position, but I did not read it over coffee at breakfast.

The drill instructors ordered us to stand at attention at the end of our racks and wait. The drill instructors walked into the squad bay, some walking to the east and west windows, looking out the window and remaining on guard. We waited. Another five minutes passed before Senior Drill Instructor, Staff Sergeant Medina, walked into the squad bay. The room was silent. It had been silent already before he walked in–so silent, yet it felt as if you could hear the thoughts of everyone in the room. When a heavily occupied room is *that* silent, the sounds that take over just add to the anxiety. I could hear my own respiration, then the sound of someone shifting his weight, the leather groaned as it creased slightly. Every recruit was in suspense, and unable to speak. Each knew that *something* was going on–nobody had a clue what it could be, except that it was *bad*.

Staff Sergeant Medina paused halfway into the squad bay and casually looked around at his junior drill instructors. Staff Sergeant Medina pulled out a newspaper. Meticulously opening it to an inside page, he brought the newspaper up to reading level and began to address the room. "Effective *immediately* ...," he began. His mouth formed a scowl as he spoke. He read every line, word for word with perfect enunciation. He was in no hurry. He walked up and down the line of recruits as he read. Other than his voice, the only sound we could hear was the *click clack* of his boots taking methodical steps in front of one recruit, then on to the next random recruit.

The content of the article was very relevant. The Commander-in-Chief issued a *direct* order to all drill instructors never to strike or assault a recruit. After he finished reading, he paused. Folding the newspaper in half, he glanced about the room, from one junior drill instructor to the next, and then set the paper on the footlocker near him. Out of my peripheral vision, I saw the junior drill instructor at the east window nod subtly to Medina.

It came without warning. The recruit standing in front of Medina was the first to go down. Medina slugged him, threw him on the ground, and began screaming at him an inch from his face. As the recruit struggled to stand, Medina had already dropped another recruit, randomly selected a few steps from his first. I heard the heavy thud, the impact from his fist slamming deep into a recruit's abdomen, the grunt of pain, gasping, screaming, and hitting the floor just like the last. Medina was standing directly in front of me. Like a demon, his eyes were scanning the faces in front of him. Unpredictable and devastating. His hands reached in front of me, and as I braced for the punch, it landed on the Marine next to me. He went to the ground hard. I could feel his body slam onto the ground next to me. The other drill instructors had joined in. We stood still and waited for the unpredictable, random attack.

It stopped as suddenly as it started. The drill instructors returned to their previous positions, and Medina waited for the last man to stand at attention.

"Did anybody see or hear *anything*?" He asked, addressing the entire platoon.

"No Senior Drill Instructor Medina!" Platoon 1042 replied in unison. Some struggled to stand while concealing the searing pain. Nobody questioned the incident. In fact, there was *no* incident. We were Marines and no politician would tell us *how* to be Marines. Some of the men had never been in a fight in their lives. If we were in war, would they have my back and could they count on me? A tactic like this–no matter how offensive to civilian taste, had its utility. Marines stick together, Marines fight together, Marines never leave another on the battlefield and MARINES DIE TOGETHER IF NEED BE!

After I graduated boot camp, I attended the Infantry Training School, known as ITS. This was similar to boot camp, except we had weekends off and we could now use the title, *United States Marine*. I was lying in my bed, awake and thinking about how much boot camp had changed me from the self-doubting, shy man who would often defer to others. I had put on twenty pounds of pure muscle. I learned how to use voice commands to take control of a situation and how to walk with confidence. Still I did not want to be that person who turned out brainwashed. We have all seen them. They cannot separate military life from their private life. *Not me*. I decided I would walk off base without saluting a single officer. As a Marine, I was required to salute an officer if I saw him, so I got creative. Basketball had been on my mind lately. It was always on my mind, when I could relax enough to reminisce.

I saw some basketball gear at the PX–Air Jordan's, shorts, and a tank top. Decked out in only the best basketball attire money could buy at a Marine Corps PX, I searched for the path most likely to cross an officer–or two–on my way, and no, I did not salute a single officer along the way. Starting Friday at five o'clock pm–1700 hours, until Monday morning at five-thirty, we were free to spend our time as we chose. We all heard about Hollywood from movies and television, seen the stories about sunset strip, Hollywood Boulevard, and the walk of Hollywood stars. Four of us decided to pool our money together and rent a room over the weekend so we could have that *California* experience.

Instructors in ITS warned us that there were any number of sketchy people out there just waiting for naïve Marines to ambush. There was the set-up, usually a pretty lady, then a signal to the wolves waiting in the shadows before the ambush. For Marines caught in this common scenario, they often found themselves badly beaten, stranded, and without cash or identification. Although this was all very new terrain for me, I liked to think I was sharp enough to smell a trap when I saw one. My casual stroll down the famous streets of Hollywood opened my eyes to a very different world. There were so many people sharing the same sidewalk, people from every lifestyle and every ethnicity.

Once back at the hotel, we decided we had to check out the club scene. As much as we were interested in seeing all the famous sights, we had one thing on our mind.

California girls. MTV videos, the big screen, and celebrities–all points of interest–but California girls were always front and center of Hollywood's appeal. In 1986, if you wanted to look the part, you had to borrow wardrobe advice from Don Johnson. I had every obligatory accessory–the black pants, white muscle t-shirt, shiny black dress shoes, and of course the long sleeve, silk, collared and unbuttoned shirt. I looked like I walked off the set of *Miami Vice*, which was the goal.

I stopped off at Bank of America for some cash before hitting the first club. These clubs were like nothing I had seen before. The dance floors were sprawling, with DJ's that knew what they were doing. The music was loud and pulsed through your chest–you could move with it without even trying. Mostly, I just wanted to dance, so that is what I did.

When the evening came to a close, I had danced, talked to more pretty girls than I had ever seen in one place, and drank my share of beers. I thought I would have one last drink, and sat up at the bar next to an attractive Asian woman. She asked if I would buy her a drink, so I ordered two. As I opened my wallet to pay, she scanned the wad of twenties and looked past me to where there were a number of rough-looking thugs hanging out near the other side of the room. Two men closest to me were black, tall, and built like trucks–the other two were Asian, and slightly smaller, but still very rough looking. A possible fifth man stood off to the side, looking around suspiciously as if he was involved in their scheme, but trying just a little harder to be discreet.

I knew already what was going down. I did not see how she did it, but I have to assume she sent them a signal, because as soon as my wallet was open and she looked up, four that I could see, started walking slowly in my direction.

They had warned me about this very scenario. I knew there was only one way out of this. I was in top physical condition and I had the training to handle myself in a fair fight. There was nothing fair about the gang about to encircle me. I had to think fast.

My drink was sitting on the bar, half-full. I politely excused myself and told her we should dance when I got back. She smiled and nodded. There was nothing warm in her smile. It would matter how I carried myself, how I managed my pace, and how relaxed I appeared. I had to look as if I had no concern other than making it to the bathroom on time. They figured I would be back. I was careful never to make eye contact with any other patrons in the bar as I made my way to the bathroom in the back. There was a side door right across from the bathroom. The bathroom door swung open, and I felt a momentary sense of relief that I had made it that far. I was not using the bathroom, though; I needed to get out that side door before I lost my opportunity. I made a quick step across the hall, pushed the door open, and sprinted the second I was clear.

I was out. Adrenaline and reality had kicked in. I was their meal ticket and they were not pleased. I only had a few minutes to get away before they realized I was not coming back. It turned out to be even less than that.

As I put distance between the bar, and myself I could already hear shouts and footsteps behind me. I was right to get away. The same four or five men, who looked so sketchy in the bar, were now in a full chase behind me–yelling at me to *stop*! "Come back!" *Were they kidding*? I chose to *run*. It was over quick–none of them felt up to a run.

Illustrations

Grandma Ellen Conway Garvais, me, Grandpa Charlie Garvais Lawrence and Marie Sullivan

Japanese Military Hokkaido counterpart insisted on us getting a picture together. Operation Valant Blitz Marines 1989

Duane Garvais Lawrence United States Marines- Gulf Company-25 Airborne - Assault Climber - Radio Operator - Police Chaser - 0311 and Marine Security Forces Charleston South Carolina

Airborne @ a club with the boyz, LCpl Chiaravalle, LCpl Stillmunks and LCpl Brian Johnson 1989 1990 Camp Pendleton California.

LCpl Hodgson Garvais Lawrence
1st Battalion 2nd Marines Gulf
Company 25 cleaning my squad
automatic 5.56 Weapon in the
jungles of Okinawa 1989 Airborne

KennyGarvais Lawrence United
States Air Force

Gulf Company 25 San Mateo
United States Marines 1990

Most decorated division! Gulf
Company

Marine Corps Gulf Co 25 MPHS
Alumni Greg Chariavelle Brian
Johnson

Marine Corps Book Camp 1986
Platoon 1042

The Military ship we arrived on.
Operation Valiant Blitz

Picture balling at Okinowa! The brother running with me is none other than Cpl Smallwood. Yep the same Cpl Smallwood I fought with then relied on to graduate Assault Climbers Course Sc

Nothing but net! Balling on the courts Okinowa 1989

German Shepard Tania Dog Tags early 80's

One of my best friends LCpl Danny Urias from Compton California. San Mateo 1989 and Okinowa 1989. Gulf Company 25

Top picture was taken during climb up Big Face Assault Climbers school during Cold weather training - Bottom picture was taken to show the elevation we reached during the course

Showing off the muscles Semper Fidelis Okinowa right after receiving my office hours running from the Military Police across the entire Camp Schwab base. (They never caught me)

Marine Corps M16-A2 Assault Rifle!

Kenny Garvais Lawrence

Mom's Drive In

Garvais Dustin Perrit rest area
Stevens Pass 1991

Thunderbird Drive In

Big Scoop

MPHS 85 Yearbook

MPHS 85 Yearbook cover (1)

MPHS Alumni Rob Martoff
Marshal Leaf (RIP) and Rod
Vesenmeyer

Duane Hodgson Garvais
Lawrence. Marie Hodgson
Sullivan and Marcy Hodgson
Petzold. My sister's taken when I
was Sophomore and Marie was a
Senior at Marysville Pillchuck
High School

Angie Wallace Kim Antak MPHS
30

MPHS Champion Wrestlers

Marysville Middle School Track
and Field

111

Marysville Middle School Track
and Field Champions

Danielle hall Peterson

MPHS 30 year peeps

MPHS peeps Sam Grow, David
Spencer Jr and Matt Tully

James Sterba De Stanton MPHS

Kim Howard MPHS

Kurt Halvorsen being Kurt!

Lynette Carlson Karin Earnst
Chavis Chris Kutz

MPHS classmatesMPHS Alumni
might remember my high school
muscle car!

MPHS 30 year Eddie Moss,
Connie McKee and Sam Grow

MPHS Alumni my high school
muscle car! 1971 Chevrolet
Monte Carlo, 4 bolt main Holly
350 double pumper carburetor,
Muncie 4 speed

MPHS Lane Shinnick Kelly
Boston

MPHS Rainer BEER

THE infamous Polaroid picture
taken at the rest area in Ohio the
day after I spent the night in jail
for a DUI trying to led the Cops
away from Hurtle.

Party in the back lol

My 1987 Pontiac Formula
Firebird, Boyd Rims, Dual
exhaust, T Tops, 5 speed 305
muscle car United States Marines

Sandi Staples Daniell Hall MPHS

Some things never change!

Susan Herring Paula Vanderpool
MPHS

Z MAN!

Tony Aubry Sam Grow Brad
Stuller

Top: Deaken Sullivan, pictured with
me
Bottom: Ralph Marcy Petzold
wedding

Kirk Sunitch - Baseball, Ron Hoffman - Wrestling, Lane Shinnick - Basketball, Tim Gross - Wrestling
Hall of Fame

My beautiful mother Mary McDonald Wenger, aka: Thriftway Mary. She worked many years at Hearth's Thriftway Also picture my awesome little sister

St Paul Chapel New York City 2013. Tina Cline, LoVina Louie, Mariah Boyd, Daisy Marie Garvais Lawrence, Northstar Garvais Lawrence

Chapter 8: San Clemente, California 1990

The following story illustrates just how much fun, and trouble, in which we could find ourselves. Greg Chiaravalle contributed this story, and I am presenting it in his own words.

To Duane Garvais Lawrence, (KD Lawrence),

This story like many of our stores begins back in the day. We were young Marines serving our time with the greatest fighting battalion of all time, 2nd Battalion, 5th Marines, 1st Marine division. A battalion authorized to wear the French Fouragutte as a result of combat readiness and honor in WWII. We had just moved from our location near the town of San Mateo near the town of San Clemente. We loved being Marines, and we loved hanging out and enjoying all the sun surf and nightclubs of Southern California presented to young marines.

This story begins one night in the year of 1990. KD and I decided to hit the club to show off on the dance scene. Me? I don't dance even though I carried the nickname of "Plastic Man," so named by KD Duane Garvais because of my long legs, arms. I did however enjoy the partying scene and drinking, laughter etc. KD Duane Garvais I fondly nicknamed the MONCHICHI for the lovable Monchichi doll and its head of hair. KD could flat out dance, I mean the dude had rhythm and it was not uncommon to see him show up African Americans on the floor, busting out the Roger Rabbit, the Running Man, Kid n Play, Cabbage Patch, MC Hammer, you name it KD killed it!

Anyhow, the "trouble" began right from the start that night, as I was only 20 years old. KD was over 21. Our partners in crime, Patrick 'Still Monkey" Stillmunks was on guard duty working the armory that night and our other brother, Brian "Da Bri" Johnson also known as Calvin & Hobbs (For the faces he could make) was not to be found that glorious night.

Now Stillmunks was a good-looking young man, how good looking you ask? He was so good looking he looked just like me, well the photo on his Nebraska Driver's License did, so much so that I had been using his license to get into bars for some time now, tonight would be no different!

Flash forward to a night of dancing and drinking at the local bar and club in San Clemente California, a great time we had! Now this isn't a story of what one should do, very much the opposite, but we were young,

117

dumb, and full of come as the Corps says. We used to have a strange game that the person that seemed to be the most drunk was given the duty to drive the rest of us Marines back to the base! The thought was that Marine would be the most careful and diligent to see us through and get us back to base.

The club was closing and a mass of young people were dumping into the club parking lot to hoop up, go get some afterhours chow and head back to base to get some much needed shut eye. Well after exiting the club KD and I made our way back to KD's muscle car, a 1988 red formula firebird T-Top 5 speed. We were in the process of chatting up the ladies, trying to get some play, some digits etc. Then it was time to bolt, head back to base. Before doing so I had need to relieve myself to that evenings cocktails, so I stepped up to the front of the car near the bushes to do so. KD had settled to rest against the firebird car door and while we were BS about the night's events a local police cruiser pulled up, shined its spotlight on KD and I both. I quickly finished my business and turned my attention to the police officer who was now getting out of the cruiser to talk with KD and I.

The local police I'm sure have seen a great many drunk marines while on patrol, had probably encountered many situations and events, BUT tonight they were in for a real treat, the comedy duo act of Plastic Man and Monchichi!

The officers asked us for our driver's license or ID, I of course provided the good-looking Nebraska driver's license of one Mr. Patrick J. Stillmunks, since I was underage and I did not want to get into any trouble. The officers took our ID cards and made several phone calls radio calls then walked back to talk to us both. The officer asked me where I was heading. I being very quick of wit and alcohol replied "To your wife's house for breakfast" I awoke a few minutes later in the back of his squad car in handcuffs looking out the passenger's side window.

I saw KD shaking a set of car keys in his mouth saying very loudly, "You can't arrest us because the keys were not in the ignition!" KD said this over and over, getting louder each time. After several minutes of this little comedy act, KD was quickly detained, handcuffed, and placed beside me in the back seat in the same police cruiser.

I looked at KD and said "HEY BUDDY"!

The local police rather than book us for being morons and assholes, took us to the main gate of Camp San Mater to drip us off with the Marines. Now this was a Godsend because we maybe saved ourselves from further

118

trouble or killing someone! This however wasn't the thoughts KD and I had that night. We were both worried because as far as the Cops knew, I was Patrick Stillmunks and my drunk buddy KD. Well we got booked on to our Units guard shack, now mind you this is the same guard shack that ONE Patrick Stillmunks was currently housed in the armory. The Sergeant on duty recognized me as I was from H&S Company, he did recognize the name of Patrick J Stillmunks. So at the moment of him seeing the name he yells into the armory to our right real loud.

"Hey Stillmunks" There is a white dude out her with the same name as you and man even looks like you. At that very moment the armory door opened wide by another Marine and KD and I and Stillmunks all locked eyes laughing, knowing our carefree days of drinking could be over!

–Greg Chiaravalle

Chapter 9: Charleston, South Carolina, August 1986

It dont matter what tribe you from
we all one nation under the Son,
we da fried bread snackin, 49 crashin,
feathered out beaded up pow wow packin
– Lil Mike & Funny Bone, "Do the Rain Dance"

After graduating from Infantry Training School, I and thirty-five other Marines received a call to report to the health clinic. We had orders to fly to Rodman Marine Corps base located on the Panama Canal. I had never heard of that base before, but I did know from history how significant that stretch of real estate was to the United States and our entire hemisphere. The security of commercial shipping between North and South America was completely dependent on keeping the Panama Canal safe.

I stood at attention, boots together at forty-five degrees, thumbs by the seam of my trousers, and body locked. We were to have our sleeves rolled up, as the nurses were administering vaccinations. I stepped up to the nurse, who held a gun with as many as six different vaccines in each gun. There was one to my left shoulder and one to my right shoulder, for twelve very painful injections.

Everything happened so fast. I was at the staging area, where we boarded the buses–the first leg of the journey to Panama. I had not told my mother, my girlfriend, or anyone else in my family. I sat on the bus with the other Marines looking out the windows at the commotion starting to take place on the cement platform. Several ITS instructors were shouting and walking in a stressed manner. One of them boarded our bus and read twelve names aloud. My name was among them. "Get off the bus and go to bus number twenty-five!" he shouted.

I grabbed my sea bag and boarded number twenty-five with the other Marines. Once we sat down, the ITS instructor boarded the bus and explained that we were being *redirected* to Charleston South Carolina, Naval Weapons Station, Marine Security Forces. At that time, the United States was involved in a direct conflict in Panama, and Marines were injured or killed as a result. Were it not for the Creator's intervention, I would have been in the middle of an armed conflict in that region.

Looking out the window as our plane approached the Charleston airport, I could see the lakes, streams, and trees that reminded me of growing up in the Seattle area. It was August 1986, and this was my first visit to any of the southern states. The plane came to a stop and I was eager to step outside finally. All the movies and photos I had seen of the south did little to prepare me for the real thing. With my bag in hand, and waiting my turn to exit, I looked out the windows at the Charleston airport.

My lungs were the first to notice the difference between Charleston and Seattle. I immediately found it difficult to breathe; the humidity was competing for dry, cool air that I was so used to all my life. *Only in a sauna have I ever experienced this kind of heat and humidity*, I thought as I descended the steps to the pavement below.

Once I stepped foot on the hot pavement, my only thought was to get inside the airport and out of that intolerable humidity. The main doors were just ahead. As I got closer, I saw an older African American man sitting in a chair just outside the main door. I quickly opened the first set of doors, when the man looked up to me and said, "Hey boy, you isn't from around here is you, boy?" I smiled and shook my head, *no*. He had to have noticed my struggling to breathe as I ambled that short distance to the main door. "You'll get used to it, boy!" He said and laughed.

"Thanks," I replied. I hoped he was right because this was miserable. I did not have to wait much longer before I was boarding another bus en route to Marine Security Forces Naval Weapons Station, Goose Creek, Charleston, South Carolina. At the main gate, they checked our identification before we travelled another ten miles to our barracks. The duty station was unique and played an important role during World War II. Once the bus came to a stop, I grabbed my sea bag and exited the bus with my fellow Marines. Staff Sergeant Grant called us to attention, at which time he took roll and assigned us to one of three platoons. Staff Sergeant Grant assigned me to the First Platoon, then dismissed us and instructed us to report to our respective platoons.

Once I joined my platoon, our Gunnery Sergeant put us into formation, and conducted his best attempt at a welcome speech. The first thing I noticed was that our Gunnery Sergeant had only nine fingers, and that he wore a permanent scowl on his face. I learned at that time that we had a four day weekend commencing immediately–not a bad way to start the first day of my new assignment.

I located my room, unpacked, and made my bed. My excitement about the unexpected time off began to diminish as I realized that I was in a state I knew nothing about. Ten miles from the gate without a car, I would not be going far. I sat on my bed and thought about it. I heard a sound coming from outside—one that I knew well. In fact, I no longer had much concern about how I would use the next four days. *Thump, thump, thump, thump…*

I got off my bed and opened my second drawer where I kept my basketball shorts and tank top. I finished tying the laces on my Air Jordan's and promptly left my room in search of the basketball court. I saw a Marine on the court, wearing Air Jordan's and a baseball cap on backwards. He had dark hair and eyes, and grinned at me as I approached. "What's up, brother?" he asked.

"Can I shoot some hoops with you?" I replied.

"Sure!" He shook my hand and introduced himself. "They call me Stallion, but my name's Don Giambra." I gave him my name and we started a game of one-on-one. Little did I know at that moment, that Stallion would become one of my best friends to this day. From watching him shoot, I could tell he was good. I wondered if I could beat him, though. He scored the first shot—a midrange jump shot. I tied it up with a layup in the next play. I ended up beating him ten to six.

I asked if he wanted to go again, and he asked for the basketball. Once he got it in his hands, he dropkicked it over the fence, laughed, and said, "I'll be right back." When he returned, we played again, and this time, I beat him ten to five. Stallion repeated his ritual of dropkicking the ball over the fence. When he returned, he asked, "Are you playing as hard as you can?"

"No," I replied.

"How am I gonna get better if you're takin' it easy on me?" He asked, glaring at me. I really liked this Italian from Buffalo, New York. We had the same likes and dislikes. We were both competitive and shared similarities in our style.

We played another game, and I won again—ten to three. This time, I had played about ninety-five percent. Expecting to see the ball fly over the fence again, he asked, "Got anything planned tonight?"

"Nothing," I replied.

"Swing by my room around seven, and we'll go out." His room was located in the headquarters building. We agreed to meet up later, and I returned to my room, where I showered, dressed in my favorite pair of Levi's 501 button-fly jeans, a black Van Halen t-shirt, and sneakers. It was six forty-five, so I left my room and walked over to the headquarters building.

I found his room and knocked. The door opened–an African American Marine by the name of Lance Corporal Peter Ward invited me inside, and behind him, I saw Stallion and five black Marines drinking beer around a coffee table. Peter Ward shook his head, "Oh hell no, Stallion! He is *not* going with us!" he said and walked to the other side of the room. Unsure at first what caused that sudden reaction, I looked at Stallion. He knew.

Smiling, he addressed the other men in the room. "Guys, this is Hodgie."

"Who's Hodgie?" I asked.

"You are Hodgie," he said smiling. This was a reference to the popular cartoon, *Johnny Quest and Hodgie*. He went around the room, introducing each man–Troy "Money Edwards, Pete Ward, Angel Cartagena, Rubin Diaz, and two others. As introductions were in progress, I overheard a number of comments–clearly sarcastic, about my Seattle attire. That was the cause for all the fuss. When I compared my attire to how everyone else was dressed, I stood out. I was feeling good about my clothing choices before I left my room, but I was in new territory and there was a significant difference in style.

Stallion walked me over to his wall locker, and handed me a pair of black eel shoes, black slacks, white muscle t-shirt, black long-sleeve shirt with collar, three gold rings, and two gold rope chains. Armed with all the latest trends, I went into the bathroom to change. I stepped out of the bathroom when I was done, and there was an almost instantaneous response. Everyone who had previously shook his head *NO*, nodded his head in approval. I found a mirror on the wall and decided to look for myself. *I look like a pimp!* I thought. It was a completely new look for me, but it earned me a cold beer and a warm welcome into the group. A cool mix of *Rodney O* and *Joe Cooley* "Cooly High" came to life bumping through the speakers, courtesy of the Techniques Turn Tables and Stallion.

I was on my third beer, and the small talk quickly redirected to more pointed questions about where I was from. People still considered Seattle a smaller city back then. It did not set the trends like LA or New York. I discovered almost everyone in the room grew up in large cities, like Chicago, New York, Detroit, and Los Angeles. Hip-hop was relatively new–artists such as *LL Cool J, Run DMC, Grandmaster Flash*, Fat Boys,

Beastie Boys, Sheila E, KRS1, Kool Moe D, and *New Edition* were exploding. The first big screen movie about hip-hop, *Krush Groove*, was an instant hit, making millions and reaching an even larger audience. Hip-hop was new to me, but I loved it. I was a big fan of the eighties rock bands, like *Ratt, Van Halen, Judas Priest*, and *Scorpions*. Even though hip-hop and eighties rock were different, I found a common love for the rhythm and beat. The men in the room all had a clear preference for hip-hop, but they at least had an appreciation for both.

We were off to the bars. We had to take two cars for all of us to fit. As we pulled up to the club, I saw a sizable crowd waiting to get in. Even in the evening, the humidity began to dampen my clothing. I needed to get inside as soon as I could.

The line at *JW's* wrapped all the way around the club. I still had a buzz by the time we made it to where the line formed. I was not thrilled about the long wait, but it was not as if I had somewhere else to be. When we got to the line, my friends led me past everyone and we walked directly past the people in the back of the line. As we approached the front of the line, I could hear the rhythm and music coming from inside. This was unlike any club I had been to before. An energy and excitement seemed palpable, pulsing in the air. We continued walking past many people in line. I was not surprised to hear comments from people in line, growing frustrated as they watched us bypass everyone.

At the entrance, there were three very large men guarding the chain that separated the people in line from the entrance. "Who the *hell* are you?" asked a man standing next to me. I was speechless. I had no idea what to say—until I watched the last of my posse walk past the three large bouncers and disappear into the club. Ignoring the question, I raced up to the front entrance and reached for the chain.

"*Where* do you think you are going?" a bouncer asked as I felt large hands grasp my shirt and pull me back. I begin to feel panic.

"I'm with my *homies!*" I blurted it out. I had no idea what I was supposed to say or what my friends said to gain entrance ahead of all the people standing in line. He did not believe me. He pulled me back farther as I watched my friends walk deeper into the crowd. "Guys! *Help*! Money, Stallion! *Help me out!*" Money Edwards, Stallion, and Ward turned around. Seeing my predicament, Stallion called out to the bouncer.

"Damn Homie! He's with us! That's *Hodgie*." The bouncer let me go immediately, and smoothed out the crease in my shirt where he had made a firm grip. It was that simple.

"Sorry about that, Hodgie, *my homie*! Have fun!" He unclasped the chain and directed me into the entrance. As I scanned the scenery inside, I noticed a very different demographic than what I was used to in my ninety-seven percent white school. The music was loud, pumping out the latest hip-hop and everyone was on the floor or mingling with drinks in hand. The club had at least fifty per cent African American patrons–two women for every man! I saw a Marine at the front of the bar. He had red hair, freckles, and short in stature, with the typical Marine build. I stood next to him and ordered a Rainier Beer. The bartender had a puzzled expression on his face.

"What does that mean?" he asked not knowing about the popular beer from the Pacific Northwest.

"You know–like the commercial with the motorcycle! *RAAIIINNNNEERRR BBBBBBEEEEERRR!*" I replied. I figured that slogan would make perfect sense to him. How could it not? Rainier Beer commercials were as common as *Frosted Flakes* or *Pepsi,* as far as I was concerned. I just confused the bartender more.

"I still have no idea what the HELL you're talking about!" he said as he laughed. I ordered a Bud Light since the Marine with red hair was drinking one. After I finished the beer, the red-haired Marine offered to buy the next round, and I accepted.

"I'm Frank Lane," he said.

"Duane Hodgson," I replied. We made small talk as we drank our beer. He asked where I was from and what kind of music I liked. I imagine I was an enigma–decked out in my pimp attire and talking about how much I loved the Scorpions, Def Leppard, Aerosmith, AC/DC, Led Zeppelin and other famous rock n' roll bands. We finished the second round, and I bought the third.

"Which platoon are you assigned to?" he asked.

"First Platoon," I responded. "I'm glad, too. I've heard that it's the best platoon on the base and that their commanding officer is young, energetic, and motivated." He smiled and nodded.

"That's great!" He replied. We finished our round and I explained that I needed to excuse myself.

"Thanks for the conversation. It was nice to meet you; I'll probably see you around. I came with a few other Marines and I need to make sure I don't lose them–they're my ride back."

"It was nice to meet you too, Duane. I'm sure we will run into each other very soon." We shook hands and I returned into the mass of people dancing and mingling. I rejoined my friends after dancing and we returned to base a few hours later.

When the weekend was over, I reported for inspection in front of First Platoon headquarters in camouflage fatigues neatly pressed, my boots spit-shined, and M-16A2 rifle thoroughly cleaned and at parade rest as we waited for Sergeant of the Guard Grant to call us to attention. I went out of my way to make certain I left no detail unchecked. Sergeant of the Guard Grant and our Commanding Officer would be inspecting us–this was my opportunity to make a good first impression.

Sergeant Grant was taking his place in front of the platoon. "Detail Attention!" Another Marine arrived. Sergeant Grant exchanged salutes with the Marine, but I did not have a clear line of sight. I figured it had to be our Commanding Officer. Sergeant Grant and our First Lieutenant began inspections. The morning breeze was cool and crisp, even though I could feel the humidity already starting to saturate the air. The sound of M16A2 hand guards slapping repeatedly as Sergeant Grant went down the line. Soon, Sergeant Grant was standing in front of me, and it came time for the pivot.

I was standing at attention after making the pivot, and face-to-face with our First Lieutenant, the man who would lead us into combat if we were called to war. The First Lieutenant had the final authority over any issues that might arise while assigned to Marine Security Forces First Platoon. I quickly brought my rifle up to point arms, smartly snapping the M16A2 rifle into position. The Platoon Commander assumed control to inspect my weapon. I let the weapon go and brought my hands back to the seams on my fatigues. My weapon actually started to fall when the Lieutenant grabbed it.

Looking up at me, he said, "Good morning, Marine!"

As I was about to reply, I realized I was looking at the face of Frank Lane, whom I had talked with at the club and drank a few rounds of Bud Light. He inspected my rifle and handed it back. As I brought my weapon back down to parade rest, I thought how thankful I was that I had been positive–if not complimentary–about the Marine Corps, my new assignment, even my new commanding officer, Frank Lane. I had a feeling that Sergeant Grant and First Lieutenant Lane liked me–always a good thing when a new Marine depends on superior officers for recommendations and guidance.

After inspection was completed, Lieutenant Lane dismissed us and turned the platoon over to Sergeant Grant. Standing five feet ten inches and weighing two hundred twenty-five pounds of lean muscle, Sergeant Grant was as solid as a brick wall. Etched into my memory like a best friend or favorite teacher, he made a lasting impression on me. He was African American and did not treat any Marine differently based on the color of his skin. He based his judgment on a Marine's ability to complete his mission, act as a member of the team, and cared about his fellow Marines.

After taking over the platoon from First Lieutenant Lane, Sergeant Grant dismissed everyone in the platoon except for those of us who were new. My name was among the new Marines Sergeant Grant asked to remain after he dismissed everyone else. He called us to attention and delivered a welcome speech–explaining what our mission was, what he expected from us, and what the Naval Weapons Station required of us. We were guarding warheads stored inside *The Area*–numerous nuclear warheads, and it was our mission to protect that weapon at all cost against any threat–including terrorism, sabotage, and all perceived threats. Our mission also included the protection of all civilian contractors and employees who worked in the area. We would accomplish our mission using sheer force. We were equipped with M16A2 rifles, gas masks, full body armor, and standard H-Gear, which enabled us to carry two additional magazines of ammunition. Our team leader kept the M16A2 equipped with a grenade launcher. Our response team would respond in the Marine Corps' *Peace Keeper*, a heavily armored assault vehicle fitted with a fifty-caliber machine gun.

Once our four days of duty was completed, the First Platoon would leave the area after the Second or Third Platoons relieved us. We would have two to three days of training and inspections, and then the weekend was ours. Every fourth weekend in the month, each platoon received a four-day weekend as long as the platoon was functioning correctly and passing all training requirements. I liked what I heard, and the four-day weekend made it even better.

The speech was over and Sergeant Grant gave the "at ease" command. He called out five names, all of whom were the newest Marines assigned to the First Platoon. Upon hearing my name, I stepped forward with the other four Marines. Sergeant Grant directed us to the green lawn behind him. Once we stood on the grass, he ordered us to shed our weapons, gas masks, and body armor. He had a slight smile on his face as he waited for us to remove all our gear and set it behind us on the lawn.

"Come on! Rush me!" he ordered. We were perplexed. His words were clear enough, but we could not help but feel hesitant as we looked at each other, searching for clarity. Sergeant Grant stood there in front of us. His muscles bulged out of his t-shirt, and he raised his hands high in the air. "Come on! Rush me!" he repeated the order. We began to form a circle around him, but nobody wanted to be the first to jump Sergeant Grant. Finally, I decided to go for it–rushing him from behind, I was hoping to catch him off guard while one of my fellow Marines kept him busy from a different direction. There was no way I would be able to take him without help.

I sprung from behind him, planning to jump on his back while the other Marines joined in. It did not go down quite like that, though. Sergeant Grant spun on me, grabbed me by my wrist in midair, and threw me to the ground. I hit the grass and rolled several times before regaining control. As I rolled, I struck my head on the flash suppressor on one of the M16A2 rifles. Blood streamed down my face from the cut on my head. I jumped back in–some Marines were just hanging on as he swung them around, while others went airborne, landing on the lawn. As each Marine landed on the ground, he returned to try again, no matter how futile it seemed.

"Attention on deck!" Suddenly, we heard a voice call out. We all snapped to attention, watching as the Marine Corps Captain approached. Sergeant Grant saluted the officer, and we heard the command, "At ease." The Captain surveyed our group, and then focused on me, seeing the blood streaming down my face from the gash in my forehead. Stepping closer to me, he asked, "Marine, how did you cut your head? Did Sergeant Grant initiate a wrestling match with you and these other Marines?" I fixed my eyes on the Captain, sensing that he was not what he appeared to be, and that God was warning me to take care in how I responded.

"No, Sir!" I replied. He focused his glare, and it became immediately clear that a short answer would not suffice. "We all decided to play around, wrestle, and see who was *King of the Mountain*. I slipped and fell … must've hit my forehead on a sharp object on the lawn. Sergeant

Grant was calling us to attention when you appeared, Sir." His eyes were squinting in the South Carolina sun as he listened to my explanation.

"Are you sure about that, Private?" He asked.

"Yes, Sir!" I replied. He then approached the other four Marines and engaged them in the same line of questioning. Receiving the same answer, he gave up. Sergeant Grant called us to attention and saluted the Captain.

"At ease," said Sergeant Grant. I relaxed my posture and wiped the blood out of the corner of my eye, where it had begun to pool. "Marine, why did you not tell the Captain all the details of your injury?" he asked after walking up to me.

"It was none of his *business*," I replied. "And *since when* do officers get involved in the day-to-day operations of the enlisted personnel?" I continued. Sergeant Grant smiled wide and nodded.

"Let me tell you, Marine, as long as *I* am the squad leader for the First Platoon, I will take good care of you." Sergeant Grant was a man of his word.

From that day on, my schedule and assignments reflected his gratitude for my thoughtful answer to the Captain's line of questioning. I received the best posts, including a full sixteen hours off between eight-hour shifts inside the area we patrolled. Two fully armed security force Marines staffed each post, equipped with M16A2 assault rifle, gas mask, full body armor, and Kevlar helmet. The Marine Corps required each of us to pass a complete security clearance through the Personnel Suitability Reliability Program (PSP). This was no ordinary background check. The Marine Corps sent two federal investigators to my hometown of Marysville and to the Tulalip Indian Reservation to interview my teachers, neighbors, friends, and family members.

The Marine Corps required each of us to pass a physical fitness test every three months. This test consisted of a three-mile run, pull-up and sit-up tests. I earned a perfect score on my test in boot camp, three perfect scores after boot camp, and two perfect scores while in Infantry Training School. Another fitness test was due, and because the climate was so different from that of the Pacific Northwest, I had concerns that I might not do as well. The extreme heat and humidity combined to render breathing almost impossible, especially under the stress of physical exertion.

The Marine Corps expected us to complete eighty sit-ups in two minutes. That had never been a problem for me before, and it was not a significant worry—I usually completed eighty in just over one minute. It was time for the pull-up test. In the past, I could complete twenty-two to twenty-five pull-ups before reaching muscle exhaustion. That day, I completed twenty pull-ups. The three-mile run was my primary concern. This was the test that would be most affected by my ability to fill my lungs with air, and in this humidity, I was unsure if I was capable of doing that. I had been running five miles or more to prepare for the test.

My platoon lined up for the three-mile. I started at my usual pace. When I reached the one and a half mile marker, the Sergeant called out my time–seven minutes fifteen seconds. I knew I was keeping the right pace to complete the three miles in less than eighteen minutes, as required to pass the test. I slowed considerably. The humidity and heat took its toll–I passed the finish line at seventeen minutes five seconds, which gave me a perfect score of three hundred.

Over the next month, I settled into the routine. I was on guard duty four days, then training at our barracks for the next two days. We had weekends off, including a four-day weekend every four weeks. Life was good. I made many friends from all races and backgrounds, but I found myself hanging out with my homies more and more. The circle of friends that Stallion had introduced to me became my best friends during that time. We fell into a consistent routine–my favorite part was the time we spent on the basketball court. One of us would bring a boom box, pumping out *MC Hammer*, *LL Cool J*, or *Run DMC* to name just a few. We played full court basketball, as the speakers thumped the latest in rap or hip-hop. At that time, I was able to jump high enough to dunk the ball, as long as I timed my steps correctly. Except for a few black players in our circle of friends, I was one of the few who could jump high enough to dunk the ball. I got even better as I practiced my jumps, enabling me to make a few put back dunks, timing my jump for the moment the ball came off the rim, then slamming it back into the basket. This accomplishment was currency in earning status with my homies. It did not take long before they were talking to me in the same manner they did with each other. The edgy humor in our banter was like nothing I had experienced before, and they treated me as an equal among their tight group of friends.

"Man, your mama is so *fat* she uses a dippy dumpster as her lunch box in elementary school," said Pete Ward to Money Edwards.

"Ya mama's so *stupid*, I told her it was chilly outside and she went out and got a bowl and spoon," Money countered.

"Hodgie, ya mama's so *fat*, she sat on a rainbow and made skittles!" Ward said to me, still trying to catch his breath from laughing so hard at the previous mama joke. Clearly, I knew I would have to learn some mama jokes quickly if I intended to keep up. It felt good knowing they accepted me enough that they would insult my mama. In the 1980's it did not seem like people were as worried about offending each other. If these men did not like you, they would not make the effort to insult your mama or your personal attributes.

We were on the court playing basketball in the hot South Carolina sun, when the shuttle bus pulled up with a group of new recruits to the base. The door hissed as it opened. We stopped our game to watch the Marines step off the bus. Several of the recruits walked toward the main building to report, as we continued with our laughter and edgy comments.

We resumed our game. One of those privates, Pete Blassimgame, stood six feet four inches, with very long arms and legs. Pete started walking over to the court where we were playing. He wore blue jeans, a large white cowboy hat, new leather cowboy boots, and a shiny belt buckle large enough to serve four eggs, sunny side up with enough room leftover for some bacon strips. He leaned against the light pole; his cowboy hat tipped slightly upward, his boots crossed, and a long blade of grass dangling out of his mouth. He looked like he walked off the set of *Bonanza*.

This hardly went unnoticed. Ward could stand it no longer, the basketball was in his hands, and he hesitated before passing off to Stallion. He stopped. The court was dead silent, and if I did not know better, I would have thought all motion had stopped as well. Pete Blassimgame maintained his relaxed posture at the light pole as Pete Ward began to stride toward him. My friends had a diverse range of facial expressions as each observed the spectacle about to unfold. This new Marine was the prototype of all cowboys. His manner was as much a part of his presentation as was his attire. Pete Ward stopped directly in front of Pete Blassimgame.

"Whatcha doin', *Cowpoke*?" Ward asked, as he looked Pete up and down in a deliberate fashion. Every one of us on the court broke into laughter–my ribs hurt from laughing so hard. Eventually, we quieted, and Pete casually removed the blade of grass from his mouth.

"Well, I was watching you little fellas run around here playing this here basketball and I thought to myself, some of these little fellas are pretty good, but Pete, you had betta get your *Air Jordan's* on an' show 'em how *Texans* play basketball!" He said in a Texan accent. I was not expecting to

132

hear that, and I could tell from the looks on my friends' faces that they were not either. Once the shock faded, we jumped right in, ribbing him relentlessly.

"Oh hell no–I *know* you did not just say that!" said Money.

"Well, ya better go get your shoes on, Cowboy! " Ward said.

With a merciless onslaught of laughter and verbal assault following him, he went directly to the main building to report in, unpack, and return with his Air Jordan's. When he returned, Pete was dressed in a tank top, basketball shorts, and a new pair of red Air Jordan's. We wasted no time starting a game with our new player. We were intrigued by his style, relaxed confidence, and witty comebacks.

Pete proved his basketball proficiency within the first few minutes of the game. He had great post-up moves from either block near the basket, and his accuracy in the mid-range jump shot was dead on. Pete had the skills and coordination to use his height to his advantage. Even better than his basketball skills, though, was his ability to fit right in to our group with such ease. This six-four, white Texan was running ball and talking smack with five black guys, two Puerto Ricans, one Indian, and one Italian.

Our typical routine was to play a few hours of basketball, return to our rooms to shower and get dressed, and then walk up and down the hallways visiting with other Marines while we made plans for the weekend. The NCO club offered seventy-five cent beers, and one-dollar mixed drinks. Located by the chow hall, it was a great place to shoot pool, have a few cheap drinks, and try to hook up or just chill with our friends.

The NCO club was the place I learned to dance. I am not talking about the generic moves I saw in my hometown or even in the Seattle area. The style of dance in 1986 was changing rapidly; MC Hammer and Bobby Brown took their moves to an entirely new level. Being Native American, I had natural rhythm.

My homies and I were at the NCO club. They were out on the dance floor showing off their moves to the ladies, while I stood at the bar and watched. Something about these new dance moves struck me and I burst into laughter as I watched Money Edwards and Pete Ward incorporate moves from Hammer and Bobby Brown. That did not sit well with either of them–maybe I should not have been looking *directly* at them as I laughed, but at least I was not pointing.

"What's so *funny*, Hodgie?" Ward asked. I was leaning against the bar, a beer in one hand, and trying to conceal my laughter with the other.

Ward and Edwards looked at each other in bewilderment as they waited for me to stop laughing and respond.

"That dancing is funny!" I replied. They smirked.

"You think you can dance like that?" Money asked.

"Sure! That's easy!" I said. Ward and Money laughed.

"Put your money where your mouth is, Hodgie." Ward was quick to challenge me to show my talent on the dance floor. They directed me to follow them to the dance floor. The DJ played MC Hammer's hit, *"Turn this Mutha Out."* As I walked to the dance floor, I watched other couples dancing this new style that Hammer was making so popular. I was from Seattle, Washington and grew up on rock n roll. The three or four beers that I drank were just enough to give me a good buzz, and lose the inhibition that tends to destroy the natural rhythm of hip-hop. I hopped up on stage with the rest of the crowd and took a few seconds to study their moves.

Copying their moves, I fit right in with my African American friends who might have had some initial skepticism to anyone *not* black being competent at dancing hip-hop and rap. Once I found the beat, and I was feeling confident in my moves, I realized just how fun this was! While I was dancing, I glanced at Edwards and Ward. They had a surprised look on their faces as they watched me. The song was over, and I stepped off the stage to rejoin my friends. As I approached them, Ward and Edwards were shaking their heads.

"I'm callin' *bullshit*, Hodgie," Ward said. "Somebody taught you how to dance, Bro!"

"No, they didn't!" I replied. "I'm just listening to the beat and havin' fun!" After that, I had no problem finding a dance partner. Most of the people in the club were African Americans, and I was one of the few men who was not black and could follow the rhythm. The southern belles of South Carolina appreciated a man who could dance, who had a sense of humor, and who liked to party. We spent the remainder of the night dancing, drinking, and talking with these beautiful southern women.

My experiences during this time were similar, I believe, to what many other people my age were experiencing in college. My decision to join the Marine Corps was a good path for me. Others in my class chose to further their education in college, and I respected their choice as much as I did my own; however, I did not feel that college was the right path for me. I knew that I had no interest in listening to a liberal professor preach his own political ideas, while repackaging the information to support his ideology.

To make my point, I would suggest that anyone look at how public schools present Native Americans to students. Non-tribal historians are teaching history about tribal people. They have no direct experience in the ways, culture, language, or community of my Native American brothers and sisters. Most of the real history and ancient ways are contained in ceremony and only taught by respected Elders to people who have demonstrated the wisdom and trust to learn and accept these ancient ways. The textbook authors and education administrators fashion a version of history about an entire nation of people from the point-of-view of their former military *adversaries*. When the history books talk about customs or events that occurred over a hundred years ago, it is clear that the writers received their information from the U.S. Army, which had declared war on the tribes who inhabited the land coveted by the U.S. Government. Over 100 Million Native Americans from different Indian Nations died in these wars! *A literal Native American Holocaust.* Not only is the information inaccurate, it is irresponsible and offensive.

There are few–if any–historians, authors, or educators, who can offer an accurate version of history from the perspective of the people about whom the material is written. Imagine if the North Korean government wrote *our* American history textbooks and had complete discretion as to how these textbooks depicted Americans. Accurate information about tribal people in North America is in short supply in our education system. I have been acquainted with many people over the years who still think Natives live in teepees, say, *"How"* (for Hello) while holding our hand up, palm forward.

During the years I was in the Marine Corps, God was watching over me, protecting me, allowing me to experience life, and to be molded to His purposes even when I was feeling burned by life. God was preparing me for a twelve-year career in law enforcement–the next step in my life. The endgame is this book, which will outline and show the reader how the Creator can use a very flawed and prideful man to reach others. I present the subsequent stories to you, the reader, for the sole purpose of detailing what a *knucklehead* I was!

My assignment at the Naval Weapons Station in South Carolina was fun, and it was a good experience for a young man. It was also ten miles from the main gate to our barracks, which meant that, without a car, I was limited in my ability to spend my free time off base. My troubles began when I met with another young Marine from the state of Ohio, Private First Class Russ Hurtle.

Hurtle was cool, he liked to party, and was always on the move. Even better, Hurtle had a green Chevelle! We became friends while I was at NCO club hanging out. One weekend, while I was drinking beer at the NCO club, Russ walked in. We shot a game of pool and ordered a round of beers. After we finished our game, he asked me if I wanted to go to downtown Charleston with him. I was quick to take him up on the offer. Anytime I could find transportation off base, I rarely passed it up.

I was a lightweight when it came to drinking. Hurtle and I stopped off at local store and bought a six-pack of beer, then continued on our way to the city. It was dark when we arrived downtown and stopped in a parking lot.

"Stay with the car," Hurtle said to me as he stepped out. "I'm going to meet somebody." I had four unopened beers at my feet, rock n roll on the stereo, and was already starting a very good buzz. I did not think too much about having to stay with the car in downtown Charleston while my new friend walked into the darkness to meet some mysterious person. In fact, from the relative safety of my hometown and the Tulalip Indian Reservation, I did not immediately jump to the conclusion that something nefarious was at play.

I had one beer left when Hurtle returned to the car. I had no idea how much time had passed. I noticed he was carrying a bag with him, and he pulled his hat down low as if to conceal his identity. Hurtle opened the door and tossed the bag in the back seat. We drove off to another location about two miles away and Hurtle parked the car and shut off the engine.

He reached into the back seat and retrieved the bag. Tipping it upside down, he shook the bag until he had the contents heaped in a pile on the seat. There were about twenty wallets and purses! I did not expect to see that. Russ could sense I was in shock. As he calmly put on a pair of latex gloves, he explained how he had been doing this for over a year, off and on. I watched as he opened each item, searched it quickly for cash or other valuables, and then returned the wallet or purse to the bag. Once he completed this process for each wallet and purse, he threw the bag out the window.

Hurtle counted the cash he stole, and then tried to give a portion of it to me. I refused, but not in an adversarial manner–more accurately, I casually *declined* the generosity, even though I was *freaking out* inside. We were off to the bar in Myrtle Beach, South Carolina.

We were on a four-day weekend. Myrtle Beach was famous for its sandy beaches, beautiful women, and the best beer. By the afternoon, I had drunk a lot of beer and was feeling very good. Hurtle drank a few beers also, but he was not nearly as intoxicated as I was by that time. We sat on the patio outside, and talked to some girls. Hurtle excused himself from the conversation, and walked away. I did not think too much about it at first—I was having too much fun partying.

A short time later, I saw Hurtle walking across the parking lot. He walked past his green Chevelle and up to a new 1986 Red Jeep Wrangler, equipped with large tires and roll bars. Hurtle jumped into the Jeep—*that* caught my attention. He was jostling about and looking around the interior. We were in a busy, well-lit parking lot where patrons had a clear line of sight to everything taking place in front of me. I was nervous.

I excused myself from the table of girls, and walked outside to the parking lot. Hurtle laughed when he saw me approaching the Jeep. I was not laughing—I had a bad feeling about this. "What are you doing?" I asked. "Whose Jeep is this?"

"Hodgie, this Jeep is *badass*! Look—the keys are in it!" He wore a sly grin as he cleverly deflected my question. Before I could reply, he started up the Jeep, tossed his Chevelle keys to me. "Grab my car and follow me!" The keys took an eternity to land in my hands—as if time had slowed, a common experience that I have had during moments of crisis or heightened fear. Hurtle popped the clutch and sped away in a cloud of dust. I stood there in shock, watching him race out of the parking lot in a stolen red Jeep. I was a United States Marine assigned to a state I knew nothing about, with a fellow Marine who had an obvious larceny problem. I was also standing in an open parking lot, where numerous bar patrons were chatting and walking around. My face would be the one identified if I waited much longer.

I snapped out of it. I had to get out of the parking lot fast, and avoid any additional exposure to this crime. I walked over to the green Chevelle; I feigned a casually confident stride, which probably came off as stiff and controlled. My heart was pounding, and my mind raced with thoughts about all the different ways this was a bad thing. I needed to get clear of any responsibility in this as soon as I met up with Hurtle. I was driving out of the parking lot at a medium speed—I did not want to attract attention, but I also did not want to linger in view any more. My thoughts raced, as I turned left on the road leaving the parking lot. *Is it too late for me to get out of this? Did the owner report the Jeep stolen yet? Did anyone see me?* This was new territory for me. Traffic tickets and drinking too many beers was the extent of my involvement with law enforcement. This was a serious crime, and they could charge me as an accessory, even though I did not ask to be part of this, and Hurtle failed to give me any warning about his larcenous hobby. I was on the main road, keeping watch to see if Hurtle kept going or pulled over.

About one mile from the bar, I saw the red Jeep Wrangler parked off to the side. Hurtle was standing next to it outside. I pulled up, applied the brakes suddenly, emitting a small cloud of dust around us. Hurtle was grinning wide as he watched me emerge from the Chevelle.

"What the *hell*, Hurtle!" I yelled as I walked toward him. His perpetual grin was not an appropriate response to placing a friend at risk of incarceration. He had to know that. Yet, I wondered.

"This is a *beeeyuuuteee!*" He said gesturing to the shiny new Jeep. He continued smiling as he lauded all the amenities of the Wrangler. "You *have* to drive this, Hodgie!"

"Did you steal that Jeep?" I asked. I was exasperated.

"Well, the keys were in the ignition, so it's not like I broke in and hotwired it. " He was completely unaffected by the gravity of what he had done, or what consequences could result for both of us. I was beyond the point of having a rational conversation. He did not exactly make that a viable option, with his perma-grin and evasive responses. Unable to reply, I just shook my head and looked at him.

"You *do* know that you cannot keep this Jeep. Right?" I asked. "If we get caught, we're gonna get kicked outta the Marine Corps!" He continued to smile. "I had nothing to do with this, and I really don't appreciate your getting me involved in a felony!" He could tell that I was unraveling.

"Calm down, Hodgie. *It's ok.* It's gonna *be* ok. I got a friend in Ohio who'll take this Jeep, and there'll be no risk to either of us." He was doing his best to settle my nerves, but that was the wrong answer.

"I want *nothing* to do with this! If you get caught, I'm not covering for you!" I do not know how I could have made myself any clearer, but nothing I said had an impact.

"Look, don't worry about it. I *got* this. I need you to drive my car to Ohio, but you will have no part in moving the Jeep–from this point on, there is *nothing* for you to worry about. All I need you to do is be there to pick me up after I drop it off." He had this way about him that was so convincing. I knew this was a bad idea, and that the only way I could really avoid being an accessory, was to have nothing more to do with this at all, including the trip to Ohio.

"I am not driving the Jeep under any circumstances!" He nodded ok. I did not feel right about any part of his plan, but as long as I never touched the Jeep, I believed I would be a little safer.

I agreed to follow him in his Chevelle back to base. When we arrived at the barracks, we packed enough clothes for the trip, and retrieved some cash for gas and food. It was my first year in the Marine Corps, and I was associated with grand theft auto. It was not my idea, and I did not agree to this in advance, but I knew the police and judge would never see it that way.

We finished packing for the trip. Hurtle led the way and I remained a few hundred yards behind him at all times. I was close enough not to lose him, but it made me feel better putting physical distance between us. The sun was out. I was young and trying to do something productive with my life, and once again, I was involved in something questionable. The Creator was always there, looking out for me, and allowing me to experience some trials along with all the blessings.

We had been driving for about two hours. I still had a buzz, and I was drinking an occasional beer along the way–more to calm my nerves than anything else. Hurtle looked to be having the time of his life. The wind was blowing through the Jeep and I could hear music blaring from his speakers. I glanced again at my rear view mirror.

I broke out into a sweat and I felt my blood run cold. It was a South Carolina State Patrol, and he was catching up to us fast. My mind raced. I had to remind myself what I would do if a trooper pulled over the Jeep, what if he pulled me over. The sun had set and darkness crept over the skyline. I did my best to remain calm as I watched the trooper come closer. I wondered if Hurtle even knew he was behind us. The trooper switched lanes and inched up alongside me, passing me gradually. I started to relax, thinking that he would just move past both of us.

The state trooper sped up suddenly and returned to the right lane in front of me. He was directly behind Hurtle and speeding up closer behind him. If the owner had reported the Jeep stolen, the trooper would know when he ran the plates. By this time, there was almost no possibility that the Jeep's owner had not noticed his new Jeep Wrangler missing. As much as I wanted to believe that I was innocent of wrongdoing in this scheme, I knew better. The trooper would run the plates, discover it was a stolen vehicle, and arrest us for grand theft auto. After that, the Marine Corps would court-martial us for committing a felony and for conduct unbecoming of a United States Marine. My involvement at this point was indisputable. I had to do *something* fast.

I felt sweat gathering between my palm and the steering wheel as I dropped the shifter into third gear and pushed down hard on the accelerator, turning up the volume as Bon Scott belted out the lyrics of "Highway to Hell." Hurtle had maintained this car. It was smooth and had ample power. I shot past the state trooper and my buddy, Hurtle. I watched Hurtle and the state trooper fade in the distance through my rear view mirror. Seconds later, the red and blue flashing lights of the trooper merged in front of Hurtle's new Jeep.

I continued to drive, ignoring the trooper as long as possible. I wanted to make sure that he focused on me, and not on Hurtle or the Jeep. When I was a little farther down the road, I pulled over and waited. He pulled up behind me, exited the patrol car, and reached for his weapon. This was not going to be easy. I watched in horror, as he drew his gun and ordered me out of the vehicle. He shouted orders for me to lay face down on the pavement. I could feel the cold metal of handcuffs clamp down tightly on my wrists. He proceeded to search me.

The trooper stood up after he completed his search. "Why didn't you stop when I tried to pull you over?" he asked.

"I'm sorry, officer. I didn't see you right away. I was rockin' out to *AC/DC*" He ran field sobriety tests, which I promptly failed. He put me back in handcuffs and escorted me to the back of the patrol car. I heard a familiar voice.

"Excuse me, officer. Where are you taking *my friend*, Hodgie?" It was Hurtle! The trooper shut the door with me handcuffed in the backseat. I could not believe what I was seeing. After taking these extreme measures to take the spotlight off Hurtle, he pulled up behind the trooper in the STOLEN JEEP WRANGLER and engaged in a conversation with him while I sat handcuffed in the back. I turned to watch. Looking past the lights, I saw Hurtle shooting the shit with the trooper, and just beyond them, I could see the red Jeep Wrangler parked behind the patrol car. I could not believe what was happening.

The trooper returned to the patrol car, and drove me to station where I was booked into jail. Still buzzed from drinking the past two days, they took my photo, fingerprints, and threw me into the drunk tank. The cell was filthy, and held about a dozen older people who were clearly inebriated or passed out. An open pit toilet stood in the near corner from me. An older man had decided to lie next to the toilet–a few inches more and he could have used it for a pillow. That sight alone made my stomach convulse. Whether that spot was his preferred real estate or just the location where he passed out, I have no idea. I cannot imagine anyone *wanting* to be near that hole–it smelled *horrific* and the sight was enough to sober up anyone.

That turned out to be a very unpleasant night. I hated the idea of being in jail, and being stuck in the same cell with a bunch of drunks just added to the misery. One of the men in the cell with me talked continuously. He followed me everywhere I tried to sit, and told me his life story. It was difficult enough to try to sleep, but having someone talking nonstop in your ear is intolerable.

The morning finally arrived. I heard my name called out. "Duane Hodgson!" It was the jail officer.

"That's me!" I stood up abruptly.

"You made bail," he said. I walked to the cell door, as he jiggled the keys in the door and opened it. I wondered who bailed me out as I walked down the hallway. I had no idea, as I prepared to leave the station, if I still had a career in the Marine Corps, or if they had arrested Hurtle. The ringing in my head from the merciless hangover was not helping. The hallway connected to the reception area of the police station.

I could see the bright morning sun shining through the windows. As I passed through the doorway to the reception room, I heard a familiar voice. "What's up, Hodgie?" It was Hurtle. My thoughts immediately focused on the Jeep Wrangler. *Where did he park the Jeep?* Hurtle was smiling at me when I emerged from the hallway. I looked over his right shoulder through the window. Hurtle had parked the Jeep right in front of the police station.

I felt numb and sick to my stomach. The jail officer handed me my wallet, identification, and personal belongings. As we walked out of the police station, Hurtle was laughing and patting me on the back. He seemed completely unaffected by any of the events that had taken place.

We pulled out of the parking lot in the stolen Wrangler, and picked up the Chevelle. The rest of the trip took twelve hours, and it was largely uneventful compared to everything I had already experienced. I did not even care if they arrested us after that. I figured that God had to be looking out for me and that if I was supposed to do any serious prison time, it would have happened already.

Hurtle was in front of me the whole way to Ohio. As I followed in the Chevelle, I listened to my favorite tunes–Van *Halen*, *AC/DC*, *Scorpions*, and *Def Leppard* just to name of few. I realized that nobody was going to believe me if I told this story. I would not have believed it myself if it did not happen to me.

We were just past the Ohio state line, and it was time to take a break. We pulled in to the rest area. I jumped up on top of the red Jeep Wrangler wearing my yellow Marine Corps t-shirt, red Marine Corps shorts, and hat. I stood on the spare tire on the back of the Jeep and Hurtle took a picture, using his new Polaroid camera. The unprocessed photo shot out of the camera, and he waved it in the air to accelerate the developing process. We drove the rest of the way to our destination–Hurtle's friend had a house in a rural area. He parked the Jeep in a hay barn and that was the last I ever saw of the 1986 red Jeep Wrangler.

I continued to work out during my assignment at Charleston, South Carolina. In fact, I *still* work out, at the age of fifty–often at the Benewah Wellness Center on the Coeur d'Alene Indian Reservation. I ran three to five miles and sometimes as much as ten miles, every workout. As a Lakota Sioux, running is in my blood. My grandfather, Charlie Garvais Lawrence was very gifted in music and athletics.

I remember a story that my grandfather, Charlie, told me when he was running the one hundred yard dash. It was the nineteen twenties or early nineteen thirties at the time. As he crossed the finish line, the fair worker who was tracking their time, muttered under his breath, "There's something wrong with this clock!" Another fair worker who was standing nearby overheard him.

"Why?" He asked, with a puzzled look on his face.

"Because if this clock *isn't* broken, Charlie is just off the *Olympic* qualifying time for the one hundred yard dash!"

Chapter 10: Jump School, Fort Benning 1987

Saw little mama from across the floo' & I was like
Dang she know how to rock the floo'
– Mike Bone, "VIP"

I am very grateful for the blessings that God gave me. My athletic gifts and my desire to improve were instrumental in saving me from getting *Office Hours* punishment in 1987 while stationed in South Carolina. I graduated from Marine Corps boot camp, Infantry Training School, and already had a perfect fitness score on six out of six tests.

I met a young woman at JW's (no need for names). I was a very typical young man at the time. I chased girls, and pursued activities that allowed me to meet even *more* women. Some of the women I met, turned out to be very good friends. I developed relationships with others. The young woman I mentioned was someone with whom I developed a relationship.

I brought her to the *E Club* on base to shoot some pool and drink a few beers. We planned to stay a few hours inside the Enlisted Club, and then we were going to head out on the town. It started with a few drinks, but turned out to be many more than we planned. She was in no shape to drive home, and being the smart young Marine that I was, I chose Don Giambro's room in the Administration Building. I had good reason for choosing Stallion's room.

The Captain of the Day *never* checked the Administration barracks on Saturdays. I escorted her to Stallion's room, and the two of us went to sleep. We woke up in the morning to the sound of the door opening. Don was in Myrtle Beach for the weekend–not due back until the next day. Since we were both sleeping, and neither of us had clothes on, we did not respond in time to hearing the door. I heard a loud voice in the darkness.

"Officer on deck!" I peered around the naked young woman toward the direction of the voice. Standing in the doorway, with the morning light radiating from behind him, I saw Captain Belcourt. I scrambled to my feet, pulling the blanket with me in my attempt to salute the Captain. I realized at that moment, that I had completely uncovered the young woman when I pulled the blanket with me.

Captain Belcourt's eyes wandered to where the young woman was laying and his ears immediately turned bright red. He regained his composure with some difficulty. "Report to Office Hours at thirteen hundred hours in your Dress Alpha uniform … *sharp!*" He turned and left the doorway, allowing the door to swing shut behind him. I could hear his footsteps fade away as he walked farther down the hallway. The young woman began to apologize. I could tell that she felt bad. I assured her that this was my fault, and that I knew the consequences of my actions.

That seemed to help a little–she was more relaxed and smiled at me. We decided that there was no point in wasting a perfectly good morning. I could not change the events or the consequences. We took our time getting out of bed, showered, and ate breakfast. Later that morning, I escorted her to her car. We gave each other a hug, and she kissed me on the lips. "Call me later, Love," she whispered in my ear.

I returned to my barracks. Reality kicked in and I thought about all the horror stories other Marines had told me about standing before Commanding General Burns. I had only been at the Naval Weapons Base for about nine months, and I was already about to stand in front of Commanding General Burns for Office Hours.

Other Marines who had been through this experience reported the same story. They were *"burned by Burns."* I learned that Burns was notorious for stripping Marines of their rank and docking pay that they would never see again. I had just made the rank of Private First Class, and now, there was a possibility that Burns would demote me to Private, which meant loss of status as well. There was a name given to Marines who lost their rank in this manner–*"shit- bird."* No Marine strived to earn a name like *shit-bird.*

I got dressed in my Class A Marine Corps uniform, taking extra care that I was squared away, ironed, my shoes were polished to a shine, and my face was clean shaven. I took one last look in the mirror before I stepped out of my room. I shut the door behind me, took a deep breath, and walked down the deserted hallway toward the Officer's quarters of the barracks. My footsteps echoed off the cinderblock walls as I began to see Captain Belcourt standing in the room just outside the Commanding General's office.

I remember Captain Belcourt as a strong Christian man, who spoke frequently about his faith. He wore black-rimmed glasses, and he had the appearance of the stereotypical nerd in school; he was the computer geek or the speech and drama club enthusiast–all prime targets for bullying by the stereotypical jocks.

"Private First Class Duane Hodgson Garvais reporting for Office Hours, Sir!" I saluted Captain Belcourt. He returned my salute and spun on his heels, pivoting toward the Commanding General's office, and walked in, closing the door behind him. I waited outside, expecting Captain Belcourt to summon me inside at any moment.

That moment never seemed to arrive. Even though my wait was not likely more than ten minutes, it seemed like hours. The door finally opened, and Captain Belcourt called me into the office. I walked in, measuring my steps and keeping my eyes forward. I was absorbing the surrounding interior in my periphery. The first thing I noticed as I passed through the doorway was the rich woodwork everywhere; the United States Marine Corps spared no expense in obtaining the very finest wood from every corner of Mother Earth. The desk was massive, bookshelves lined with leather-bound tomes about military strategy, historical battles, and philosophy stood behind the Commanding General's desk and alongside the adjacent wall.

I came to a halt about two feet from the Commanding General's desk. With my eyes locked, I said in my best, assertive voice, "Private First Class Hodgson Garvais reporting for Office Hours, Sir!" I remained at attention as the General scrutinized me from my boots to my midsection, and up to my face and head. The light from the lamps directly over me reflected the shine of my boots–I was grateful that I had paid close attention to detail before my arrival.

The General returned his gaze to the folder he was looking at when I walked into the office. *It has to be my personnel folder*, I thought. The smell of expensive cigar smoke mingled with the aroma of fresh coffee. The silent wait was nearly intolerable. The General's eyes followed the pages in front of him, occasionally flipping to the next, then back to the previous. His mouth was moving as if he was muttering to himself. Whatever he might have been thinking or mumbling, it was inaudible. He paused from reading, and looked up at me suddenly.

"Are you *fucking* kidding me, Marine?" He yelled. It was time for me to review the past events. I snuck a girl into the barracks, clearly against all policy and regulation. Many Marines had done this many times before, and in all likelihood, it was probably happening somewhere else on base right now. Something seemed out of place. The General's reaction just did not seem to match the crime for which I was accused. A nightmare scenario unfolded in my mind over the next few seconds as I waited.

I had been setup. Someone *framed* me for something to avoid taking the blame. It was an *atrocity*, a moral offense to the sensibilities of every decent American, or maybe, it was something provoking the deepest revulsion imaginable, like a mass grave–that might be over the top, but still, I knew that bedding a beautiful, naked woman in a Marine barrack could not evoke such emotion by itself. Whatever *it* was, I reasoned, involved far more than anything in which I could have been involved.

The Commanding General slammed my personnel file on his desk. Looking up, he had a faint smirk on his face. The smirk evolved into a smile, then a chuckle as his eyes narrowed, and he focused his gaze on me again. That was a slightly more reassuring reaction–maybe if I was setup, it involved a heinous prank perhaps.

"Was she *worth* it, Hard Charger? Was this young lady worth you being brought into my office to face potential punishment?" He asked. I was confused about the General's reaction to my misbehavior–one minute; it seemed that I was witnessing the disintegration of my military career after only nine months. The next minute, I sensed an unmistakable softening of his expression. This was a critical moment in my short-lived military career, and I did not intend to waste the opportunity. Respect and honesty would have to take center stage in my response.

"Sir! Hell Yes! Sir!"

"Well, at least you have a set of *balls*, and you know how to *use* them," he muttered. Captain Belcourt was visible out of the corner of my eye. I could see that he was in shock.

"Marine, do you mean to tell me that you have eight, perfect three hundred physical fitness scores in a row?" He asked.

"Sir! Yes, Sir!" I replied.

"Marine, now that's what the hell I am talking about! This is what being a Marine is all about and your physical fitness scores show the commitment to the highest standards of my beloved CORPS! How would you like to go to Jump School?" He asked. His tone had changed dramatically from when I first stepped into his office.

"Sir! Yes, Sir!" I replied enthusiastically, not completely certain that I heard him correctly. The Commanding General leaned back in his chair. He lit a cigar that was resting in an ashtray off to the right side of his desktop.

"You are going to *Jump School*; now get the *FUCK* out of my office!" The conversation, if one would call it that, had ended as far as he was concerned. His attention no longer focused on me, he returned to my personnel file, shut the cover, and set it in front of him to the front of his desk. The sweet aroma of cigar smoke was swirling above him. In the Marine Corps, there is a standard, unwavering rule that Marines speaking to a superior officer must salute, and repeat verbatim the superior officer's last phrase back to him before the Marine leaves his presence.

"*Sir! I am going to Jump School and get the FUCK out of your office! Sir!*" I replied as I saluted, spun on my heels, and walked briskly out of his office.

As I passed Captain Belcourt, I saluted him. He was speechless. I noticed that he had a pair of *silver jump wings* on his uniform. I could relate to Captain Belcourt's bewilderment, as I was still in shock about the meeting that had just transpired with the General. How many times before had Captain Belcourt witnessed an *entirely different* outcome for a Marine in my situation?

I quickly changed out of my Class A uniform, replacing it for basketball tank top, shorts, and Air Jordan's. I walked over to the E Club. When I entered, I noticed that a number of Marines, who had been talking, suddenly went silent upon seeing me. Looking around, I decided to head up to the bar. I ordered a Bud Light, and scooted the bowl of complimentary pretzels closer. The television behind the bar featured a local

Talk show. Nobody else appeared to be watching, so the bartender set the remote control next to me with my Bud Light.

Conversations in the room gradually began to resume; however, there was no doubt that I remained the focus of their attention. I scooped a handful of pretzels as I flipped through the channels. I was well aware that the Marines sitting nearby were staring at me. I ignored them, knowing exactly what they were dying to find out. I let them stew a while longer, and smiled at them after I took another sip. It was too much for them. They could take it no longer. Three Marines who were sitting at a table a few feet away scooted their chairs out, and headed up to the bar next to me.

"Hodgie, what happened at Office Hours?" Asked Lance Cpl Angel Cartagena.

"The Commanding General threw the charges *out*, and I am going to Jump School!" I said. I raised my hand to let the bartender know I was ready for another Bud Light. Rubin Diaz looked at Angel with a puzzled look on his face. The bar went completely silent. I could feel the gaze of everyone in the bar looking and waiting to hear more.

"Well, what really happened?" asked Diaz in disbelief.

"Did the *old man* take your rank and pay?" Cartagena asked before I could even respond to Diaz.

"All the charges were thrown out," I said smiling. "The old man crumpled up the papers, and threw them out." I did a charade motion, imitating a decrepit old man crumpling up papers, gagging on a stogie, and throwing the wad of imaginary paper at an imaginary trash bin. "Then, he asked me, *was she worth it*?" I did my best imitation of a pretentious, gruff old curmudgeon. "So I said, Sir. Hell yes! Sir!" Angel and Rubin burst out laughing.

"No way!" Said Rubin.

"I kid you not! I thought I was gonna get my *ass* kicked, from everything I heard about Burns, but he just smirked, looked at my personnel file, and asked me if it was true that I had eight perfect scores out of three hundred on my physical fitness tests. So, I said 'Sir Yes, Sir!' Then he asked if wanted to go to Jump School, and I said, 'Hell yes, Sir!' So guess what, guys? I am going to *Jump School*!"

"*Raahh*!" Rubin, Angel, and the other Marine initiated a deafening cheer as soon as I finished telling my story.

I was off to Jump School at Fort Benning, Georgia with Lance Corporal Cassadenia. The United States Army runs the Jump School, and all Army recruits have the opportunity to attend if they choose. The Marine Corps, however, rarely sends Marines to Jump School unless they are higher-ranking officers–a Private First Class or Lance Corporal would not typically ever see Jump School in his future. With this understanding, I realized that Commanding General Burns had given me a rare opportunity. I was not going to screw this up.

The Marine Corps does *not* tolerate failure on any level. When the Marine Corps sends a Marine to a special training program or school, there is no option to quit or flunk out. Failing a training program results in a blemished personnel file, and a Marine's military career is *over*. I was not entirely sure what Jump School entailed, but I had an idea that it involved jumping out of a *perfectly good* airplane. No matter what they asked of me, I knew that I had to do it right.

When we arrived at Fort Benning, the bus drove us under the big jump wings entrance to the base. Once off the bus, we walked to our barracks to report in to our platoons. As we walked, I observed an army recruit walking with his arm in a cast.

"What happened to your arm?" I asked.

"I broke it on my *second* jump," he said. We continued on our way. Not long after we passed the army recruit with the broken arm, we saw another recruit walking. This recruit was struggling along with his leg in a cast.

"What happened?" I asked.

"I broke my leg on my fourth jump," he said. His face winced in pain as he struggled to balance himself on his crutches. *Hmmm*, I thought. We were almost to our barracks when we saw another recruit–with his *neck* in a brace! Naturally, we had to ask *him* what happened.

"Oh, I hurt my neck on my first jump," he replied.

"Uh, what's the best advice you can give us so we don't get hurt?" I asked.

"Keep your feet and knees together, slightly bent and don't look at the ground! If you can do that, you'll be ok and survive Jump School. Oh, and one other thing," he said. "Be prepared to run, run, run, and run!" We nodded and smiled. Inside, I wondered if I would regret this assignment. Although, I doubt that I had a choice when I was standing before General Burns. I was there to face punishment that could have resulted in loss of rank, a blemish to my record, and forfeiture of pay. My future in the Marine Corps was in jeopardy. Had I declined the offer to attend Jump School, my career would have been brief.

Lance Corporal Cassadenia and I reported to the barracks, received our assignment orders to Sergeant Airborne Jackson's "*stick*"–which was the term they used for platoon. We decided to do some recon. As we met others in the platoon, we asked what they could tell us about Jackson. The responses ranged from a smirk, a laugh, to shaking heads. Cassadenia and I settled in after unpacking. The morning would arrive early–wakeup call was at five-thirty. We were about to learn why we saw so many in our platoon shake their heads when we asked about Sergeant Airborne Jackson.

Morning arrived, but only for Cassadenia and me. It was five o'clock–not five-thirty, when we heard his voice reverberating through our sensitive eardrums. The unexpected assault on our slumber felt like an ambush–Jackson's percussive enunciation of each syllable echoed off the interior of my skull. Scrambling to attention, we came face-to-face with Sergeant Jackson. He had penetrating eyes, and the veins in his forearm bulged like a roadmap. He wore a pair of black military-issue glasses, and a black baseball cap, from which the name, "Black Hat" derives.

All Airborne School instructors wore the black baseball caps, with a brass rank insignia and parachutist badge in the front. His lips parted in a sneer, as he ordered both of us to the push-up position. We dropped to the push-up position–all I could see were his perfectly polished shoes.

"Do you know why I like having Marines in my Army Jump School?" he asked.

"No, Sergeant Airborne Jackson!" we replied in unison.

"Because I can *fuck* with you guys more than others and *you* can *take* it," he said as he placed a steaming hot cup of coffee on Cassadenia's back, who was still in the push-up position. "Don't you *dare* spill my coffee, *Marine!*" He pulled up a recliner, placed his spit-shined boots on Cassadenia's back next to the steaming coffee cup and opened the morning newspaper. Sergeant Jackson continued to read the newspaper for the next *half hour*–making Cassadenia and I trade places until it was time to wake the rest of the airborne class.

The thirty-foot tower was the hardest part of Jump School. Physiologically, the human brain recognizes thirty feet as the critical point of imminent death. This height is hard-wired into our brains and all humans have this feature. Once the brain detects this height, agonizing and inescapable panic arises–only through a highly competent training strategy can this panic diminish. The reasoning for setting the tower at thirty feet made sense to me after I learned that. If we could overcome the fear of jumping from thirty feet, we could jump from a real airplane. The Airborne instructors told us, that when we get into the simulated doorway of the C-130 airplane inside the thirty-foot tower, they would tell us to jump one time, and *only one* time. The instructors warned us that failing to jump would result in *dismissal* from Jump School. *Any* hesitation after the command to jump would result in failure. Ten to fifteen percent of Jump School participants did not make it past this phase. In our class, we lost fifteen people who either hesitated or failed to jump.

Cassadenia and I looked at each other as we ascended the steps of the tower toward the simulated C-130 doorway. We both knew that we *had* to jump without hesitation. No matter how panicked we felt, we could not allow fear to take over or we would be sent home, and if that happened, we could forget about a career in the Marine Corps.

I tried to calm myself, as it got closer to my turn. There was no other way out of this. I walked up the last few steps. The instructor hooked me into the parachute harness, and clipped my harness to the steel line that descended from the tower to the ground. In the brief time it took for me to take my turn, several people had already refused to jump and waited for their dismissal papers before they returned to their previous assignment. Cassadenia had just jumped. Although his response was not fast, he successfully completed the jump without hesitating.

I stood in the doorway, placing my hands in the proper position. I looked out into the clear, blue sky. That is when I felt the instinct to step back, *get away*, remove my gear, and leave. I had beads of sweat forming on my forehead and neck, and my heart was racing. I heard the Jump Master talking to me–he ran through a series of commands, preparing me, and then it came–"*JUMP!*"

I forced myself to react against my instinct and against my sense of self-preservation. Using my hands, I pushed myself through the doorway and jumped into the empty space. It was *over*. I landed in the soft sand below, successfully completing the test. Cassadenia ran up to me, laughing and excited as both of us passed. I unhooked my harness, as I watched the fifteen participants who did not pass walk back to their barracks to receive their papers. I felt bad for them, knowing what awaited them when they returned. It was human instinct to recoil at that height. I never saw them again.

We completed five jumps, including the "night jump." In that test, the *LEG*–the name for recruits who had not earned their wings yet–was required to jump out of the C-130 or C-141 jet plane with a full pack of military gear, including the M16A2 assault rifle. There was so much gear, and the weight of it all was so heavy, that while waiting for the plane, all the LEGs were laying on their backs to take the weight off–which made us look like a bunch of turtles!

The night jump was the hardest, because the recruit cannot see the ground. Many recruits received injuries on this jump. I fell through the night sky at thirty feet per second, after jumping out of the plane. A civilian jumper lands softly on his or her feet, by comparison, and in most cases, walks off the drop zone. In the military, however; the parachute is designed to get the soldier to the ground as fast as possible (30 feet per second) without breaking body parts, but that all depends on keeping one's knees together, slightly bent, and looking up at the sky. I landed with a resounding crash. The impact knocked my helmet off, but I had no injuries! Other jumpers were not so lucky. We lost another five recruits on the night jump.

On graduation day, the instructor called our stick to attention. The Officers stepped out to present the coveted jump wings to the graduates. Earlier, Lance Corporal Cassadenia and I agreed that we would *not* receive our Blood Wings in the ceremony. Blood Wings is a tradition in which the graduate hands the silver jump wings to the officer with the back off the metal points. The officer slams the jump wings into the graduate's chest. The metal pins, which are about one inch long, would normally fit nicely into the back, fastening the jump wings to the uniform. The metal points pierce the graduate's chest, just above the heart. It does not take a lot of imagination to see how the term, Blood Wings came about.

We watched as the Army Officers went through their ranks, asking each of them if they wanted Blood Wings. To our surprise, not a single Army recruit agreed to get their Blood Wings in the first rank before us. Suddenly, the door to the squad bay opened and a Marine Corps Captain, with his double silver bars on his collar, walked at a measured pace toward the line of newly graduated Jump School class. Cassadenia and I had a feeling he was looking for us. After saluting the Army Jump Master, his eyes scanned the platoon as we stood at attention. He locked eyes on us, and spun quickly on his heels, heading directly toward us. He stopped in front of Lance Corporal Cassadenia.

"Marine, congratulations on your accomplishment, graduating from Jump School in keeping with the highest traditions, mission, and values of the Marine Corps," he said as he returned Cassadenia's salute. "Would you like your Blood Wings, Marine?"

"Sir! Yes Sir!" I remained at attention, eyes straight ahead as the Marine Corps Captain prepared the Blood Wings. I could hear the determination in Cassadenia's voice–he was ready. Then I heard the sickening sound of a fist hitting him in the chest, and the silver jump wings driving into his chest. Cassadenia's whole body moved back a step into the ranks behind him. He recovered, then snapped back to attention, saying, "Sir! Thank you Sir!" I chuckled inside. Unlike the movie, *Full Metal Jacket,* in which the graduates at Jump School held helmets full of beer, and chugged the whole helmet upon graduation, we had no helmets, and no beer. There was also no way I could refuse to get my Blood Wings now. The Captain pivoted and faced me. I saluted him, and awaited the greeting.

"Marine, graduation from Jump School is an honor. You have represented the Corps in the highest degree of honor, integrity, and perseverance. Would you like your Blood Wings?"

"Sir! Yes Sir!" I replied. I handed him my jump wings, and he removed the backings exposing the long sharp twin points.

"This Marine is quite a bit bigger than the other one," he said under his breath. He reared back and set his body weight in motion. The blow struck me square in the chest. As he pulled his fist back, I could see blood on his knuckles as he struck the jump wings, pushing the one-inch points into my chest. I felt the two points hit a bone in my chest as I landed on my ass in the row of soldiers behind me! I scrambled to my feet, snapped to attention, and saluted the Captain.

"Sir Thank you Sir!" I said. He saluted me back. Spinning on his heels, he was gone. Sergeant Jackson called us to attention, and then dismissed us one final time, as Airborne!

Cassadenia and I hugged each other–we were full of excitement and adrenaline. We looked down at our uniforms–blood had soaked into a widening circle on our chest area. I grabbed the jump wings with my fingers and began to tug at them. They made a strange sucking sound, as they reluctantly came loose from my chest.

After graduating Jump School, we returned to the Naval Weapons Station in Charleston, South Carolina, and back to our platoon. Over the next six months, I continued to guard the nuclear warheads, train in the woods on our training days, then once a month, we received a four-day weekend, the same schedule I enjoyed before I started Jump School. The four-day weekends allowed us to spend time in the sun and in the clubs at Myrtle Beach. This was one of the benefits to signing up for the Marine Corps–I could see places, exotic locations, and meet a diverse cross-section of the American population while I advanced my career.

Chapter 11: Daytona Beach 1987

Pow Wow Pow Wow
We keep it bangin like them drummers at a Pow Wow
Pow Wow Pow Wow
We got ya moving like them dancers at a Pow Wow
Turnt UP aayy Loud as it Go, I got my suds workin like they on my
payroll
– Lil Mike & Funny Bone, "POW WOW"

As I look back to those years, I have the hindsight to recognize the protection, teaching, and refining through life's lessons that our Creator, YHWH provided. Through all the partying, drinking, fighting, and driving like a maniac, I was always safe, even though I had to learn some uncomfortable lessons along the way. The dark times in my life, whether self-inflicted or dealt to me by chance, offered learning opportunities that would teach skills I would desperately need later in life. When I think of the gifts I have, or the skills I learned in a moment of desperation, I obtained them during a time of extreme hardship. Athletics were a healthy outlet in my youth, which later came to my rescue in the Marine Corps. I was desperate in my determination to make the high school varsity basketball teams. I refused to say no, and I made the team after two consecutive disappointments. That taught me that I could learn to improve if I worked hard enough, put in enough time and effort, and used my intelligence as much, if not more, than my strength.

Lance Corporal Robbins and Private First Class Bracken accompanied me to Daytona in the spring of 1987. Robbins was entertaining; he liked to party, drink beer, and tell stories. Bracken, on the other hand, was quiet and shy. He had a dry sense of humor, and liked country music. While Robbins and I were on the dance floor, Bracken was content to sit at the table. He was too shy to ask anyone to dance.

We arrived in Daytona Beach during Spring Break. MTV started a tradition, an open invitation to America's college students, primarily attractive women, to descend on this town in Florida. It was an opportunity to view in one place and one time, all the stylistic trends that were sweeping the country. *Vixen* was hot. The Beasties Boys, a hip-hop staple, was in town performing such hits as *"Fight for your right to party"* and was on concert tour with *Run DMC.* New wave band, Squeeze, performed *"Great Balls of Fire."* Between the second week of May and the third week of April, a delegation of America's youth participated in some of the strangest contests conceivable, while the rest of America's youth enviously followed along, courtesy of MTV.

I had seen this before, but only on television. That year, I was in the center of the celebration, experiencing the craziness instead of watching from the grainy screen of my analog television. Crowds of young and beautiful people were drinking, dancing, and competing for a chance to be one of MTV's five-second celebrities. It was almost surreal to see the very same scenes in person as I had on television or the cinema–beautiful young women dancing everywhere I looked. Sunbathers covered the beach, while others lifted weights–but only those with the right build and cut were on display. The eccentrics were easy to spot, as were the eye-catching, body painted women who teased the brain by disguising body parts with ingenious decorations or themes. Bike Week shared Daytona Beach during the same time as Spring Break, necessitating the creation of a new task force by local law enforcement. As far as I knew, there were no citywide riots–perhaps a few, harmless bar fights, but with that much alcohol flowing through that many people, it went smoothly.

Robbins, Bracken, and I walked around, taking in the sights as we drank beer from one location to the next. Some of Bracken's family lived in the vicinity, and planned to meet up with us at a local bar. We found a table near the front of the bar and sat down. College kids packed the bar. It was standing room only, with every imaginable demographic–bikers, Marines, stylish kids on break from college, and young people who have never set foot on a college campus, but loved the party atmosphere of spring break. Our beers arrived at the table.

"How 'bout a shot?" Robbins asked, addressing both Bracken and I.

"No, thank you–hard liquor hasn't done me any favors, just gets me in trouble," I explained. I was doing just fine with beer. As if he did not hear me, or more likely, he decided I would change my mind, Robbins ordered a shot for all three of us, and kept them coming. Between the two of them, I knew my shot would not go to waste.

As it turned out, Bracken was drinking his shot, and the shot intended for me. I discovered that a little later. Even though I declined the hard liquor, I did not slow down my intake of beer. The sharp pain of an overextended bladder reminded me I was due for a trip to the bathroom. I excused myself from the table, and headed to the bathroom–Robbins and Bracken continued to slam shots of whiskey, while another three waited on deck. It was no easy task winding my way through the crowd. Once I found the bathroom door, I pushed it in and walked up to the urinal.

Another Marine walked in right after me and stepped up to a urinal to my left, just as I finished relieving myself. Zipping up my pants, I took a step back. The door slammed open. Before I could even turn around, a body slid into the center of the bathroom across the floor, and the man hit his head on the adjacent wall. I looked at the Marine next to me and nodded as the man struggled to his feet. We both knew what we needed to do. Opening the door and quickly ducking my head, I saw the *blur* of a fist swing above me. A man standing on the other side of the door had hit one man hard enough to send him through the door, and he was waiting for more action as we attempted to leave the bathroom. The other Marine punched him solidly in the face, and I kicked him in his midsection, sending him backwards on his butt. Looking through the doorway, I watched the entire bar gripped in a fight. Just like the movies, this was chaos–*every man for himself.* Pool balls flew through the air, landing hard, knocking people out as they made a direct hit to the head or face. One stalky man held a chair over his head and brought it down fast, crashing over the back of a biker, whose beard hung just above the floor–he was on all fours, and desperately trying to stand up. The chair put an end to that. I saw shoes, high heels, and pool sticks propelled through the air, striking those not alert enough to duck. My only thought at that moment, was to find Bracken and Robbins, and get out of that bar before the police arrived.

I punched, received punches, and shoved my way through the crowd. As I got closer to where our table once sat, I saw Robbins exchanging punches with a large kid who looked to be part of the college crowd. I recognized this kid when we first arrived. He was with his girlfriend at a table, who was very nice looking. My peripheral vision caught a glimpse of movement under the table where I stood. I pulled back the tablecloth. It was Bracken! He had a nosebleed and looked terrified. I motioned for him to crawl toward me. Together, we moved closer to Robbins, and the three of us pushed and punched our way to the front door.

Once we got through the door, we piled into Robbins' car, and sped out of the parking lot–at that point there were no flashing lights pulling up to the bar, but the sound of sirens were audible and getting closer. Pumped with adrenaline, all three of us were feeling the mix of excitement, anger, and danger. Robbins accelerated well past the speed limit. I felt uneasiness, like a nudge, that Robbins needed to slow down. I asked him to ease up on the gas, and go the speed limit. We had been drinking, and after a bar fight like that, the police would be keeping their eyes out. As soon as Robbins eased up on the pedal, a line of ten or more police cars, lights flashing and sirens blaring, passed us heading the opposite direction, toward the parking lot of the bar. We escaped some real trouble that night. As we got a few miles down the road, we began to relax.

"What happened back there?" I asked. "What started that fight in the first place?" Robbins and I had nosebleeds, split lips, and a few bruises starting to form. I know that we caused more injuries than we received. Bracken had no noticeable injuries. Still no answer to my question. The car was silent. "What happened?" I asked again.

"It's Bracken's fault." Robbins said with a faint smile. His fat lip kept his smile to a minimum. "While you were gone, Bracken told me he'd be right back. He got up, walked over to that table where the big college kid was sitting–you know the one with the blonde girlfriend we all noticed." I nodded, looking over at Bracken in disbelief.

"Yeah, I remember them." I said.

"He tapped on her shoulder, tipped her chair back, and lip locked her until her boyfriend pushed him to the floor. Well, when the fight broke out, the big guy *totally* disappeared. The fight was *on* after that!" Now that made sense. Even before I escaped the bathroom, I just had this *feeling* that we had some part in starting the brawl–I guess I had *Robbins* pegged for starting the fight. Bracken seemed more the type who might cry if a girl talked to him, let alone tip her chair back in front of her boyfriend and give her a kiss!

Chapter 12: Korea

Children, listen to the discipline of a father and give attention to know understanding, For I gave you good instruction, Do not forsake my Torah, For I was my father's son, Tender and the only one in the eyes of my mother, then he taught me and said to me, Let your heart hold fast my words..
    —MISHLE (Proverbs:4)

It was 1989 and I had just received new orders. I was transferred to second Battalion, First Marine Division, Gulf Company. My company received orders to participate in a training mission in Japan and South Korea, where we were to train with our counterparts, exchange information, and prepare for any possible confrontations with North Korea.

My company received orders to participate in a training mission in Japan and South Korea, where we were to train with our counterparts, exchange information, and prepare for any possible confrontations with North Korea. It was here that I received my second written warning during my career in the Marine Corps.

My company participated in a joint exercise with the Hokkaido Japanese Army. We provided radio support and updates on enemy movements, strength, and positions. In one of the many mountain's that surround Korea, my platoon was embedded deep in the sand and trees, taking turns watching the roadways that weave in and around the rice patty plantations throughout the Korean landscape. As Fire Team Leader, and responsible for about four Marines, I reported any and all developments to my Team Leader, and carried the Squad Automatic Weapons, or *SAW*. This bad boy could fire one thousand rounds of 5.56 millimeter ammunition per minute.

Our orders for this training exercise were clear. We were positioned and assigned as recon, to watch and report enemy movements on this strip of road back to base command using our secure military radio. Positioned halfway up the hill, I had a clear vantage point from which to view activity below, and to a certain extent, any traffic coming from within my line of sight. Even though this was a training exercise, our orders and our obedience remained as rigid as if we were in a wartime scenario. Once we hunkered down, we were to remain concealed. We were the eyes and ears of the United States Marine Corps, for that particular stretch of roadway at least.

The weather was typical for Korea–high humidity, bursts of rain, then sun, then more rain. When I was not soaking wet from the last downpour, my clothes dripped from sweat and the humidity that hung thick in the air. It was afternoon, and with the rain in abeyance, the warmth of the returning sun began to heat the droplets clinging to my face. Hidden from sight in my camouflage in the hillside, I saw the daily school bus rounding the corner to its usual stop below us. The near continuous rainfall and humidity had rendered the dirt roads a sticky mud that clung to the tires and spattered clumps as it struggled to grip the path. The bus came to a stop, as it had predictably these past few days. Schoolchildren of various ages stepped off the bus, chatting with each other as the bus closed the doors behind them.

The sound of a second vehicle caught my attention. Speeding down the road from the same direction from which the bus had just come, a truck approached with increasing speed. With the children now off the bus, it inched forward at first, and then picked up speed as the driver shifted down. The children regrouped in the road, preparing to go their separate ways.

I could hear the engine from the truck, by that time. Instead of slowing down, it revved even louder, fighting the pull of sludge-packed ruts, causing it to swerve from side to side as it kicked up mud behind it. I turned my field glasses back to the bus stop. The children remained clustered in their group. While most still stood together in a group, some had begun to make their way toward the edge of the road, as they carefully avoided the deepest patches of mud and standing water.

From my position, I could hear them laughing and talking to one another, oblivious to sound of the truck's engine coming from behind them. Helpless to intervene in the horror that unfolded before me, I shouted at my fellow Marines. Careening toward the children, the truck, in its final moments, lost all control. Without slowing or attempting to avoid them, it barreled into the group of unsuspecting school children, sending several hurling through the air and landing in the mud to the side. The truck had struck the main group of children. The shock of impact was eerily silent. There were no screams or crying at first, just the thud, and sound of tires frantically trying to find traction in the muddy ruts. As my squad gathered around me, an indescribable sound of agony filled the air below.

Children lay strewn about the road, writhing and crying. Some could not have known what struck them, their attention consumed by conversation with their peers. As a Marine, and a human being, I knew what I had to do.

I radioed my squad leader to come to our position immediately. Once the Corporal arrived, I explained the events that had occurred as he surveyed the scene through his field glasses. I watched his expression as he examined the scene below. He radioed base for help. There was no answer. It was everything I could do to restrain myself from running down the hill to give aid, but I would have been in violation of a direct order, and there was no ambiguity in our orders. We were to remain in our positions, maintain concealment, and report enemy movements *until told otherwise.*

After another unsuccessful attempt to contact base and our platoon leader, the Corporal came to the realization that immediate medical aid would not arrive from base. "What do you think, Lance Corporal?" His eyes, fixed on mine, already resolute in our course of action.

"We get our asses down there *ASAP* and help them!" Nodding as I spoke, he called for a fire team consisting of four Marines. After we gathered for a quick briefing, the four Marines, medical personnel, and I raced down the hill to the scene of the accident. The children were still crying and talking in their native language. The truck struck three of the children directly, two of whom had minor injuries; however, the third child had a broken arm and was lying in the mud screaming in pain. We secured the scene, provided first aid, and treated all of the children for shock. The Corporal directed me to break the command for radio silence, at which point I reported the incident to the rest of our Company. Soon, more reinforcements arrived. Medical personnel stabilized the children and transported them to the nearest hospital.

Three days later, I received news from my squad leader that our command was writing us up. According to the Corporal, the command contended that we were in violation of disobeying a direct order and command, to remain silent and concealed as the recon element in the training mission. Through our actions, we disobeyed a lawful order, and our actions compromised the mission. There never seemed to be a question as to whether we were making the correct decision. According to the creed and motto of the Marine Corps, *to Protect Life, Liberty and Rights, Foreign and Abroad, God, Country, Corps, always faithful, Semper Fidelis,* we did exactly that–the lives of children were at stake and we had the opportunity to determine their fate.

When I enlisted in the Marine Corps, I intended to make this a twenty-year career. I was a good soldier, worked hard and trained with all my effort. Now, for trying to protect the lives of innocent children, the Marine Corps saw things differently. If protecting the lives of innocent children warranted disciplinary action, *then what the hell was I doing in the Marine Corps?*

"I, Duane Hodgson Garvais Lawrence, do solemnly swear that I will support and defend the Constitution of the United States against all enemies, foreign and domestic; that I will bear true faith and allegiance to the same; and that I will obey the orders of the President of the United States and the orders of the Officers appointed over me, according to the regulations and the Uniformed Code of Military Justice. So help me God."

My decision to lend aid to injured children was not part of our recon mission, to remain silent and concealed in this training mission. It was just that–a *training* mission. By jumping to their aid, we had disobeyed a direct, lawful order, and technically speaking, command had the right to issue punitive measures if they chose; however, that step was unnecessary. Real children suffered serious injuries as we looked on. Had we *not* come to their aid, imagine what the children's parents (and every Korean citizen) would have thought about Americans as they watched us ignore their screams and pleas for help. We fully understood the importance of following orders. We also remained true to the creed and motto of the United States Marine Corps, an oath to which I and everyone else in the Corps had sworn.

We continued training with our Japanese counterparts. By the end of the training, both U.S. Marines and the Japanese equivalent got together for a barbeque and celebration. Our training mission lasted about thirty days. Both sides were ready to let loose and party hard. In the Marine Corps, we train hard, work hard, and when time comes to party, we do that with even more energy!

Throughout my time in the Marines Corps, I had come to fantasize about hitting an officer, and getting away with it. Those who have struck an officer did so out of rage and lack of impulse control. The consequences can be severe, and even in the best-case scenario, it would not be worth it. One could lose his rank or spend time in the Brig. My goal, however unorthodox, would require and equally unorthodox set of circumstances in order to pull it off.

162

Both the Japanese Army and U.S. Marines met together at a large hall, complete with a dance floor, more food than one could imagine, and several kegs of beer. The Marines brought Budweiser, small bags of potato chips, Doritos, and other popular snack foods. The Japanese Army brought sake, and chips that somewhat resembled our potato chips, except they were made from seaweed, dried squid, and fish.

As the evening progressed, the beer and sake flowed; toasts were made, Americans switched from beer to sake, and the Japanese soldiers drank American beer–a mistake for some. I was fortunate that I chose to stick with what I knew best, American beer. I had a very good buzz by this time, or as we used to call it, *head change*. I entered the large common area, through the gathering of Marines and Japanese military, beer in hand, and buzzed. A small group of higher-ranking Japanese military personnel walked toward me, and as they came closer, I could see that their leader focused his gaze intently on me.

More accurately, he was fixated on my uniform. I wore standard issue Marine Corps uniform for daily use, camouflage trousers, green t-shirt, and short-sleeved top. On my collars and just above my left breast, I wore my prize possession–the silver jump wings that signaled to all other military personnel that I had completed the training in Jump School. The group stopped in front of me. The leader began speaking to his friends in Japanese. I noticed his change in pitch as he spoke and made various gestures. His eyes returned to gaze upon my set of silver jump wings.

I could not understand them, and when I spoke, none in the group could understand me either. I noticed how polite they seemed–even when I could not understand their language. After only a few short exchanges, a crowd began to gather, as if they could sense that an event was about to occur. Another Japanese enlisted man offered to interpret.

I learned that the leader of the small group was a General! A plan began to form in my mind as I learned how the General was so enamored by my silver jump wings. I explained to the interpreter the process for obtaining the jump wings, including the rite of passage, known as *Blood Wings*. The General wasted no time telling the interpreter that he would gladly take part in whatever process was required to earn the jump wings. In return, I would trade my jump wings for his insignia rank of General. The interpreter and General discussed this in Japanese and quickly agreed that we had a deal.

The feeling that one has when someone or something is watching can be so overwhelming it cannot be ignored. This was such a moment. Looking to my right, I saw my Commanding Officer, watching, his hands over his forehead as if he had a headache. I knew that I was on dangerous ground. My Commanding Officer must have sensed where this was headed as well. Despite the effects of alcohol, I had the wherewithal to explain, in clear detail, to the Japanese interpreter the full extent of this process, lest I find myself in the brig, devoid of rank and pay.

In as vivid and clear language possible, I explained once again that the General would need to complete the required five perfect parachute landings first. As I received confirmation that the General understood and agreed so far, I continued to describe the removal of the backing, the metal pins, the punching of the wings into his flesh above the left breast, and that it would *hurt*!

I watched carefully as the interpreter relayed the information to the General in Japanese. Without understanding even the basics of their language, I had to rely on the universal human language of facial expression and emotion. The General remained intently focused as the interpreter spoke each word and phrase. His face remained stoic, smiling occasionally, and then nodding in fascination, as I assume he was being told about the Blood Wings ritual, he held eye contact with me, nodded, and smiled. His eyes widened as he listened. There could be no doubt that the interpreter had done his job. Only a thorough description could elicit such a perfect reaction. Then, without hesitation, the interpreter stopped speaking, and the General nodded in agreement.

The crowd buzzed with conversation. Japanese and English conversations mingled in the air. Excitement and anticipation were evident even in a language about which I knew nothing. Both American and Japanese personnel formed a circle around us. The Japanese General and his Commanding Officer approached me and bowed. I snapped to attention and saluted them each, and both returned the salute. I watched, as the General reached up to his shirt collar, and removed the backings from a set of four bronze stars. Smiling, he reached over to me and pinned the stars on my collar. A number of my friends began shouting, laughing, and yelling, as did many of the Japanese soldiers.

All the Marines who had earned their jump wings came to the front of the circle, standing in a line about five feet apart, The Japanese General joined us up front, as we showed him how to conduct and execute a

Parachute Landing Fall, also known as PLF. We practiced this several times until the General signaled that he was ready to complete his initiation. We all gathered together and performed the five required PLF's, jumping in the air, landing with our feet and knees together, slightly bent, and with our eyes fixed above to the ceiling as we hit the ground, and rolled safely to a stop. Having completed the requisite jumps, the General proudly awaited his coveted ceremony.

As the General awaited the Blood Wings rite, I considered that, not only would I have my opportunity to hit an officer; I would be hitting a General! We stood up together and I saluted the General. He returned the salute and bowed in our direction. Our Commanding Officer was, by this time, very nervous. Knowing how Marines can be when they have been drinking too much and letting off steam, he had every reason to be concerned. Before continuing with the rite, I explained the process one last time to the interpreter, making certain that my Commanding Officer and everyone else in the vicinity could witness my detailed explanation. As before, the General watched me intently, his eyes almost glowing as the interpreter explained the vivid details of metal pins being punched into his flesh. Nodding and smiling enthusiastically, his eyes gleamed as he agreed in his native language.

My fellow Marines gathered close, as they watched me remove the jump wings from my uniform, remove the backing, and expose the quarter inch pins. The General snapped to attention as I approached him. I came to a halt in front of him, saluted him and he returned the salute. Through the interpreter, I congratulated the General on performing the five basic PLF's correctly, which qualified him to receive his jump wings. His face was glowing as I gently placed the jump wings into his uniform just above his left breast and stepped back. Keeping my balance steady with my right foot, I pulled my fist back as everyone looked on. The room was silent. Even up to that moment, I doubt that many of the Marines in the room believed that I would follow through with this last step, punching the jump wings into the General's chest.

I came forward with my fist, making a direct hit on the jump wings. I could hear him let out a gasp as my fist reverberated through his body. He fell back several feet, and slid to a stop about ten feet behind him. The room was still, and time paused as if to prolong the suspense.

The General jumped to his feet, jumped in the air, shouting and screaming while pointing to his new jump wings. The crowd of Japanese and American soldiers all screamed and yelled, patting each other on the backs, laughing, and celebrating. The General approached me, snapped to attention, and saluted me, after which I returned the salute and we shook hands. My Commanding Officer, meanwhile, stared in disbelief and shook his head. This was the icebreaker for the remainder of the evening between the two fighting forces. Setting an entirely new tone, we spent the rest of the night drinking, arm wrestling, laughing, and eating. Formation was scheduled for 0900 hours the next morning. It soon became apparent that this would not be a practical goal.

Most of the forces suffered intolerable hangovers, and many passed out in some of the most unusual places. I tried to locate an unoccupied portable latrine, but after finding passed out soldiers in the first thirteen, I was lucky to find the next one open. The two Commanding Generals had a conference, and set an amended time of one o'clock pm for formation. After that long night of drinking, most of the soldiers from both American and Japanese forces arrived with ashen faces and found sunlight very difficult to handle. This was, by far, the most memorable formation in which I have participated during my military career!

Chapter 13: Assault Climber School

"I forgive you" —Emcee One 2006 Rockin' the Rez Coeur d'Alene Tribe

"Yo, I was mad. I wasn't asked to come into this world, unplanned parenthood from this bad little girl. So I stand in this land that doesn't understand loving, dreamed of being great, but told I would be nothing."

Gulf Company 2/5, San Mateo, California
United States Marine Corps 1989

Shortly after arriving at my new duty station, the Second Battalion 5th Marines Gulf Company (2/5), I made another lasting impression with my Platoon Commander and First Lieutenant. The Second Battalion 5th Marines are the most decorated battalion in the Marine Corps–and the *only* battalion authorized to wear the French *Fourragère* on their uniforms. Our motto, "Retreat Hell," seemed to fit perfectly during this time in my life.

I was told to, once again, report to the Company Commander's office. Dressed in my razor-sharp, pressed green combat fatigues, my spit-shined boots, Lance Corporal Insignia on my collar, and my prized set of silver jump wings pinned squarely just above my heart, I reported to my Company Commander. *Déjà vu* set in as I watched him flip through my military training records, muttering to himself, and glancing back and forth through the numerous documents. Standing at attention with my eyes fixed straight ahead, I began to wonder why he called me into his office. I had been with Gulf Company fewer than six months and kept myself out of trouble as far from trouble as possible. *Had I been set up again?* I wondered. *Why am I here?* I had my answer as soon as I asked myself that question. The Commander looked up at me, fixing his gaze on me as if to size me up.

"Lance Corporal Garvais Lawrence, welcome to the most decorated battalion in my beloved Marine Corps! Here at Gulf Company two-five, we are hard chargers, take no enemies, trained killers, and *go-getters*! Your accomplishments speak highly of your commitment to the Marines. I see you have letters of appreciation and that you've achieved over eight straight perfect three hundred physical fitness scores. That in itself reflects perseverance, drive, focus and the willingness to go the extra mile." As I stood there, locked at attention, my mind was racing. *What was he getting at? Why did he call me in here?* The good news, I thought, *was that it appeared I was not in trouble!* As I stood there at attention, I realized that my mind had begun to wander. I was so perplexed at this odd meeting that I lost my focus on what he was saying. Hearing his words brought me right back into focus. "Lance Corporal Garvais Lawrence, I am offering you the chance of a lifetime, a position of honor, integrity, and commitment–*if* you graduate, that is. How would you like to go to Marine Corps Force Recon?"

Wow! This seemed very familiar! But this time, something was different. I could, once again feel that familiar warning from Creator God warning me this was not the path he wanted me to be on, and I was not to accept. Now, of course, the Commanding Officer and my First Lieutenant were not expecting my forthcoming reply.

"Sir, with all due respect, I have to decline your invitation to attend the Marine Corps Force Recon training, Sir!" The bright anticipation on his face disappeared as soon as the words echoed off the walls of his office. The expression on his face had been that of someone presenting an expensive gift, full of the joy of giving, and not prepared for the possibility that this priceless gift could be refused.

"What the hell did you just say? I cannot believe what I am hearing! I have Marines training year round just to achieve the minimum cutting score required to take the test for Recon, and here you stand, having multiple perfect scores, and only ONE is required just to try out for Recon, yet you are telling me 'no'? WHY THE HELL NOT?" I almost felt bad for him. It almost seemed that I had hurt his feelings with my response. He was trying to do something *nice* for me. From his perspective, my response might have even appeared ungrateful or unappreciative.

"Sir, permission to answer truthfully, Sir!"

"Go ahead." He shook his head slightly. His voice sounded more like a growl.

"Sir, because my idea of service is not being flown out to a third world county, inserted under the cover of night and ordered to kill a person or persons whom I don't know. And if caught, the United States Government declines to help or even denies knowing me, Sir!"

"Get the FUCK out of my office, Marine!" I saluted my Commanding Officer and I repeated his last words, as required.

"Sir! Get the fuck out of your office! Yes Sir!" I spun on my heels and exited the office. As I walked back to my platoon, I thought about what had just happened. My declination to join Force Recon had nothing to do with my physical ability or capabilities. No, it was the spiritual warning that I had felt inside. Something I had come to recognize as a reliable, pure, and outside intelligence had given me all the information I needed to make my decision. When I listened to this spiritual nudge in the past, I was always grateful I had obeyed. Every time I failed to heed the warning, I regretted that decision. This time, I decided, I was not going to make that mistake. But trying to explain *that* to your company commander!

After I arrived at my platoon, a group of Marines came up to me and asked about my visit. I described my experience, play-by-play. Some of them laughed, some listened quietly, and others just shook their heads as if I had lost my mind. One of those was an African American Marine by the name of Corporal Smallwood. He was from St. Louis, Missouri. Smallwood was very committed to the mission of the Marine Corps.

Obviously, my declination to attend Force Recon did not sit well with him. In fact, it only furthered his initial dislike for me, which began when I arrived to the company wearing jump wings, and when I beat him one-on-one on the basketball court in front of our peers. "Well, that was a smooth move, Garvais. I'm sure the Commanding Officer was impressed by your decision not to attend Recon." A sneer formed on his face as he shook his head.

"Stay out of this, Smallwood. It's none of your business. Do you want me to kick your ass again on the basketball court in front of your homies?" I knew he wouldn't like that dig.

"How 'bout we just go outside and see who kicks whose ass, Halfbreed!"

"Break it up! Let's finish our training so we can all get some R&R!" said the Sergeant.

About two months later, our company was to attend "Cold Weather Training." I was not looking forward to this at all. We had all observed other platoons coming back from Cold Weather Training –many with blisters on their faces, courtesy of the subzero temps in the high elevation of the mountains. Nobody was looking forward to this mandatory training, and it was clear from the demeanor of our company as we established our camp at the base of the mountains in the high winds, which subjected us to the biting wind chill factor.

I had just finished cleaning my makeshift quarters inside our big tent. As it turned out, my squad leader was Corporal Smallwood. You can probably guess how that worked out for me. I seemed to get all the hard details, and it seemed like he was on my ass no matter what I did. The tension had been building up over time, and I could feel the corners of my mouth tighten with every order he issued. Over the years, I had learned to recognize this as a sign that I am becoming dangerously close to expressing my repressed anger toward someone. Some people turn red. Others frown. When I am building up a high level of rage inside, and I am doing everything in my power to keep from exploding, I can feel the corners of my mouth tighten. I knew this was not a good sign.

I just completed sweeping the areas around the tent when Corporal Smallwood came around the corner and began to yell at me. That was my breaking point, and I yelled right back at him. I do not remember exactly what words were spoken, but the tension over time had finally reached a climax. This was my breaking point. To anyone watching, it must have been a great sight! Corporal Small stood facing me with his fist cocked back as his other hand grabbed my shirt. I was holding his shirt with my left hand, and was in the process of landing a devastating hook to his body when we both heard the dreaded words, "Officer on deck! *Attention!*" Everybody froze, including Smallwood and I, who were still holding each other's shirts in our hands. "That's real good. Real great. Smallwood and Garvais Lawrence, just great!" The Marine Corps officer stood shaking his head, his jaw clenched tight. "Report to the LT Office in ten minutes ASAP!" Turning on his heels, he spun and walked out. The tent room was silent. Smallwood and I looked at each other, finally releasing our grips on each other's shirts and started to prepare to report to the LT Office.

As we approached the door to the Platoon Commander's Office, Corporal Smallwood looked at me and said, "This is my fault and I will take the blame, Duane." With that, we walked into the room, up to the desk, saluted, and stood at attention. Our LT was smirking, and even chuckling to himself as we stood at attention. He had both of our personnel files in front of him.

Looking up from our files, he said, "Well, boys, seems like neither of you *like* each other much. That's just good, real good because both of you are going to Assault Climbers School, where you both have to rely on each other. If you do not, and you keep fighting with each other, you will not graduate, and depending on the circumstances, one or both of you could be killed. That is all. Don't fail and don't disappoint me. You are excused. Good luck as this training is very intense and critical to the mission of the Marine Corps."

Lance Corporal Smallwood and I walked back to our platoon in silence. I'm pretty sure he was not pleased and was thinking the same thing I was. *Awesome! Now we don't have to attend Cold Weather Training!* Each company selects two hard chargers (Marine slang for "motivated, physically-fit, kick-ass Marines") to attend the Assault Climbers course during the Cold Weather Training. My second thought was, *how am I going to repair the damaged relationship between Smallwood and I?* One minute we were just about to throw down, as only Marines can do, and the next minute we were standing tall in front of our platoon commander, being selected to complete the Assault Climbers course–one of the most challenging ropes courses in the military.

The United States Marine Corps Assault Climbers course is based in Fort Ord, California. The company attends Cold Weather Training while the two selected Marines from each company attend the Assault Climbers Course. At the end of the training, the Assault Climbers meet up with the platoons who have just finished Cold Weather Training at dusk. The Assault Climbers set up a rope ladder system by free climbing to the top of the cliff, relying on each other in a two-man climbing system. For example, Corporal Smallwood and I stood at the base of the cliff preparing to begin our climb. Prior to this, we both completed the rigorous training, which consisted of multiple smaller climbs, and we had to demonstrate the ability to tie ten different knots, eight of them while blindfolded. The two-man system means that I would start climbing up the cliff, and would continue to do so until running out of rope or until I could not climb anymore.

The Marine (me) would then tie an anchor system into the cliff, which would have to hold my partner (Smallwood) and me as he climbed. This climbing system allowed the two-man team to reach the top of the cliff, but each man's life depended on the skill and training of both men working in concert.

As Corporal Smallwood and I prepared for our final climb up what we affectionately referred to as "The Big Face," we both knew this climb would be different and more difficult. This time, we would be climbing a cliff much bigger and taller than we had ever attempted before. It would also be taking place at night. The darkness would make it more difficult to see potential obstacles, and we would be hammering pins into the rock and stringing up a rope so that the platoon could follow us. I had no idea that I would have *another* close brush with death!

171

The process of setting up the rope for our platoon to follow us was tedious, long, and tiring. Corporal Smallwood and I had been awake all night climbing Big Face, trusting each other, the system of two-man anchors, and the pins, chocks, and ropes we used while setting up the rope for our platoon to use. Our fellow Marines and leadership were counting on us, and we certainly did not want to fail or disappoint. We made it to the top, finishing out our rope ladder. After making last minute checks, Corporal Smallwood and I repelled back down the cliff to await our platoon and leaders.

As we waited, Smallwood and I laughed at how we were once enemies, and now we had actually become friends. Having to rely on one another through this training developed a sense of absolute trust. The sound of footsteps announced the arrival of our platoon commander and NCO.

We quickly briefed them on the established rope ladder, showing them the starting point at the base of Big Face. After a quick planning session, Gulf Company arrived and we began to tie each Marine onto the rope ladder system, snapping each on securely with the locking pin, then off they went up the cliff. About two hours later, after the entire company had made it up to the top, Corporal Smallwood and I began the equally long and dangerous climb back up Big Face, taking down the rope system as we went.

I remember being exhausted, both mentally and physically, as I approached the top. The brief light before sunrise was starting, and Smallwood was already on top. I only had a few more pins to take out. I could see the top. It was almost within reach. That's when it happened.

The last pin was seated in the rock. I remember reaching for the pin, and as my hand fumbled on it, I was gripped by fear. I had no back-up! *No way to stop me or catch me if fell.* I missed the pin, and knowing that nobody was around, I did the only thing I could do. With my other hand, I reached up and grabbed a slight crack in the rock face, which swung me into the rock, face first. My lip was bleeding. Then, to my horror, I realized that my momentum was going to cause me to fall!

I was tired when I reached for that pin. Exhaustion and sleep deprivation had taken their toll on me. Knowing that nothing was there to catch me if something went wrong suddenly took control of my conscious mind. That realization, together with the exhaustion, only multiplied the sense of panic that flashed through my mind. I was not about to go out this way, but the momentum caused from swinging over to the crack in the rock had made a bad situation even more deadly.

I anticipated that the unthinkable was about to happen. That sensation of impending death, falling from such a terrific height, is difficult to explain. Time seemed to stand still during those last few seconds, just before Corporal Smallwood reached down and grabbed me by my helmet. I managed to throw my hand straight up, grasp his hand and he pulled me up over the ledge.

Chapter 14: Okinawa, Japan

It aint no shame in my game, we bang Christ Name in this thang,
No Change still doin the same, Christ 4 Life we will remain
– Mike Bone, "Holla"

The flight to Okinawa was long. We flew over miles of ocean from the United States to a small military base in Japan. Once we arrived, we rode by truck to Camp Schwab–not my first choice, as it was the farthest point of the island, but it was on the beach and views were unbelievable! The water was warm and clear. Most of the Marines there bought snorkeling gear, and spent most of their down time swimming, snorkeling, and watching the colorful fish and abundant sea life in the warm waters.

When we were not in the ocean, we trained in the surrounding jungles, preparing for warfare. The humidly was like nothing I had experienced before, not in the South, and certainly not in Washington State. Our uniforms were drenched in sweat within the first five minutes of every jungle training exercise. Sweat pooled in our gas masks during training. When the exercise was over, we tipped our masks over and sweat poured onto the ground.

On Okinawa, if I was not in training, there were only a few options to consider–snorkeling, shopping at the military PX store, and eating seafood at the local restaurants, playing basketball or going to the gym. Of course, we always had alcohol at our disposal in case we were determined to get in trouble and suffer the predictable hangover.

During my time on Okinawa, I managed to remain sober for five months, working out with my good friend, Danny Urias–from Compton, California. Danny and I had a routine. On our days off, we visited the PX in the morning, ate at Yakisoba, our favorite local restaurant, then lifted weights, and played basketball until it was time for the military theater's double feature.

I owe Danny a lot for encouraging me not to party, being there to talk to when I would have otherwise turned to alcohol. On the other side of Okinawa, there was a partying town called Kenville. We made several trips to Kenville, but it was during the day, and we spent our time sightseeing and shopping in the local stores.

I learned that my beloved Grandfather, Charlie Garvais Lawrence, was not doing well. I made a special point to visit him in 1986 just before I enlisted. He was eighty-five years old, and almost full Sioux from the Assiniboine Tribes of the Fort Peck Indian Reservation in northeastern Montana.

Charlie married my Grandmother, Ellen Contway, from the Fort Belknap Indian Reservation. Their children included my father, Kenny Garvais Lawrence, Ron Garvais Lawrence Sr., Darlene Garvais Lawrence, and Elaine Garvais Lawrence Moomaw. My grandparents were well respected in the small communities of Omak and Okanogan, Washington, just off the Colville Indian Reservation. They made their final home by the old sawmill on the Colville Indian Reservation in Okanogan County, Washington in a singlewide trailer on the property of their oldest daughter, Elaine.

My grandparents grew up in the depression era. Charlie was one of the two best fiddlers in the county of Okanogan. When Charlie was young, he tried out for a fiddling gig in Nespelem on the Colville Indian Reservation. Charlie had to ride a horse over Desetual Pass in the winter in order to audition for the gig.

Back in those days, money was scarce. When Charlie was selected for the job, his family was very excited because he would be paid a dollar and twenty-five cents to fiddle at the dances, and he was able to eat as much food as he could. Charlie had a full time job already, so this additional income was very helpful to cover expenses for the family. Charlie was very talented, but he did not read sheet music. He could listen to a tune and repeat it perfectly after hearing it once. He played by ear and from his heart.

While in his late twenties, Grandpa Charlie often competed in athletic contests at the local fair. During this time, contestants paid an initial entrance fee, and if they won, they received a prize. Grandpa was a talented athlete, and his unique style and abilities were legendary in that small community. Grandpa Charlie registered for the one hundred yard dash at the fair one year. When the officials called for the contestants to line up for the race, Charlie took his place among his competitors. At that point, maybe few if any, noticed anything different. When the officials fired the gun and the contestants took off in a sprint, many were amazed to see Grandpa take the lead while *barefoot*! When he crossed the finish line, the official pointed at Charlie and remarked that he was just under the qualifying time for the Olympics in the one hundred yard dash!

Grandpa Charlie was an honorable man, talented in music and athletics. He led a remarkable life, providing for his family through some of the harshest conditions imaginable. He played music with his family, passed these gifts on to his children, and spent many weekends fiddling while other family members sang and played guitar.

The news came by phone. When Grandpa Charlie passed away, I was filled with sadness and grief. After I hung up the pay phone, I thought about all the times I visited him as a child in his singlewide trailer. I still remember walking into the trailer–my grandmother met us at the door. A petit and beautiful Indian woman, she would meet us at the door with a huge smile on her face. She glowed with love and joy at the sight of her grandchildren. Grandpa would stand from his chair, his face chiseled from years of hard work. His heritage, directly tied to the Crazy Horse Clans, was clearly visible throughout his features.

Neither Charlie nor his father was enrolled in any tribes; however, there was no question from looking at him that he was an *Indian*. Since neither Thomas nor Charlie was enrolled, my father and I were also not enrolled in any Native American Tribe. This would turn out to be very critical later in life. My Native American ancestry would be the subject of a federal court trial, and the outcome would determine if I would be prosecuted for crimes that I did not commit.

Grandpa Charlie retired from two different jobs. After he retired, he returned to work after the second retirement and continued to show up for several more years *without pay*, just because he enjoyed being a productive member of society and he enjoyed working. We have a picture of Grandpa posing when he was about sixty-five years old. His stomach was flat and ripped, his arms were cut, and his biceps were huge. Our cousin, Blake Marchand recently posted a photo of himself on Facebook, and I immediately recognized the striking resemblance between Grandpa and my cousin.

Walking back to the barracks on Camp Schwab, I was in shock. I felt the inescapable need to return, and pay my respects, even though I was in Okinawa, a rock in the middle of the Pacific Ocean thousands of miles from the United States of America. I needed to return home, to say goodbye, pray for him, for our family, and be there for Grandma Ellen. As I approached my barracks, I remembered that only "emergency" leave requests were granted, because the government considered our deployment a *National Security* issue. At that point, though, I had no reason to doubt they would grant my request. I located my Platoon Sergeant and submitted my request for leave.

The next day, my Commanding Officer summoned me to headquarters. I arrived at his office, and saluted my Commanding Officer. He gave the command, "at ease" and I relaxed to parade rest. My Commanding Officer peer over my leave request and asked me, "Why do you need to go home for leave?"

"My grandfather was very important to me. I need to be there for my grandmother and family ... this is *very* important to me." How difficult it felt to have to explain in words the true importance of taking leave to say goodbye to my grandfather. I did everything I could to explain the important role he played in my life, how much I respected him, and the close relationship we had.

"Well, your request for leave is too long, and I have to deny it." His response was matter of fact

"If I fly home, attend the funeral, and fly out the next day, would you approve it?"

"No. It is denied, for *National Security* reasons." That was that. His response was as cold as he was, and his rationale for denying my shortened leave was baseless.

I was livid. There was no way that I bought his reason for denying my request. I found it impossible to believe that one Marine's absence from training for three or four days for funeral leave would put the security of the United States of America on the brink of collapse. I did not have my real father in my life—Grandpa Charlie was as close to that relationship as I would ever see.

That weekend, we were on Liberty status, beginning around five o'clock Friday afternoon until seven o'clock Monday morning. One of the soldiers in our platoon, L/Cal Edwards decided this was an opportune time for us to party hard. Edwards was from the South—he loved hunting, fishing, and spending time outdoors. He was an enrolled Cherokee tribal member and sported a pronounced southern drawl.

I had abstained from drinking any alcohol for the past five months, and worked out every day instead. After three beers, I felt a strong buzz. Along the way, we picked up a bottle of Crown Royale. Edwards started drinking the hard liquor, and passed it on to me. This was a huge, and potentially fatal, mistake.

Native Americans have been exposed to alcohol for only a couple hundred years. DNA indicates that we are not equipped to process alcohol the same as our Caucasian brothers and sisters. Depending on how one looks at this, it could be either good or bad. When I was in high school, my friends would be on their third or fourth beer and thinking about where they were going to get another six-pack, while I was still drinking my second beer and had a solid buzz. This was one of times, however, that not being able to handle a lot of alcohol worked against me.

L/Cal Edwards and I sat on the beach, admiring the clear waters and feeling the breeze coming off the water. Edwards tipped the bottle back and handed it over to me. "Let's be *blood brothers*!" Just like in the movies, when two men cut their forearms and press their open cuts together, they form a bond between them for life. Naturally, this sounded like a great idea.

.

"Hell Yeah!" I took another drink of Crown Royale and passed it back. Life was good. The sun was out, I had one hell of a buzz, the ocean was beautiful, and I did not have to go to work the next morning. If I could go back, I would tell myself to enjoy the view and the friendship, eat some food, and pass out. Unfortunately, that is not what happened next.

As the sun began to set, the men from my platoon kept talking about how messed up it was that my leave was denied. This reminded me how angry I was when the Commanding Officer denied my funeral leave to pay respects to my Grandfather due to National Security. When I drank alcohol, it exacerbated whatever emotion I was feeling at the time. If I was happy before I started drinking, I was a happy drunk. If I was sad, I became a very sad drunk. When I was angry before I started to drink, I was an angry, fighting drunk, and my decision-making abilities were not able to keep out of trouble in most cases.

The sun looked like a giant fireball over the ocean as it set. My anger at that point flamed as I thought about the officer who denied my leave request. If I could not go home to honor my grandfather, and pay my respects to this Lakota man whom I loved dearly, then I was going to have my own way of honoring him–by thumbing my nose at my superiors.

I stood up and started to walk toward the Officer of the Day headquarters. My friends, sensing what I was about to do, tried to stop me and convince me sleep it over. By that time, I was in a rage. Nothing could stop me from doing what I thought was right. As I walked closer, it did occur to me that I could get into some serious trouble for my actions, but the combination of hard liquor and being denied leave for National Security reasons continued to dominate my thoughts. The door to headquarters was within reach, and I fully intended to give my Commanding Officer a *piece of my mind*.

I pushed the door open and looked around. I saw the Sergeant sitting behind a desk. It was a typical military room with all the necessities and *nothing* more. The walls were sparsely decorated with pictures of the Commanding General, various officers, and of course, a picture of the Commandant of the Marine Corps. That only added to my uncontrollable rage.

I stood in the doorway, drunk, no shirt, wearing shorts, and dripping blood from the cut on my forearm, courtesy of my new blood brother. I staggered up to the Sergeant's desk. "Write this down!" I demanded, my finger stabbing his desk as I spoke. Another door opened and a Marine Corps Captain, looking startled, stared at me in disbelief. I looked back at him and repeated, "Sergeant, write this down in your damn book!" The Sergeant stood up from his desk.

"That's a Captain you are talking to, Marine!"

"I don't give a *damn* who he is, write this down!" I retorted in a loud voice. The Marine Captain picked up the telephone. Even in that state of mind, I knew he was calling the military police. That only enraged me more. I ran up to the desk and told the Sergeant, "Write this down NOW!" Finally, he obliged and picked up a pen, waiting for me to dictate the message. "Tell the Commanding General he can kiss my RED ASS for not letting me go home on leave to see my Grandpa laid to rest. KISS MY ASS!" After he finished writing, I quickly read it and signed the message with my signature. I had a sudden feeling of satisfaction. In the distance, I could hear the sound of sirens approaching.

Instinctively, I turned on my heels and ran out of the building into the cool night. I heard shouts from the Captain and the Sergeant as I ran down the road. Even though I was very intoxicated, the excitement and the sound of sirens sobered me up enough to evade them. I was in top physical condition. There was no way they were going to catch me.

I decided that I would do my best to avoid capture that night. As I ran, I felt like my grandfather was with–it gave me strength and purpose. The moon provided adequate light, so I took a back road near the chow hall, which would lead me to the other end of Camp Schwab. I had no idea where I was going.

A police car rounded the corner in front of me. I ducked into the bushes near the road. I watched as the police cruised by, shining his spotlight back and forth in the surrounding foliage. I continued this pattern for the next few hours–running, ducking under cover, into a building, or behind a military truck.

Eventually, I ended up on the far end of Camp Schwab in the Motor T Division. My buzz had nearly worn off. I was hungry and thirsty from running all night.

Somehow, I found my way into a barracks. I located a room in the far corner of the open squad bay, where I discovered a refrigerator filled with all the fixings for a sandwich. I made the best triple-decker bologna sandwich–sparing nothing. I used an entire package of bologna, Kraft cheese, mustard, mayonnaise, ketchup, lettuce, and anything else that happened to be in the refrigerator at the time. My hunger was ravenous, after all the adrenaline, physical exertion, and drinking.

The next morning, I woke up on a cold, cement floor with a blanket covering me. My head was swimming. I tried to look around, but the light was overwhelming. The veins in my head felt as if they were ready to burst with every heartbeat. The sight of dried blood caught my eye. Memories began to cascade in no particular order. The cut to my forearm … my blood brother … *Crown Royale*. I fought the dizziness and tried to stand. I forced myself to look around the room, despite the sharp pain brought on by each ray of light. I saw a large Marine, a Sergeant, standing in the doorway, watching me with a smirk on his face.

"Well, you must be the Marine the *entire* base here in Okinawa is talking about, huh?" I was standing now, and it took everything I had to maintain my balance. "I was sleeping when you walked into my cubicle. I watched you look around–you were laughing, then you walked over to my refrigerator and–*I swear*–you made the BIGGEST sandwich I have ever seen! You ate that down, then you fell asleep. Couple other Marines from my unit and I put two an' two together, and figured you were the Marine on the run from the MP's. Man! You must've ran about five or six miles to get to the other side of the base, and avoid capture! We decided to let you just sleep it off and let you handle it when you return to your platoon." As he spoke, more memories flooded back. I started to remember running from tree to tree, jumping over fences and military equipment. In my head, I could hear the police sirens behind me, as I ran.

It was hard to believe the Military Police did not catch me. They were very capable, and for the most part, it was true–*they always got their man.* After a brief visit with the Motor T Sergeant, I offered to pay for the food I ate. He declined to accept, telling me that it was "on him." He even thanked me for putting on a good show for the base, and for the enlisted personnel. I was, it turned out, a type of hero for voicing my thoughts, telling off the officers, and escaping into the dark, humid night of Okinawa.

I started the long walk back. I thought about my actions, and wondered if I should have been feeling remorse. I did not. I still felt anger at the manner in which the Marine Corps was treating me. In my two years of service, I had always stepped up to the challenges, fought many battles physically and mentally. Anytime the officers needed a warrior to battle against other Marines in the battalions, I stepped up and represented my platoon and my company. I had secured thirteen consecutive perfect physical fitness scores, which reflected favorably on our commanding officer, our company officer, and of course, our platoon commander. All I asked, was to take a three or four day leave so I could be home with my family and pay respects to my grandfather and help my grandmother, yet the Marine Corps refused.

As I walked, I decided at that moment, that I was not going to reenlist in the Marine Corps. I had planned to make the military a career, by serving another twenty years, but now, all that had changed. I continued walking and thinking about my grandfather. I thought about how hard he worked to take care of his family, sometimes working two jobs–one full-time and one part-time job. I really love this man. I loved his sharp facial features, how he would hug Marie and I when we came to visit him, how he sat in his chair, chewing Red Man tobacco and spitting into his container–always nearby. I grinned as I remembered the sparkle in his eye when we asked him to play the fiddle, how it seemed to be a reflection of pure love. He always jammed with the fiddle under his chin. He never read music–just played from his heart and soul.

I reached my barracks. Opening the squad bay door, I walked down the middle of the open squad bay. It was obvious I was in trouble. The question remained, *how much* trouble was I in? My fellow Marines looked at me as I walked. Some had that boy-are-you-in-trouble look on their faces, others were laughing, and of course, my boys were just stupefied. That day will be forever burned into my memory. I was suffering a merciless hangover, dehydrated, and facing an uncertain future.

I went directly to my rack and crashed out for as long as I could. I knew that, eventually, the Platoon Commander would summon me to his office. I was surprised when evening arrived, and still, I had not been summoned. I recovered with some very badly needed sleep. The feeling of having Office Hours hanging over my head did not seem to be helping my mental state. I was not aware at the time that the story of my antics was growing all over base. The story about telling the Commander General to *kiss my red ass*, evading capture all night, and making a legendary triple-decker sandwich from the Sergeant's refrigerator made its way through the entire base. How many who heard that story relished the idea of doing the very same thing themselves?

I reported for Office Hours the following week. Arriving in my best Class A uniform, I reported to the Commanding Officer's headquarters to have the charges read to me. This time, I sensed that the outcome was going to be different from my previous Office Hours at the Naval Weapons Station in South Carolina. My Platoon Commander was unusually quiet as the Commanding Officer peered over the detailed report of my drunken actions. I had to imagine how the conversation unfolded between the Officer and higher-level brass when they had to report my signed message to the Commanding General–"...*kiss my red ass!*"

The Commanding General finished reading the report. I stood at attention, waiting for his next comment, or move. He asked me if I had anything to say, or if I wanted to explain my actions. Referring to my personnel folder, he cited all the accomplishments in my brief, three-year career in the United States Marine Corps. "I see you graduated Jump School, Radio Operators School, Police Chaser School, Assault Climber's School, two Letters of Appreciation, the Meritorious Mast, and thirteen perfect physical fitness scores running consecutively... and *now this*?" I paused to reflect on my actions and how, even now, I had no remorse.

I explained, very calmly, how I had a special relationship with my grandfather, and that I became enraged when the Marine Corps denied leave for me to pay final respects to the man who was the closest I had to a father. I felt that I was a damn good Marine and that I always tried to be the best I could, follow the Motto of the Marines, "Semper Fi," and that now, I felt as if the Marine Corps had let me down. The Commanding General listened as I wrapped up my response.

He reached for his cigar, taking a large draw, as he pondered the report. The smell of cigar some floated through the humid Okinawa air. He pushed his chair back and looked up at me. "Lance Corporal Garvais, taking into consideration your outstanding service record, and the untimely death of your Grandfather, I hereby sentence you to twenty-five days of Barracks restrictions, twenty-five days of extra Kitchen Duty, and a two hundred dollar reduction in pay for two months. You will begin serving your punishment starting this Friday. You are excused."

I saluted, pivoted, and walked out of the Officer's quarters returning to my squad bay. My fellow Marines were amazed to discover that my punishment was so light. There was an expectation, I believe, that I would be sentenced to the brig or have a reduction of rank. My Platoon Sergeant approached me, shaking his head, and chuckled. He looked me squarely in the eyes. "You are one lucky son of a bitch or God is watching over you! Your punishment could have been really bad, it's a huge offense to tell an officer to kiss your ass! Then, to top it off, he commands you to start your sentence this Friday, right?"

"Yes, Sergeant." He shook his head.

"We are going on an extended movement this Friday for about two weeks or twenty-one days. Those count on the days you have to serve, so you will only have *four days* of actual punishment! Man, that Captain and Commanding General must really like you!" I thought about what he just explained. God was watching out for me. I joined my Platoon for twenty-one days and only had to serve four days of the punishment.

I returned to my routine with Danny Urias working out and staying sober. Toward the end of my time there, new companies began flying onto the island to replace us. While in the chow line, I heard a voice that felt like a punch in the stomach. *"Hodgie, is that you?"* I looked toward the voice and saw the familiar face of Russell Hurtle! The same dude who stole the Jeep a couple years back in South Carolina. My blood went cold. I did not know what to say or do. Glancing through the line where Hurtle stood, I saw my fellow Marines, a number of high-ranking officers, and no possibility that anything Hurtle said would go unheard. "You know, Hodgie, I still have those twenty-five hundred dead presidents set aside for you." The words cut through me. I knew that he referred to a felonious act committed without my consent and against all my protests, but having no sense of discretion, a concept with which he was completely unfamiliar.

"I have no idea what you're talking about." I was irritated and I could only hope that he would get the hint.

"Don't you *remember* that Jeep we grabbed and brought to Ohio?" No way. It was inconceivable to me that he could be that dense. It was just as I had suspected a long time ago. This man was not all there. Three years later, he was still talking about the Jeep that he stole, and had no reservation implicating me. This had to end.

I motioned for Hurtle meet me outside the chow hall. We stepped into bright sunlight, as I looked around nervously to see that nobody was nearby or within earshot. Hurtle sill had that crazy look in his eyes that I remembered so vividly. Before I could say a word, he began talking about the Jeep, how he and his friends from Ohio made a huge profit off it by parting it out. He seemed so proud of his accomplishment and how much money he made from it. At that point, he added that he still had my cut, the twenty-five hundred dollars he had allotted to me for my involuntary role in his scheme.

I interrupted him at that juncture. "Look, Russ, I do not want the money, and I had no part in taking the Jeep. I was drunk. Do you remember how this went down?" I regretted asking him, since he never seemed to hear anything I said. In the past, every time I tried to explain that I wanted nothing to do with stealing the Jeep; he just interjected how perfect his plan was and how fortunate he was to find such a nice Jeep with the keys still in the ignition.

"Yeah, I remember, Hodgie. *We* ..." I cut him off before he could continue. I had to know that he really understood I did not approve, and that I was not comfortable with stealing or profiting from the theft.

"*No*, *we* did not steal the Jeep, Russ. I only went along as far as I did because I was drunk and I was getting a ride with you at the time. *Please*, you need to stop talking about this, especially around other Marines! I can't take the money, ok?" He stood there, absorbing what I said. Then, a smile crept over his face, his eyes brightened, and he nodded.

"Ok, Hodgie! You got it!" He raised his hand and we gave each other a high-five. Maybe he realized this was a larger share for him if I did not take the cut. I was just relieved that after all this time, he finally seemed to understand that much. By clarifying this point with Hurtle, I successfully relieved my nerves. I had no way of knowing at the time that this clarification would later save me, when I took a polygraph test for employment as a law enforcement officer.

Since that day, I have not seen or heard from Hurtle. Our company finished deployment at Okinawa shortly thereafter and returned to the

United States. Each of the new locales that I visited taught me something new. Spending three months in a third world country taught me to appreciate the blessings I have right here in the USA.

The day finally arrived when my enlistment was up in the United States Marine Corps. I had been talking about this for the past year, planning where I would go and how I would spend my new freedom. I thought about a trip to New York City to visit the *Italian Stallion*, Don Giambra, or simply take a long road trip. But first, I had unfinished business.

I invited Greg Chiaravalle, Brian Johnson, Pat Stillmunks, and any other Marines who wanted to party, to meet at Huntington Beach for our *Getting Out Blast!* We spent the next three days drinking beer, more beer, and again, more beer. All I remember about those three days was that I actually became *bored* with drinking beer, and that all I really wanted to do was go home to Marysville, Washington.

I drove home alone. The road trip took eighteen hours to complete, and when I arrived, I discovered that really, not much had changed during the time I was gone. I took a job at Bates Abrasives, located in Sedro Wooly, and for about two years, everything went well. I made money, worked the day shift, and returned home around three in the afternoon. I continued to party. I went dancing at clubs, such as the Black Angus in Lynnwood, where I was suckered into a dance-off.

While in the Marine Corps, I learned many new dance moves. I found it easy to mimic the moves I saw, and the new hip-hop style was especially my speed. That night, we went to Black Angus with my sister, Camille Desatuel. We tore up the dance floor.

After a while, I noticed that couples were leaving the dance floor. The DJ was loud and kept pumping out tunes. I did not pay much attention to what he was saying, but I did notice that there were only three couples remaining on the dance floor, not including us. The crowd was electric. Soon, it was just two couples left–us and an African American couple. I realized at that point, that we were in the middle of a dance-off. The crowd shouted as we danced, sometimes chanting "MC Hammer and Rico Suave!" I soon realized they were referring to the other man on the floor and me. He was good! Then, he hit a move I had never seen before, and one that I could not copy. It was game over. He won first place, and I won second place, for a prize of hundred-dollars. Not bad for a small town boy who grew up wearing *Levi's 501 button fly jeans* and hard rock t-shirts!

MTV defined a generation that brought music videos into our living rooms. This movement inspired what is now called a second invasion of British music with the introduction of super groups, such as *Duran Duran, Free Cell, Flock of Seagulls, David Bowie*, and many others. It later paved the way for hip-hop music videos with a show called, *"Yo! MTV Raps"* with Ed Lover and Dr. Dre. Artists, such as *Big Daddy Kane, KRS1, New Edition, LL Cool J, MC Hammer*, and Bobby Brown found huge success. The biggest group of that time was Run DMC, who made music history in their awesome team-up with Aerosmith on *"Walk This Way."* This video brought both groups together in their joint crossover hit.

I began to learn how sneaky alcohol could be. There were fun times when I drank, and for that very reason, I continued going back for more. It is the fun times that we remember when we drink. In reality, more bad times follow heavy drinking than good. There were countless times that I could have killed others or myself due to poor judgment while intoxicated.

My sister, Camille, and I drove up to Mount Vernon to check out one of the clubs in the area. My former girlfriend from high school was a *Bud Light girl*, meaning that she would promote the brand by wearing Bud Light attire with several other girls, while interacting with patrons at various clubs. We were on good terms, and I was looking forward to seeing her there.

Once we arrived, we ordered some beers. I scoped the scene, looking for someone with whom to dance, while Camille mingled with some of the men. My girlfriend arrived shortly after. I watched her perform her routine with the other girls as they promoted the brand. I danced with her a few times, and she seemed happy, but as the evening continued, I lost track of her. Camille and I continued to drink and mingle with the crowd until it was closing time.

As we exited the club, I could clearly tell that I was in no shape to drive anywhere. Camille seemed to be ok, so I let her drive my 1988 Formula Firebird, complete with T-tops, Boyd rims, and Toyo tires. At that time, this car was very nice!

As we drove away from the club, I started to notice that Camille was intoxicated as well–the car was weaving back and forth between the lanes. I told her to pull off I-5 at the next exit, a side road several miles before Arlington and unoccupied by any other motorists. Since neither of us was in any shape to drive, I told my sister we should try to sleep it off and drive home in the morning. She agreed, and we both went to sleep where we had pulled over. At least, that was my assumption.

Several hours later, I awoke to the sound of tires screeching and the motor in my Firebird revving. I saw several women and children running and screaming, dropping their bikes, and others hurrying off the pavement in terror as we raced toward them. Everything seemed to slow down as if in slow motion. I could see the horrified expressions on their faces as they scrambled out of the way. I tried to make sense of this, how it was possible that I was asleep one minute, then racing out of control toward innocent people the next.

I looked over at my sister. She was screaming as the Firebird skidded out of control. Then I saw it. First, I caught a glimpse through the windshield, and then the side window. We were racing toward a large concrete tower on the right side of the rest area. We skidded through a concrete parking curb, exploding the front right tire, then the rear right tire struck, letting out a loud crack and hiss. Fortunately, because the tires had popped, we avoided hitting the concrete tower head-on.

The Firebird skidded to a halt about twenty-five yards past the tower, and we missed it by only two feet to the left. When we came to a stop, we were looking straight at a couple sitting in the back of a green Ford pickup, with a look of disbelief on their faces. Apparently, they had jumped into the back of the truck to avoid being struck by us.

I screamed at my sister. "What the hell are you doing? We could have been killed!" She was hysterical and crying. I did not realize at the time that she had blacked out. I got out of the Firebird. People at the rest area scattered. Some left by car, others by bicycle. Everyone was in shock. I looked at the path where we skidded through the rest area. Somehow, we went right down the middle and missed every single person parked, people on their bikes, and others who were walking. God was looking out for me. The chances that we did not hurt or kill anyone were very slim.

I called a tow truck to take care of the wrecked Firebird, and my sister and I rode in the back of the truck to our house on 116th Street. When we arrived home, my dad, Ken Garvais had a look of shock when he saw the wreckage, and our disheveled state. Later, I found out that the Washington State Patrol showed up at our house, but my dad told them to leave and that I was not there. There were no legal repercussions for either my sister or me that day, but my car was badly wrecked.

After a month passed, I turned twenty-five. I sat on my bed looking up at the ceiling and thinking about my future. I had served four years in the Marine Corps, and had completed many training missions during that time. I met numerous people who made a tremendous impact on me, and enjoyed everything the nightlife had to offer in this country and even on a small Pacific island. But now, I was in the same house in which I grew up, in the same bedroom, and doing all the same things I had done before I enlisted in the Marine Corps. I wondered if I should attend college. My dad wanted me to try the community college and try the basketball team. There was always soccer, but at that time, basketball had replaced soccer as my favorite sport. I looked around the room and saw the latest issue of the Colville Tribal newspaper, which my sister received for being a member of the Colville Tribe.

I picked up the newspaper and opened it to the classified ad section. There was an ad for "Police Officers Wanted." Normally, I would have ignored it. I spent the better part of my life avoiding the police. In high school, I evaded them on countless occasions, but for some reason, I continued to read the advertisement. Testing for the position would begin in two weeks.

My mother grew up in the Kartar Valley of the Colville Indian Reservation. I had many relatives still living in the area, most of whom I did not know. As I read the ad again, I decided that I wanted to become a police officer. *If you can't beat em, join em.* I thought about my childhood in the Marysville area, and remembered that I had taken a junior law enforcement class in one of the smaller, outlying cities that surrounded Seattle. There, we learned the basics of being a police officer, and I really enjoyed the class. Somehow, I lost sight of my goal when I spent more time with friends whose influences were not congruent with law enforcement.

The Creator had a reason for everything that happened. My time in the Marine Corps prepared me for a career in law enforcement, and gave me the training I needed to excel. The next day at work, I told my boss, Tom Maurer about my new plans. Tom was someone I respected a great deal. He was easy-going, friendly, and loved life. I even dated his daughter, Nancy, for a short time. I will be the first to admit that I acted immature during that time and did not always treat her the way she deserved to be treated. Another co-worker, Dustin Perrot, was skeptical, and admittedly, I had not given anyone a reason up to this point why I would make a good police officer.

Chapter 15: The Beginning of a Long Journey

His mailbox at a home he maintains near Nine Mile Falls was firebombed, starting a small fire, on July 5, the night before he appeared before Quackenbush on the issue of whether the Spokane Tribe has jurisdiction to prosecute him for allegedly stealing drug-buying money. "I just don't understand this," Garvais said Tuesday of the court rulings. "I prayed last night, and will leave all this in the hands of God."

"BIA firing complicated by rulings," by Bill Morlin
<u>Spokesman-Review</u>, July 14, 2004

I began my career in law enforcement much in the same way I learned how to do any other job. I was focused on the policies and procedures involved in performing each task. I was excited to learn how to use the police radio, the siren in my patrol car, and all the other cool aspects of being a cop that we see in the movies. I was not prepared for the culture into which I was immersed.

Nobody prepares you for the posturing and petty rivalries that come at you from nowhere. In my case, I knew from the beginning that at least two officers in my department had an immediate resentment toward me, but I had no idea where their hatred came from. I had been warned that Johnson and Edwards felt superior to the Native tribal police officers. It made no sense to me. Why would they choose to work as law enforcement officers on an Indian reservation if they felt that out of place in the community? Their immediate perception of all Native community members was that of suspicion and contempt. The few times they showed me any courtesy at all, I felt a nudge inside to be on my guard. Those gut feelings always proved right.

Johnson and Edwards would not be the only ones to take this attitude. In a way, they prepared me for my experiences with even more insidious and dangerous adversaries in the next few years. I was raised to show respect toward authority, so even though I could see through their intentions, I felt compelled to give them respect as senior officers above me. God always makes things right, and that was exactly what happened for me, even though it took many years for me to see justice served. I had to learn some hard lessons along the way, but I am thankful today that God was always there beside me, even before I submitted my life to Him.

I learned in Marysville Pillchuck High School that I would have to fight hard if I wanted to succeed. Nothing came easy for me. I had to accept the beat downs, and get up for more if I wanted to play varsity basketball. The disappointments were almost unbearable, but the payoff was worth it. I learned how to pursue goals without giving up. The Marine Corps prepared me for the physical tests in law enforcement, and a few years later, I would see my name on the Honor Wall when I attended the Academy for federal agents in Glynco, Georgia.

As a federal agent, I uncovered corruption within the Bureau of Indian Affairs. A BIA Chief of Police and three other BIA police officers were the subjects of a criminal investigation for multiple crimes, including theft, intimidation, and making false charges against innocent tribal members. I was ambushed in one of the most devious ways imaginable. While I uncovered corruption within federal law enforcement, a sinister plan was being devised by my own commander and the corrupt agents to turn everything on me. Their plan was successful.

I did not take this laying down. Maybe if I had kept quiet and walked away at the first warning, I could have avoided the betrayals and years of pain. I was angry. I did the right thing; I performed my job without bias or favoritism. I was punished for speaking the truth. Ultimately, my first wife was lured into joining forces with those who filed false charges against me. I was betrayed at every level one can imagine. I knew that I was doing the right thing and that my refusal to keep quiet was touching a nerve. One day before I was scheduled to appear in Federal Court to address these issues, a bomb was set off at my home, endangering my current wife, LoVina, and myself. My two small children were not at home when it went off. At that time, my former wife and I had a plan of scheduled visitation, and it was her turn to have the children with her. Had my children been there, or playing near the place the explosion happened, they would have been injured or killed. This was not the first time my home was bombed after I spoke out about corruption in the Bureau of Indian Affairs and Tribal police department.

But all that is too complicated to explain in this final chapter, and honestly, most people would never believe that all the events that happened to me were true. I remember sitting across from a well-known reporter from the Spokesman-Review, who listened patiently to my winding tale of police corruption, cover-up, and near-fatal escape. Even though he admitted that I seemed credible, he could not run the story without some physical evidence to back it up. Fortunately, I had exactly what he needed. I had the circumstantial and direct evidence, recorded confessions of the BIA federal officers admitting to committing various crimes. When I think about it, if I did not have that physical evidence, I might not be writing this right now.

I served my country in the Marine Corps. I later served my community and the Colville Tribe as a police officer. My time as a Colville Tribal police officer was filled with good memories. I met some very honest police officers and worked for a Chief of Police who would serve as my role model for integrity, Chief John "Jay" Goss, Jr. Johnson and Edwards were just nasty symptoms of a much larger disease. Neither had respect for the average person on the reservation, and they had no problem using dishonesty to their advantage.

In the second book of this series, I explain my career starting as a patrol officer progressing to the North Central Washington Drug Task Force and ultimately the pinnacle of law enforcement, an 1811 Special Agent. I further began to detail how BIA federal agents engaged in theft from the Spokane Tribe of Indians, the federal government, and innocent tribal members. There are many victims in my story. Some of those people have never had their story told, yet they suffered the bullying of corrupt police officers and powerful families.

I received a mysterious phone call one day at my desk. A nervous tribal member asked to meet me in private, and begged that I not disclose their name. During that conversation, this tribal member explained how BIA federal police officers assigned to the Spokane Indian Reservation were charging innocent people with possession of drugs in order to confiscate their vehicles and other property. This person, whose identity remains a secret, was in fear for their life. The bizarre turn of events was so incredible that most people would think I was making this up. When I decided to take the BIA and tribe to federal court, I was unable to obtain an attorney, in part, because the events were more unbelievable than one would find in any suspense novel. BIA bureaucrats and their corrupt attorneys had put out the word to their colleagues that I was a troublemaker and that I was guilty of the charges they fabricated–I was blackballed. I finally did obtain an attorney, only with the Creator's hand interceding on my behalf. No attorney wants to take a case that is destined to lose, and with a team of federal agents from the BIA and the FBI working together, I did not appear to stand a chance.

I was surrounded at my home, off the Spokane Indian Reservation, by federal agents and a Stevens County Deputy (who was *not* acting on the orders of the County Sheriff Craig Thayer). Armed with a tribal arrest warrant for false accusations, they sought to arrest a citizen and federal agent who was not a tribal member OFF the Spokane Indian Reservation. Tribal courts do not have the authority to arrest non-Indians off the reservation. That did not stop this group of vigilantes. Their only hope to silence me was to assume I would resist arrest, or maybe even to claim that I had. I don't need to spell out how that would have gone down. The third book of this series will show the astonishment of a well-respected federal judge, as he listened to the details of this conspiracy. It will detail startling spiritual facts about who the Nazarene man really was, how this affects my brothers and sisters in modern day Christianity, and how these original tribal teachings can help my Native American brothers and sisters.

As a federal agent, I was trusted with guarding the second half of President George W. Bush's cabinet members during the September 11, 2001 terrorist attacks. I was in training at the FBI Academy when the Twin Towers were attacked that day. My colleagues and I were mobilized within minutes and were assigned to protect the lives of our nation's leaders at a time when we had no idea who our enemy was. Yet, my commander at the BIA allowed or orchestrated the false charges against me for theft of drug money while I worked for the Spokane Tribe as a federal Special Agent. That unbelievable insult is part of what has driven me to write my story. The ease with which a few people turned my life upside down is frightening. It all started because one person filed a formal complaint about police corruption and because I took that report and did my job without bias or favoritism. Had another officer received that phone call, somebody else would have a story to tell.

I felt incredibly insulted to think that I could not be trusted with government funds, especially after I had handled many thousands of dollars in drug money without losing a single penny. As a federal agent earning a GS12-2 salary, I had no need for the alleged money I was accused of stealing. I certainly did not need the risk.

Keith Johnson and Cal Edwards did everything in their power to catch me doing something wrong. I believed at the time that both of these officers despised me because they disliked the majority of Native police officers with whom they worked. I still believe that their actions were motivated by racism and jealousy but it almost seems like an insufficient explanation for the level of venom with which they attacked me.

While working patrol at Colville Tribal Police Services, I became aware that Edwards and Johnson both had a reputation for lying. Cal Edwards famously executed a search warrant on the wrong house during a drug raid. The family who was dragged out of their home at night–not to mention, at *gunpoint*–was not happy with Detective Edwards. That search warrant had more than a few errors. Somehow, he saw two Mexican families living next to each other, and could not decide which door to kick in. His contempt for the people living on the reservation was transparent, and he knew how I felt about that.

There were complaints about Edwards writing false statements in police reports. Like most gossip, I dismissed it as being an attempt to discredit him, and paid it no attention. I had my own opinion of Edwards, and he was perfectly capable of doing something like this, but if it was not true, I felt sorry for him. Chief Goss, who was a man of integrity and compassion, would not have allowed this to go on without addressing it. It was not long after I first heard the talk about Edwards that I learned the truth. I was passing by Chief Goss' office. As usual, I nodded to him as I strolled by. He looked up and waved me in. "Duane, come in for a minute." The Chief looked like he was deep in thought. He had been staring at the wall when I walked by, and that was not typical for him.

"What's up, Chief?" I backed up and stood in the doorway. He motioned for me to close the door. That is usually not a good sign. The first thought that comes to mind when a person starts a new job is, *what did I screw up now?*

"I received a complaint about another officer, and after I checked it out, it happens to be true." I wondered about that vacant look on his face.

"What kind of complaint?" Chief Goss shook his head slightly, looking down at his desk pad.

"Somebody informed me that some false statements were included in a police report. I looked into it and there is no question about it." He looked up at me, catching me in a state of shock.

"*No way!*" I was not expecting to hear that. I did not know what to expect, really, but I was unprepared to hear something as blatantly dishonest and dirty as *that.*

"It's true. So now, I have to decide what I am going to do about it. Normally, I would not share this information with anyone, but this is that part of the job I do not enjoy." I nodded. I could tell that he was wrestling with a decision that had no positive outcome, no matter what he did. "It was Edwards. He lied in the report, and there is no doubt that it was deliberate." I was shocked that an officer in our department would lie on a police report. I was not surprised to learn that it was Edwards. Not at all.

"Chief, I don't envy you right now." My feelings toward Cal Edwards were well known. He did not like me from the moment I pulled up to the department to apply for the job. He begrudgingly signed off on my training when I first started. That day I pulled up to apply for the job, he could not even muster a "hello" when I greeted him, or allow me room to pass when I tried to enter the front door. No, he blocked the entrance and waited for me to say, *"Excuse me"* before he stepped a few inches aside for me to squeeze past. The rumors about him and Johnson having a deep dislike of Native patrol officers turned out to be very true.

"Well, Duane, I am trying to decide if I should let him go or give him a chance to salvage his career. Something like this is *serious*, and it affects the integrity of our entire department." He leaned back in his chair. *"What would you do?"*

Edwards deserved to be fired. I had no love for Edwards and his absence from the department would result in one less racist roaming the reservation. Something bothered me, though. During the time I worked at Colville Tribal Police Services, I had met many of my coworkers' spouses and children. This was a small community. Everybody knew *everybody*. Edwards was no different. I had met his wife, his children, and they were very nice people. I also learned through casual conversation, that Edwards was the sole source of income for their family. If he lost his job, his wife would suffer, and she did not deserve to pay for his lack of integrity. To this day, I do not understand how such a nice lady could be married to a man like Edwards, but I think we have all seen mysteries like that.

My blood pressure had begun to surge slightly when I thought about Edwards deliberately falsifying a police report. *Would this result in convicting an innocent person?* I did not know all the circumstances, and I had complete confidence that Chief Goss would make sure the victim in this incident did not have to pay for Edward's dishonesty. Assuming the damage had been contained and the subject of the police report did not suffer any further consequences, it all came down to punishment. He was

196

not *fit* to have the kind of power that a police officer wields. "Chief, I'd be the first one to tell you to fire his ass. I think you know that." Chief Goss smiled and nodded. He knew. "I've met his wife, and she is a very nice lady."

"Yes, I have too, and yes, she is. I think that is part of my struggle with this."

"When I spent all that time in training with Edwards, I found out that he was the sole source of income for the family. They have kids, too. I really hate to say it, but if I was in your position, I would write something up, make sure he feels the pain somehow, but let him keep his job. And I would only do that because I have met his wife and kids, not because he deserves a break, because he does not!" Chief Goss and I both laughed. It was true that Edwards was no friend of the Tribal community. He acted as if everyone he met on the reservation was secretly against him, that he could trust no one. Little did he know that if he was in trouble, and back-up was an hour away, it would be a *resident* of the reservation who would come to his rescue. His worldview was "*us versus them*," but the reality on the Colville Indian Reservation was very different.

"Thanks, Duane. I think I know how I'll handle this." That was my cue to get back to work. I learned later that Cal Edwards was demoted from his rank as Sergeant. Chief Goss was as compassionate as he was ethical in carrying out his duties as Police Chief. I do not know all the personnel details other than the demotion, but I would not be surprised to learn that Edwards had to make some additional amends.

I felt bad for Edwards' family. Had he been dismissed at that time, I would have been spared countless problems in my career during the remaining years I worked there. Edwards had no idea that I lobbied for him behind the scenes to keep his job. If he did find out, he certainly did not *show* it.

Edwards and Johnson perpetuated a constant campaign to undermine me as a police officer while working on the Colville Indian Reservation. They jumped at every opportunity to make me look inept. Most of their antics were petty and ineffective, but when they found an opportunity to bury me, they jumped at it. During my time with CTPS, I gave neither of these clowns a reason to question my integrity. They simply believed that I was dishonest because I, like most of the people on the reservation, was Native American. That was all it took. After advising

Chief Goss to let Edwards keep his job, I have to admit that I felt betrayed by Edward's actions.

As I progressed in my career as a patrol officer at Colville Tribal Police Services, I was honored to be placed on the *North Central Washington Narcotics Task Force* (NCWNTF), which included officers and agents from many different law enforcement agencies. As an undercover agent for the task force, one of my responsibilities was to reconcile receipts for the money used to buy and sell illegal drugs in undercover operations. The protocols were very rigid and controlled for every buy. Before the criminal informant entered a house or establishment where the purchase would be made, I and another officer on the task force witnessed and signed for the cash given to the informant. The serial numbers on the cash were recorded. The entire process was audio recorded as an additional layer of security. After the informant returned from the drug buy, we met at a nearby location immediately after the operation. In the presence of the criminal informant and two task force members, we recorded the money used and the drugs were logged into evidence. There was simply no way to misappropriate funds with this system.

Keith Johnson, who enjoyed enormous pride for being included on the task force, shared a friendship with the leader of the task force. When I first met the Commander of NCWNTF, his reaction was to share a quick smirk with his assistant. The mention of my name first compelled them to exchange a glance–for a split second. Reluctantly, they took turns shaking my hand. Any time tension mounted between the Commander and I, Johnson always seemed to be *lurking* in the background.

When my time at CTPS ended, Chief Goss had already left, and I would have had to watch my back with Johnson and Edwards determined to put me in my place. They had become increasingly jealous of the awards and accomplishments I earned. After I made one of the largest drug busts in the reservation's history, their jealousy was out of control.

Johnson's daughter was present at a home that was the subject of a large drug bust, and he disobeyed my orders in how that warrant was conducted. He was deliberately told not to show up at this raid because we knew his daughter would be there. He showed up, failed to stay away from the residence where evidence involving his daughter was located. Johnson even tried to shut down the search before a large quantity of drugs was discovered in that home. That was just one of the *many* reasons Johnson developed an intense dislike for me.

One of the responsibilities I had while assigned to the task force, was to reconcile the money sheets and receipts accounting for the undercover drug money and evidence. Johnson knew the process involved. He had watched me reconcile money sheets countless times. There had never been a question about the accuracy or integrity of my handling of drug money, nor was an inquiry ever *officially* ordered.

After working several years as a tribal police officer, I took the exam and passed the application process to become a federal Special Agent for the Bureau of Indian Affairs. I made the choice to accept an assignment on the Spokane Indian Reservation. Edwards and Johnson clearly had enough hatred for me to hold a grudge over the years when I faced the darkest time of my life. They waited until I had reached the lowest point in my life to make their move.

In my assignment as a BIA federal agent at the Spokane Indian Reservation, I uncovered corruption among several of the federal BIA agents. My investigation into the corruption was highly unpopular with some members of the tribal council and with my BIA Commander. The second book in this series details the progression of this investigation–how the corrupt officers and my superior conspired to frame me for stealing drugs and drug money from evidence. After following the rules, staying true to my oath, and serving my country, I was the one who was ultimately accused of using my position to take money and drugs.

News of the false accusations spread quickly from the Spokane Indian Reservation to the Colville Indian Reservation. When Johnson found out that I was accused of taking drugs and drug money from evidence on the Spokane Indian Reservation, he wasted no time running to the NCWDTF headquarters to rifle through the receipts that I had prepared during my time there. He never did find anything suspicious. In fact, after making some of the largest drug busts in the history of the Colville Indian Reservation, not a single penny that I touched had turned up missing. The hours he spent going through receipts, evidence, and money sheets were all done without authorization from his supervisors in the department or from the task force.

Ultimately, Keith Johnson enjoyed the satisfaction of seeing me handcuffed in front of my current wife, LoVina, and children while we had been enjoying a family outing at the Omak Stampede. While I worked as a Tribal Police Officer for the Colville Tribal Police Services, Johnson was satisfied to make me look bad every chance he got. Edwards, however, reminded me of the sidekick to any *Marvel Comic's* villain. He was shorter and in terrible shape compared to Johnson. He also lacked the *evil genius* that we often associate with our favorite villains. But as a sidekick? He was perfect!

Edwards was small in stature, integrity, and charisma. Johnson had shark eyes concealed behind the veil of police-issue sunglasses, whereas Edwards was more like a snake–content to smirk, and bait his prey as he slithered through the office, spreading gossip and innuendo as he hunted for donuts. I have wondered at times, just how much joy did both of these clowns derive when they succeeded in seeing me in the back of a patrol car on my way to jail? It was Johnson, ultimately, who spotted me that day. Knowing that I was with LoVina and my two small children at the Omak Stampede, he had his chance to call my adversaries for the ambush.

The man who, at one time, had introduced me to law enforcement my first day on the job, and Edwards, his sidekick who trained me and signed off on my training, would feel the ultimate gratification. Through all the times that they tried to make me look bad and failed, they would finally have their moment of glory. I had close friends who took great risk to help me in a time of danger. My family surrounded me with love and support when the wolves surrounded me. When all the details finally came out for the public to see, I had no doubt that the Creator had protected me and restored me, just as my vision dream had shown.

Tribal Court issued a warrant for Garvais, who was arrested at the Omak Stampede by the nearby Colville tribal police and "extradited" to the BIA's detention facility on the Spokane Reservation, where he was held without bond. "The tribe's retaliatory animus toward Garvais for his investigation of a tribal member and tribal descendant could not have been more obvious," Quackenbush wrote.

by Kevin Graham, <u>The Spokesman-Review</u>,
"Former agent wins judgment against BIA"
February 19, 2010

APPENDIX
Lil Mike & FunnyBone
SupaMan
Emcee1
Soul the Interrogator
Prawphit On Point
Prayers for the Nation
Quotes by Jim Linden
Alumni of Marysville Pillchuck High School Class of 1985 who have
passed on
Salute to Veterans of MPHS

Lil Mike & FunnyBone

SupaMan

Duane Garvais Lawrence and SupaMan
at the Coeur d'Alene Casino
SupaMan is on Facebook and Twitter @Supamanhiphop
Won the MTV Award in collaboration with Taboo from
Black Eyed Peas and Emcee One

Emcee One is on
Facebook

Soul The Interrogator
Soul The Interrogator is on Facebook and Twitter @soultheinterrogator

Prawphit On Point

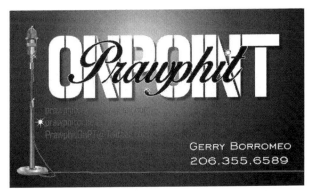

Prawphit On Point is on Facebook and Twitter @PrawphitOnPT

Prayers for the Nation

We prayed at St. Paul's Chapel in New York City 2013 to repent for the following sins of our nation:

1. City of Chicago–we felt sense of doom when we stopped there on our way to New York City,

2. Broken Treaties by the Federal Government

3. Bloodshed on our lands

4. Abortion (human sacrifice)

5. Violations of the Torah

6. Violations of the Ten Commandments

7. The real identity of the historical Jesus versus the Greek Jesus revealed

8. Exploiting women

9. The 426 deaths already on the highways in 2013

10. Drug addictions

11. Prayers for the two vans with "4 Jesus" stickers on them (Missions)

12. Alcohol addiction

13. Man inspired laws teachings

14. Media influence

15. Music influence

16. Aunt Marie Sullivan and Pat Sullivan to return to faith and Jesus

17. For the 7 people killed, 26 shot, 30 wounded incident in Chicago Sunday 2013

18. Guns, Crips, Bloods

19. Government corruption to be exposed

20. Worship of false gods and idols

21. Pride

22. Anger

23. Generational sin

24. Traditions against the written Torah

25. Translations against the Torah

26. Church worshipping on the wrong day

27. Roman Catholic Church influence

28. Christianity teaching false or misleading doctrines

29. Religions teaching false theology

30. Love of power

31. Love of money

Prayers for the Nation (Continued)

33,34,35,36,37 Failure of pastors, ministers, youth pastors, church leaders, church fathers, to teach their churches, congregations about God's Sabbath, Moses' Law and Leviticus feasts

38. Tornadoes in Denver 2013

39. Gettysburg North vs. South

40. Bloodshed on the lands

41.Ten scattered tribes of Ephraim to come forth

42. Bitterness

43. Judah (3) tribes to come to and know Yahushua the Nazarene historical Jesus

44. Ephraim aka Christianity to know and embrace the written Torah aka the historical Jesus and to understand the Oral Torah

45. Acts of jealousy

46. Acts of murder

47. Bondage with drugs and alcohol

48. Restoration of Creator's Sabbath to Christianity

49. Restoration of Moses' Law to Christianity

50. Restoration of Creator's Feasts to Christianity

51. Spirit of suicide

52. Spirit of homosexuality

53. Schools, both tribal and non-tribal

54. Our relationship and family that has passed on, that they may be received by love and grace

55. 56. 57. Repentance, restoration, and revelation of Yahusua Yeshua, the set apart spirit, the Sabbaths, Feasts as defined in the Hebrew Scriptures to be restored to all people, religions, and faiths

58. The name of "God" Yod Hey Wav Hey YHWH Yahweh to be restored, revered, and revealed

59. The new moon Sabbath to be restored

60. The Shofar to be released and restored

Quotes by Jim Linden, Beloved Teacher and Coach at MPHS
The following quotes were submitted by alumni of
Marysville Pillchuck High School

Jeff Shoemaker: A tisket a tasket put it in the basket.

Dave Spencer Jr: "All right that's enough." "When two guys were fighting." "Only PE teacher that lets fights go on for a while right, Jim Frauenholtz."

Tony Aubrey: "You two drive my Chrysler back to the school, we'll be right behind you and DO NOT SPILL MY COFFEE!"

Tyler McCoy: "Dive…..Dive… Baooga Baooga!"

Tyler McCoy: "We're running tomorrow bring your PF Fylers!"

Tyler McCoy: "Gotta look sharp, feel sharp, be sharp….BUY GILLETE BLUE BLADES!"

Duane Garvais Lawrence: "It's HARTMAN VS. HARTMAN!"

Fred Stevens: "We're gonna watch a movie today, no notes, no talks, no SLEEPS!"

Fred Stevens: "Back when MEN were MEN and sheep were scared! Are you a SHEEP?"

Rich Hansen: "Zanoni you knucklehead!"

Kimberly Rae Howard: "Run for fun in the sun HOWARD!"

Alumni of Marysville Pillchuck High School
Class of 1985 who have passed on

Todd Swinger

Marshall Leaf

Delores Moses

Chad Laughlin

Patricia Krausz

Nancy Stich

Kevin McNeal

Mike Jones

Christy Eder

Mike Miller

Craig Earl

Kevin Padgett, Class of 1984

Shannon Smith Boston, Class of 1984

Jeff Lewis, Class of 1986

Chris Paul, Class of 1987

Kevin Medina, Class of 1985

SALUTE TO VETERANS OF MPHS
As a veteran of the United States Marines, I salute and thank my fellow classmates for serving and protecting our freedoms, our way of life in the United States of America and the Native American Indian Reservations.

Jeff Essers: United States Air Force

Tony Bennet: United States Navy

KD Pedersen: United States Army

Sam Grow: United States Army

David Hodgson: United States Navy

Tom Miller: United States Navy, Marine Corps Corpsman Kilo 3/3

Don O' Flanagan: United States Marine Corps

Scott Miller: United States Navy

Laurie Clark Willis: United States Air Force

Duane Hodgson Garvais Lawrence

2nd Battalion 5th Marines Gulf Company 2/5

Airborne, Assault Climber, Radio Operator, Police Chaser

Top Rock and Roll songs 1985:

Dire Straits: Money for Nothing

Bruce Springsteen: Born in the USA

Bryan Adams: Summer of 69

Heart: Never

Huey Lewis and the News: Power of Love

Honnydrippers: Sea of Love

Tears for Fears: Shout

John Cougar Mellencamp: Small Town

Tears for Fears: Everybody wants to rule the world

Simple Minds: Don't you (Forget about me)

1985 Top Hard Rock N Roll Groups
as perceived by Duane Hodgson Garvais Lawrence

Arrowsmith

Scorpions

Def Leppard

AC/DC

ZZ Top

Van Halen

Quiet Riot

Led Zepplin

Billy Squier

Judas Priest

Top Dance Songs 1985

Madonna: Like a Virgin

Ready for the World: Oh Shelia

Bronski Beat: Smalltown boy

Expose: Point of no return

Tears for Fears: Everybody wants to rule the world

Madonna: Material Girl

AHA: Take on me

Lisa Lisa N Cult Jam with FULL FORCE: I wonder if I take you home

Jellybean: Sidewalk Talk

Mary Jane Girls: In my house

Top Country songs of 1985

George Strait: Does Fort Worth Ever Cross your mind

Reba McEntire: How blue

Alabama: (There's a) Fire in the Night

Merle Haggard: A place to fall apart

The Oak Ridge Boys: Make my life with you

Kenny Rodgers: Crazy

Hank Williams Jr: I'm for love

The Judds: Have Mercy

George Strait: The Chair

Hank Williams Jr: Ain't I Misbehavin

Top Movies of 1985

Back to the Future

The Goonies

The Breakfast Club

Just one of the guys

Ferris Bueller's "Day Off"

Teen Wolf

Commando

Weird Science

St. Elmo's Fire

Purple Rain

The previous lists of movies and songs were popular during my time at Marysville Pillchuck High School in 1985

– Duane H. Garvais Lawrence

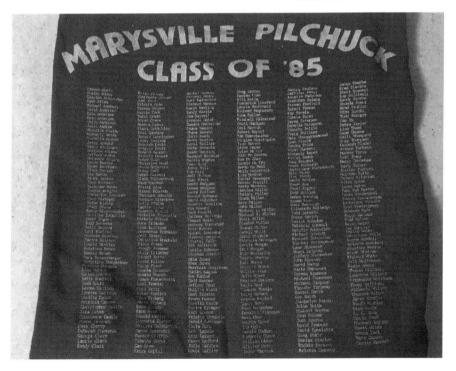

Please tune in to
"Faith & Hip Hop" Radio Show at

www.kwis883.com

Please send friend requests to my personal Facebook page for
Duane Garvais Lawrence or to the Official Facebook Fan Page for
"Halfbreed"

LoVina Louie, Founder of Rockin the Rez Program
Miss Indian World 1990

KWIS88.3 FM is a publicly funded radio station.
If you would like to make a donation, please contact Valerie Fast Horse,
Information Technology Director for the Coeur d'Alene Tribe.
Mail contributions to: KWIS FM Fund, PO BOX 408, Plummer, ID 83851

or visit the KWIS Facebook page for more information.

77591210R00126

Made in the USA
San Bernardino, CA
25 May 2018